GAUGING PUBLIC OPINION

GAUGING
PUBLIC OPINION

By HADLEY CANTRIL

and Research Associates

in the Office of Public Opinion Research

Princeton University

PRINCETON

PRINCETON UNIVERSITY PRESS

LONDON : HUMPHREY MILFORD, OXFORD UNIVERSITY PRESS

1944

Printed in the United States of America
by Princeton University Press at Princeton, New Jersey

To
George Gallup

PREFACE

WITHIN the past decade the field of public opinion research has been transformed from an academic hobby and commercial toy to a discipline of its own. The enormous possibilities of the sampling technique used in market research have been avidly exploited by American business. Newspaper and magazine publishers were quick to sense the news value of reports on what the nation thinks. And now responsible public officials have learned to take public opinion polls seriously for their contribution to modern statecraft.

The dizzy speed with which this development took place left the social scientist momentarily breathless. Vaguely he sensed that something important was happening in a domain he had come to regard as his own. But it was not easy at first to recognize in those methods, which were forecasting winning candidates or telling manufacturers the popularity of various brands of soap, a means for gathering data which the social scientist could regard as of some significance. Sometimes his irritation— irritation at the upstarts who often, neither knowing nor caring anything about traditional academic abracadabra, seemed nevertheless to carry off the honors or the cash—led him to a type of superior criticism that did little credit to his sense of objectivity. Sometimes, on the other hand, his genuine desire to learn the methods was thwarted, either because of the expense of the research involved or because of inability to get specific information on the methods used from men who rapidly found themselves in a highly competitive game and who felt for a while that they had to play their cards close to their vests.

For a time, as a result, the social scientist as well as the layman was in the dark. About this new type of research there seemed to be something mysterious, almost fake. And yet, over and over again, it demonstrated its accuracy—in the form of predicting elections, increasing sales, or discovering useful information.

By now, however, much of this earlier skepticism and ignorance has passed. Both social scientists and informed laymen have become familiar in a general way with the theory of stratified sampling. They know why the fate of the *Literary Digest* poll does not necessarily lie in wait for its more streamlined counterparts. There are no longer any major technical secrets jealously guarded. Public opinion research has become public property.

There already has been, and there undoubtedly will be and should be for many years, serious discussion of the place of public opinion and reporting in a democracy. Some critics claim that the polls are undermining the theory of representative government on which this country was

founded; some believe the polls influence legislators to such an extent
that the judgment of experts goes unheeded. On the other hand, certain
policy makers hail the polls as an answer to Abraham Lincoln's dilemma:
"What I want is to get done what the people desire to have done, and the
question for me is how to find that out exactly." Whatever the ultimate
verdict may be, it seems likely that public opinion reporting will continue
for some time to play an important role in national and international
affairs. For this reason, if for no other, it is imperative that the methods
used by those who take upon themselves the responsibility for reporting
opinion be carefully and constantly reviewed. Although it would be difficult for any unscrupulous investigator to remain long in the field, the
faith many people now have in the polls is due in no small measure to the
honesty and ability of the men who have done most to show the practi-
cability and usefulness of the mechanism.

Because the field is still in its infantile stages, the investigator today
feels somewhat as must the explorers of the fifteenth and sixteenth cen-
turies when they saw only bits of vast unknown areas whose precise
boundaries and potentialities they knew they themselves would never
fully comprehend. So many problems in the field call for some solution
that the investigator hardly knows where to begin. As soon as he begins
work on one problem, several other related and equally important problems loom ahead.

The research reported in this volume deals almost entirely with the
study of public opinion through some form of the polling mechanism.
This emphasis is deliberate. Although polling is, of course, only one of
many methods of public opinion research, it is the device which appears
at the moment to be the best yet found for gathering reliable information
of a certain type. The course of wisdom, therefore, seemed to lie in the
direction of systematic concentration upon that device.

In spite of the miscellaneous nature of the studies reported here, I
have tried to bring together for the first time in one volume some idea of
the serious problems encountered in every phase of the polling operation.
My hope is that the series of studies will advance the science of polling,
show that it is more than a parlor game, and point up some of the perils
as well as indicate some of the rewards that can be found in this new
field. The volume should discourage vague and unsupported criticism,
just as it should encourage more solid criticism by those who sympathize
with the basic problems at hand.

Part I considers some of the dilemmas that confront the investigator
when he sets about the task of posing issues. Are questions asked of a
large population always meaningful? What are some of the difficulties
of wording questions? Can we gauge the intensity as well as the direction

of opinion? What is the relative value of a single question compared to a battery of several questions?

Part II summarizes some studies in connection with interviewing. How much do the opinions of interviewers themselves influence the opinions they report? How reliably can interviewers rate some of the background characteristics of respondents? How many people refuse to answer the questions interviewers ask? What is the value of giving interviewers personal training in the field? What happens when interviewers use a secret ballot?

Part III contains analyses of some sampling problems. How does one go about choosing a sample? How does the "representative sample" of the polls compare with the true population? How much can we rely on the use of small samples?

Part IV indicates ways in which polling data may be treated to discover something of opinion determinants. What is the most efficient use of breakdowns? How can we find out whether one determinant is more important than another? How does amount of information affect opinion? What can the polls do to chart trends of opinion?

In Part V a single complete study of public opinion is reported, tracing a public opinion survey on a complex topic through its various stages from beginning to end.

From now on, research is particularly needed, I think, on methods that will increase the reliability of our *understanding* of public opinion rather than the reliability of short-time *predictions*. Statistical comparisons based on polling information afford many insights and interpretations of great theoretical and practical usefulness. But the limitations of even the most exhaustive analyses of the most intensive interviews made of representative samples of the population still leave the psychologist dissatisfied in his answer to the question of why a person's opinion is what it is. Strictly speaking, statistics on sample populations cannot tell anything final as to why people really think this or that. But statistics can disprove many false hypotheses. For this reason, the Office of Public Opinion Research is now engaged in research on case studies in the belief that the motivation behind opinion is always obscure when more than a single individual is involved. Research on larger populations should be considerably more penetrating if it is bolstered by hunches obtained from more complete studies of single personalities.

It is *not* my concern here to give any systematic account of what public opinion is, what its determinants are, or how it can best be guided under different contingencies. Before such an account can be written in any precise way, it is essential that the assets and liabilities of our present tools of research be understood, that certain new tools be devised, that we be fully aware of the value and limitations of the data we get. I hope this purely technical volume will, therefore, be a step forward toward our eventual understanding of public opinion and our conceptualization of the many forces that bring it into being.

The research here has been made possible by a foundation grant. The Office of Public Opinion Research at Princeton University was established in 1940 for the purpose of (1) studying techniques of public opinion research; (2) gaining some insight into the psychological problems of public opinion motivation; and (3) building up archives of public opinion data for the use of qualified students.

Many of the data used in the investigations reported here have been taken directly from the American Institute of Public Opinion. The data of the American and British Institutes together with the studies made by this Office and many miscellaneous investigations done by others through this Office or deposited here for safekeeping furnish us with archives of public opinion information which I believe are almost without equal. All these data, together with the published results of the *Fortune* poll, are catalogued by subject matter.

All but one of the chapters in this volume have been written by persons who have at some time been associated with this Office. Chapter 10, on the construction of samples, was especially prepared by J. Stevens Stock whose work with various government agencies provided him with specially appropriate material. So much of the work has been done in a spirit of mutual cooperation that every author owes some direct or indirect debt to his coworkers. Persons who have been associated with this Office and who have contributed to the work in some nameless way are Frederic Swift, Grayce Northcross, Mabel Rugg, Bruno Foa. Leah Catelli has done yeoman service running the sorting machines; Jennie Cortese has worked indefatigably with the manuscript; Elizabeth Deyo has been of inestimable help in managing the details of the varied projects and preparing the manuscript. Katherine Bruner assisted in the final editing. The Office is deeply indebted to staff members of the American Institute of Public Opinion for their willing assistance and their constructive criticisms. Among these persons are Edward Benson, Lawrence E. Benson, Paul Perry, Samuel Northcross, Elizabeth Bissell, and Virginia Dudley. Gordon Allport has read the entire manuscript and made many helpful suggestions.

My greatest debt in the work of the Office is to George Gallup. He has given me permission to reproduce all the data of the American and British Institutes of Public Opinion. Not only has he allowed me to use the interviewing facilities of the Institute to gather information, but he has, furthermore, encouraged me to experiment with the Institute's research tools without restriction or stipulations concerning the publication of results. The reader will see for himself that no criticism of the

Institute's methods has been spared wherever it seemed justifiable. The ideas for several of the studies contained in this volume are Dr. Gallup's. Conversation with him has helped formulate many of the problems this Office has investigated.

Although the phrase "a Gallup poll" is by now almost a household word, comparatively few people realize the amount of experimentation Dr. Gallup conducts to improve his own understanding of the mechanism he did so much to create. The public and the social scientist can be thankful that the man who wields so much influence through his reports on the state of opinion is a person distinguished for his integrity, for his lively curiosity, and for his research acumen.

H. C.

Office of Public Opinion Research
Princeton, N.J.
April 1943

CONTENTS

PART I

PROBLEMS INVOLVED IN SETTING
THE ISSUES

CHAPTER I

THE MEANING OF QUESTIONS[1]

A s MEN have known throughout the ages and as modern semantics has pointed out in detail, the meaning of even the simplest word may be slippery. When we add to the ordinary problems of verbal communication the additional problem of presenting a meaning to groups of people widely separated in background, experience, education, and terminologies peculiar to interest or occupational groups, the difficulty confronting a public opinion investigator becomes clear.

Persons who use the techniques and facilities of modern public opinion research have the responsibility of slicing issues meaningfully and then of presenting those issues to people in such a way that answers can be reliably interpreted. Even after elaborate testing on the clarity and bias of questions by the most conscientious investigator, many of the items finally included in a study may remain obscure. It seems appropriate, therefore, to begin the present volume with a study of this important and neglected problem—the meaning of questions.[2]

From the comments of others and from our own experience, we were able to select for study certain areas where misinterpretation or obscurity of meaning seemed likely, where answers to questions did not seem consistent with observable facts or with other opinions. The following difficulties were examined:

1. Questions too vague to permit precise answers.
2. Questions obscure in meaning.
3. Questions getting at some stereotype or overtone implicit in the questions rather than at the meanings intended.
4. Questions misunderstood because they involve technical or unfamiliar words.
5. Questions presenting issues not sufficiently circumscribed.
6. Alternatives provided for answers not exhaustive.
7. Alternatives too many or too long.
8. Questions whose implications are not seen.
9. Questions concerned with only a portion of the population and therefore meaningless to many people.

[1] By Hadley Cantril and Edrita Fried.

[2] The interpretation placed on answers to questions by poll administrators and investigators has been seriously criticized. The most bitter attack on the polls from the point of view of misleading questions is that of Paul Studensky, "How Polls Can Mislead," *Harpers,* December 1939. Other comments are found in R. F. Sletto, "Pre-testing of Questionnaires," *Amer. Sociol. Rev.,* 1940, 193-200; Selden Menefee, "The Effect of Stereotype Words on Political Judgment," *Amer. Sociol. Rev.,* 1936, 614-621.

10. Questions getting only surface rationalizations.
11. Questions getting only stereotyped answers.

These difficulties are, of course, most likely to occur in studies of opinion using national stratified samples where the investigator is faced with the problem of presenting an unequivocal meaning in a few words.

A specific test was designed to point up and illustrate the difficulties in each of the areas described above. In order not to place the problem in a hypothetical context, wherever possible questions already employed on national surveys of opinion by the American Institute of Public Opinion, the *Fortune* Poll, the National Opinion Research Center, or the Office of Public Opinion Research were used. It should be noted, however, that the questions used were highly selected because difficulties in interpretation of the answers were already suspected. One could by no means pick at random questions used by any careful investigator and show the meaning to be as problematical as that of the questions chosen here.

Most of the information for this report is gathered from 40 careful and intensive interviews made by three especially skilled interviewers. Since on this study, as with all studies, there were definite limitations of cost, the investigation was confined to a few people: yet every attempt was made to exhaust the relevant information obtainable from these people. The precise method used to tap each of the eleven areas is discussed below with the results.

METHODS AND RESULTS

1. *Questions too vague to permit precise answers*

Here we chose a question asked by the *Fortune* poll: "After the war is over, do you think people will have to work harder, about the same, or not so hard as before?" The alternatives provided were: "harder," "about the same," "not so hard," "don't know."

Several concepts here are vague and make interpretation of results difficult. For one thing, the meaning of the word "people" may be vastly different to various respondents. Hence our investigators asked their forty respondents: "When you said that people would have to work (harder, about the same, or not so hard), were you thinking of people everywhere and in all walks of life—laborers, white-collar workers, farmers and business men—or did you have in mind one class or group of people in particular?" Our instructions continued: "If the respondent said that by people he meant one class or group, then ask him not only which group he meant but how, in his opinion, other groups will fare in this respect?" Furthermore, the concept of working "harder" is obscure in meaning. One does not know, for example, whether it refers to working longer, making a product of higher quality, working in order to meet stronger competition, or what. Hence our investigators asked: "When you said before that people would have to work harder, did you think then that they would have to work longer hours, that there would be more competition, or that in general a higher quality of work would be demanded?" A third possible complication is contained in the phrase "as before." Do people mean before the war started, before the interviewer appeared on the scene, or what? So our investigators also asked: "And when you said that people would have to work _____ did you mean to say that they would have to work _____ than (as) now in these war times, or _____ than (as) in the old days of peace?"

The upshot of the forty interviews is shown in the following table.

TABLE I. WORKING

When you said that people would have to work........, were you thinking of people everywhere and in all walks of life—laborers, white-color workers, farmers, and businessmen—or did you have in mind one class or group of people in particular?		After the present war is over, do you think people will have to work harder, about the same, or not so hard as before?			
			Not so		
		Harder	Hard	Same	Total
	People in all walks of life	14	3	7	24
	One class	7	4	1	12
	Don't know	2	1	1	4
					—
					40
					—
When you said before that people would have to work harder, did you think then that they would have to work longer hours, that there would be more competition, or that in general a higher quality of work would be demanded?	Longer hours	6			6
	More competition	5			5
	Higher quality	10			10
					—
					21
					—
And when you said that people would have to work......, did you mean to say that they would have to work...... than (as) now in these war times, or...... than (as) in the old days of peace?	War times	6	5	4	15
	Peace times	14	2	4	20
	Don't know			1	1
					—
					36

We see, then, that to slightly more than half of our group, the word "people" meant everybody, that it meant a particular class to a third of the group, and that one-tenth of the respondents just didn't know what they meant by the word "people."

The word "harder" turns out to mean higher quality to some, more competition to others, and longer hours to the rest; whereas the phrase "as before" means before the war started to half the group and after the war started to the rest of the group.

On the basis of this analysis, it would, then, be difficult to interpret percentage results obtained from this particular question in any reliable fashion.

2. Questions obscure in meaning

A question frequently used by the Office of Public Opinion Research to test opinion in favor of a negotiated peace was: "If the German army overthrew Hitler and then offered to stop the war and discuss peace terms with the Allies, would you favor or oppose accepting the offer of the German army?" Examination of the comments made by respondents on national surveys convinced us that the question implied different things to different people and that to most people it was not meaning what we had intended it to mean.

So this question was followed up in our forty-case study by the question: "We are wondering whether the question I just read to you means

TABLE 2.   PEACE WITH GERMAN ARMY

What the question meant in respondents' own words.	Make Peace		
	FAVOR	OPPOSE	NO OPINION
Correct	2	9	
Incorrect			
German people will overthrow Hitler	9	4	
We should make peace with Germany	1	2	1
If revolution make peace	1		
Overthrow Nazi principles	1		
Peace with Hitler		1	
If army overthrows Gestapo		1	
Revolt of soldiers, etc.	1		
Don't know		2	5
	15	19	6

the same thing to everybody who answers it. Would you mind telling me in your own words what you understood it to mean?"

The results shown in the table above indicate that only 11 out of 40 people could be said to understand by the question what we had intended. Seven of the 40 could not say precisely what the question meant to them. The meaning most uniformly accepted by the others revealed an obvious confusion: respondents identified the German people with the German army.

It is significant to see that of those who opposed peace, the great majority understood the meaning of the question, whereas of those who favored peace the majority identified the German army with the German people.

The simple percentage answers to our original question, then, do not mean at all what they would appear to mean without further probing. Although most people might be in favor of stopping the war and discussing peace terms if the German people overthrew Hitler and made such an offer, they would not necessarily be in favor of doing so if on the other hand the army overthrew Hitler and made such an offer.

3. *Questions getting at some stereotype or overtone implicit in the question rather than at the meanings intended*

Here we chose for examination perhaps the most famous stereotype in the United States—the white against the Negro. A question was taken from National Opinion Research Center. "In general do you feel that right now Negroes have just as good a chance as white people to get defense jobs, or not?" In the interviews with the forty respondents this question was followed by other questions which determined opinion toward the Negro more realistically and behaviorally. Each of the questions concerning the Negro was widely separated from each of the others. Three questions in addition to that above were asked, "Do you think Negroes should be allowed to build homes in any neighborhood they want to, or do you think special areas should be set apart for them?" "Do you think that Negroes should be admitted to all colleges just like the white people?" "Do you think that colored people should be admitted to hotels and restaurants that have so far been closed to them?"

On the basis of comments and answers to the three more specific questions, respondents were divided into "sympathetic" and "unsympathetic" groups. If respondents answered in an anti-Negro direction on at least two of the three specific questions, they were classified as "unsympathetic." Comments of those we have called sympathetic and unsympathetic confirmed their opinions as expressed in answer to the direct questions. Some typical "sympathetic" remarks were: "If this is supposed to be a democracy, we are all supposed to be equal." "This should be a free country for Negroes as well as for whites." Some typical "unsympathetic" comments were: "I don't like niggers and that's all there is to it. I have seen enough of them to know they can't mix with whites." "They are an entirely different race. People just can't trust them."

TABLE 3. OPINION TOWARD NEGROES

In general do you feel that right now Negroes have just as good a chance as white people to get defense jobs, or not?	SHOULD BE ALLOWED TO BUILD			ADMIT TO COLLEGES			ADMIT IN HOTELS, ETC.		
	Yes, any-where	Special areas only	Don't Know	Yes	No	Don't Know	Yes	No	Don't Know
Just as good a chance									
Sympathetic 6	2	4	–	5	1	–	4	1	1
Unsympathetic 12	–	12	–	8	4	–	–	12	–
Not as good a chance									
Sympathetic 12	6	6	0	11	1	–	8	3	1
Unsympathetic 6	0	6	0	2	4	–	–	6	–

From this table we see that of the 18 people who were *sympathetic* to the Negro, 12 did not think the Negro has as good a chance in defense industries, whereas of the 18 who were *unsympathetic* to the Negro, 12 felt the Negro did have as good a chance.[3]

The only possible conclusion to draw here, then, is that opinion concerning the original question was affected by general prejudice against the Negro. The question is, in fact, really a fairly good index of Negro prejudice itself.

4. *Questions misunderstood because they involve technical or unfamiliar words*

The study of unfamiliar words or relatively technical terms was made around the concepts of "initiation fees" and "strict entrance requirements" as these phrases are used by labor unions. *Fortune* had asked the questions: "Which—C.I.O. or A.F. of L.—do you feel has the lowest initiation fees?" "Which—C.I.O. or A.F. of L.—do you feel has the strictest entrance requirements as regards the skill of its members?"

After our investigators had asked these two questions, they followed

[3] In this and some other instances reported below, cases do not add up to 40 because of incompleteness or inadequacy.

up considerably later in the interview with three questions also separated from each other: "The term *initiation fee* is sometimes used in connection with labor unions and other organizations. Could you tell me exactly what it means?" "Do you think that a person must have any particular experience and skills to become a member of the A.F. of L. or the C.I.O.?" "For the sake of a little experiment which we are conducting I would like you to do this. I will read to you a question which occurred in this interview. After you have heard me read it would you mind stating the question in your own words. Here it is: 'Which—C.I.O. or A.F. of L.—do you feel has the strictest entrance requirements as regards the skill of its members?' Now please say it in your own words."

A tally of the results reveals that out of the 40 respondents

5 understood correctly and volunteered the correct information before they were asked specific questions;

4 in addition to the 5 above were correctly consistent on all of their answers;

8 showed that they understood the terms "initiation fee" and were correct in their answer concerning the requirement of skill to join the A.F. of L. but did not give a strictly accurate interpretation when asked to repeat a technical question in their own words;

15 were inconsistent in that they contradicted their original answers;

8 were quite wrong or had no opinion.

It is conservative to conclude, therefore, that at least half of the people who answered the original question did not know precisely what they were talking about.

5. *Questions presenting issues not sufficiently circumscribed*

Frequently issues are posed to people in such general terms that answers are meaningless. Either one does not know to which of many possible parts of the issue the answer refers; or one is bewildered by the various degrees of conviction, intensity or interest which are possible with respect to the issue. A question asked by the American Institute of Public Opinion illustrates this situation. "Are you in favor of labor unions?"

In order to find out somewhat more accurately what the question really meant, we asked our 40 respondents six other questions listing somewhat more specific attitudes concerning labor unions.

Would you enter a store to make a purchase while the store is being picketed?

Do you think that the government should have more, less, or as much control as it has now over labor unions?

Do you think that the majority of labor leaders are honest?

As you know, a closed-shop agreement means that the employer promises to hire only union members. Do you think that there should be more, or fewer, or no closed-shop agreements?

Do you think that an employer has a harder time or an easier time with employees who belong to a union or do you think that it makes no difference?

Do you think labor unions should be permitted to go on if they get into the hands of radical leaders?

Thirty people, or an overwhelming majority of our small sample, said they were "in favor of labor unions." Only four stated they were not in favor of labor unions; six had no opinion. However, of the 30 who originally said they favored labor unions:

  8 would enter a store that was being picketed;
  8 said there should be fewer or no closed shops;
10 believed the majority of labor leaders are dishonest;
14 thought employers who had to work with union employees had a
     harder time than others;
18 believed the government should have more control over the unions;
25 felt that labor unions should be prohibited if they got into "radical"
     hands.

It seems clear then that answers to the question "Are you in favor of unions?" cannot be unequivocally interpreted. Different people mean different things when they answer the question in the affirmative. If opinions are to be meaningful, this issue, as well as many others, must be studied with a battery of questions presenting more circumscribed issues.

6. *Alternatives provided for answers not exhaustive*

The major advantage of the open-ended or free-answer question is obviously its ability to record opinion which is catalogued to the minimum degree by the investigator. When an issue has become fairly clear-cut, however, or where common sense and experience have shown that meaningful alternatives can be posed, there is little advantage to an open-ended question from the point of view of its faithfulness in reporting opinion.[4] There is even, on the contrary, a considerable disadvantage in the open-ended question from the point of view of reporting precise trends, keeping costs down, and avoiding bias in the coding of answers for statistical treatment.

With respect to issues that are not clear-cut, however, armchair attempts to design alternatives may often prove extremely misleading. This situation still obtains even if the armchair attempts have been forti-

[4] Cf. Chapter 2.

fied by considerable testing in the field. In many areas opinion is either so completely unstructured that people are suggestible to the latest conversation, news event, and columnist, or else their lack of interest, concern or information may mean that the answer they give to an interviewer is only a "top-of-the-head" answer—it means nothing except that they want to get on with the interview and get away or that they don't want to appear too ignorant.

A question used by OPOR on a national survey seemed to fit the qualifications for a bad choice of alternatives. The question, asked in January 1942 ran as follows: "If Russia should defeat Germany, which of these things do you think Russia would then try to do—try to spread Communism all through Europe, or work with Britain and the U. S. in making it possible for the countries of Europe to choose their own form of government?" The results of this survey were: 41 per cent try to spread Communism, 36 per cent work with Britain and the U. S., 23 per cent no opinion.

The 40 respondents were asked in this special study: "If Russia should defeat Germany, what do you think Russia would try to do next?" The answers tabulated below show that of the 40 respondents, only 3 could strictly be said to have answered either of the two alternatives posed by our earlier dichotomous question. Not more than five out of the 40 people, furthermore, gave answers which were strictly classifiable in any single category. Eighteen separate classifications were really needed if the answers of these 40 people were to be honestly classified so that individualistic meanings would not be lost.

TABLE 4. VARIETY OF RESPONSES TO OPEN QUESTION

1. All depends on how strong Russia and United Nations are.	1	operate it.	1
2. Continue conquests, fighting any noncommunist nation including U. S. A.	4	11. Try to defeat Japan and spread Communism in Germany.	1
3. Try to get part of Finland and Bessarabia, not any more.	2	12. Try to dominate U. S. A.	2
4. Declare war on Japan	5	13. Hope Russia would still be on our side.	2
5. Rebuild their country and mind their own business.	5	14. Try to form a democratic government in Russia.	1
6. Take back all countries Hitler has overrun.	1	15. Continue to cooperate with Allies.	2
7. Try to assume leadership of United Nations.	1	16. Spread Communism in Germany and not try to take Germany by force.	1
8. Demand that Allies put 4 freedoms into effect.	1	17. Try to communize Europe.	1
9. Try to get all they could.	1	18. Take some of smaller countries on border.	1
10. Try to take German property and		19. Can't answer.	7
			40

If one is willing to sacrifice some of the uniqueness of meaning, these 18 classifications can, of course, be combined. Such a broader classification might be:

		Response from Table 4
1.	Cooperate	15
2.	Mind their own business	5
3.	Make internal changes	14
4.	Spread Communism	2, 11, 16, 17
5.	Conquer more territory	3, 6, 9, 10
6.	Fight Japan	4
7.	Try to dominate United Nations	7, 8, 12, 18
8.	Depends	1, 13

This episode illustrates, then, in a clear-cut way the extent to which opinion can be forced when only a few narrow alternatives are provided in a questionnaire form.

7. Alternatives too many or too long

The advantages and disadvantages of using attitudinal scales in public opinion surveys are discussed elsewhere.[5] In addition to the fact that alternatives may not exhaust all possibilities, one of the chief dangers is that if several alternatives are presented to the respondent, even with cards, which are handed him and on which alternatives are printed, it is impossible for him to keep them in mind when selecting the opinion most like his own.

In order to test this problem we chose a question used by *Fortune* to get at opinion on post-war policy. "As far as America and the rest of the world are concerned, which one of these six policies comes closest to what you would like to see us do when the war is over?" After the respondent had made a choice from one of the six alternatives listed on the card, the original card was taken away from him. He was then given another card on which two of the six alternatives had been changed and one of the alternatives left out entirely. He was asked if he could tell which alternatives had been changed and which one had been left out. The second card handed the respondent, with the changes and omission, always included, however, the particular statement he had chosen. The interviewers had six cards ready and handed the appropriate one to the respondent. The original statements together with the changes used in the second presentation are listed below. All 40 of the respondents participated in this experiment.

[5] Chapter 2.

13

Original Statements

1. Stay at home and have just as little as possible to do with any other country.

2. Have as little as possible to do with any countries in Europe or Asia but form a new U. S. to include in one government all North and South American countries.

3. Use our influence to try to organize the world for peace but form no actual ties with any other country.

4. Form a new League or association with all the nations of the world and take an active part in making it work.

5. Try to form some close connection with the British Empire.

6. Form a new United States to include in one government all democracies in the world.

Changes

For 2. Have nothing to do with the countries in Europe but include in one government the Central American countries, U. S. and Canada.

For 4. Form a new League or association with all the nations of the world organizing them for peace, but form no actual ties with any other country.

For 5. Try to combine in one union all the English-speaking nations in the world.

For 6. Have the United States set up one democratic government to rule all countries in the world.

The results show that whereas 41 out of a possible 80 changes were correctly identified, only five respondents out of the 40 located correct omissions, illustrating the well-known psychological principle that recognition is easier than recall. Five respondents erroneously thought the statements they had chosen had been changed.

It is noteworthy that considerable difference in the ability of respondents to detect changes and omissions occurred with relation to the statement they originally chose. The rank order of the correct identification of changes according to question chosen was:

Statement 4	82% noted correct changes
" 1	50 " " "
" 6	43 " " "
" 3	39 " " "
" 2	0 " " "
" 5	Not chosen at all originally

When the original choices were tallied against the educational background of respondents, we find that those who chose statement 4 were the best educated of the group, 75 per cent of them being high school graduates compared to about 40 per cent of the total sample with this educational background.

It is also important to notice that the best recognition of changes was among persons who chose alternative 4, which expressed what is commonly regarded as the most enlightened point of view and the one that seems closest to the official policy of this government and the United Nations. Those who were second best in recognition were persons who had chosen statement 1, the most isolationist sentiment in the list. This circumstance gives some indication that persons who had thought most about the problem and for whom the problem had most meaning were able to discriminate more accurately alternative propositions concerning post-war participation.

It is clear, therefore—at least as far as this particular question is concerned—that the majority of respondents do not make a conscious choice of one among six alternatives which they bear clearly in mind.

8. *Questions whose implications are not seen*

In opinion surveys, answers to dichotomous questions or a simple attitudinal scale often seem reasonable enough when the straight percentages are examined. Sometimes, however, when the opinion expressed is compared with other opinions held by the same person, with comments, or with the interviewer's notes about the respondent, one begins to suspect that the implications of the question were not at all understood.

This situation has been tested on a national survey by OPOR. Again the question deals with an attitude toward the post-war world. It will be seen here that one population sample was presented a question stating two alternatives at the beginning of the interview, whereas people in the other sample were asked first whether they had given any thought to the problem as a whole; those who said they had not thought about it were followed up with the same questions asked of the first sample. In June 1942 we asked two comparable samples of the national population the following questions and obtained the following results.

One Form of Ballot:

Which of these things do you think the U. S. should try to do when the war is over:

Stay out of world affairs as much as we can, or	21%
Take an active part in world affairs?	68
Don't know or unable to choose	11

If "Stay Out" ask respondent:

If it should happen that there is trouble and other nations get ready again for war, do you think we should stay out of world affairs then?

Yes	61%
No	25
Couldn't happen	1
Don't know	10
Other	3

Suppose our standard of living is reduced when we try to get along on what we grow and produce at home; would you still think that it would be best to stay out of world affairs?

Yes	66%
No	14
Couldn't happen	6

Don't know	13%
Other	1

If "Take Active Part" ask respondent:

Have you ever considered the possibility that we might have to keep up a large army, navy and air force at great expense to help police the world if we want to take an active part in world affairs?

Yes	94%
No	6

If "Yes" ask: Do you think this expense would be justified?

Yes	97%
No	1
Don't know	2

If our trade with other countries after the war gets us involved in entangling alliances and power politics, as Europe always has been, would you still think it would be best to take an active part in world affairs?

Yes	82%
No	11
Don't know	7

Other Form of Ballot:

Have you given any thought to the role the U. S. should take in world affairs when the war is over?

Yes	68%
No	31
Don't know	1

If "Yes" ask: What part do you think the U. S. should play?

Don't know	2%
Economic and social readjustment	2
American Century; U. S. take leading part; run the world our way	42
Propose an international conference for peace	4
Active participation; vague phrases; partnership, United Nations	31
Advisory; promulgate democratic ideals, four freedoms	8
Prepare for and guard against	

next war; police world; strong army and navy	6%
Set up a U. S. of Europe	3
Clean up Washington politics	3
Stay out of world affairs, mind our own business, etc.	3
Yes, No answer, can't say, etc.	2

If "No" ask:

Which of these two things do you think the U. S. should try to do when the war is over?

Stay out of world affairs as much as we can	32%
Take an active part in world affairs	49
Don't know, or unable to choose	19

If "Stay Out" ask:

If it should happen that there is trouble and other nations get ready again for war, do you think we should stay out of world affairs then?

Yes	57%
No	28
Couldn't happen	3
Don't know	8
Other	4

Suppose our standard of living is reduced when we try to get along on what we grow and produce at home; would you still think that it would be best to stay out of world affairs?

Yes	61%
No	20
Couldn't happen	5
Don't know	13
Other	1

If "Take Active Part" ask:

Have you ever considered the possibility that we might have to keep up a large army, navy and air force at great expense to help police the world if we want to take an active part in world affairs?

Yes	82%
No	18

If "Yes" ask:

Do you think this expense would be justified?

Yes	93%
No	3
Don't know	4

If our trade with other countries after the war gets us involved in entangling alliances and power politics, as Europe always has been, would you still think it would be best to take an active part in world affairs?

Yes	61%
No	20
Don't know	19

One-third of the population admitted it had not thought at all about U. S. post-war problems. Among both samples it was possible to shift the opinion of about 20 per cent who said originally that we should stay out of world affairs, by presenting certain contingencies that might arise if their point of view became official policy. On the side advocating "taking an active part in world affairs" opinion was not so flexible, although here again there was considerable change when certain contingencies were mentioned. It is noteworthy, though naturally to be expected, that persons who said they had not given any thought to the problem proved more suggestible than the rest of the population.

Related to this experiment and on the same subject of post-war aims, five brief descriptions of possible roles the U. S. should play in the post-war world were compiled ranging from complete isolationism through U. S. imperialism to world cooperation. These alternatives were asked of a small but representative sample of 100 people. The statements and percentages are indicated below.[6]

There should be complete disarmament with all nations, including the United States, destroying their war weapons. Then all countries should share the goods of the world so there would be no difference between the "have" and "have not" nations.　　　　9%

[6] These statements are condensations of longer proposals following the same lines compiled by George Gallup and tested on a considerably larger sample. Gallup's results showed essentially the same tendencies as ours.

There should be an organization of nations with an international police force. No nation, including the United States, should have an army of its own. All nations, including the United States, should obey the new international organization which would try to keep security throughout the world. 15%

There will probably always be wars and we should not have to worry about settling problems in Europe and Asia. What we should do is keep a large army and navy to protect us from any nation that started a war against us. 32%

The Allies should form an organization to police the world, see that Germany, Italy, and Japan never get power again, and keep peace and security in the world. 19%

The United States must become the strongest nation in the world, take leadership in world affairs, and fight any nation which tries to take our leadership away from us. 25%

The important point here is that when implications are clearly stated we find in general a much more isolationist tendency than when the role of the U. S. in the post-war world is put in general terms. It is particularly clear that when cooperation is spelled out to include our cooperation with others as well as their cooperation with us, people are not so eager to follow this line of thinking. Also if disarmament is to mean disarmament of this country, if an international police force is to rule us as well as other people, we are not so sure that we want to give up our army or navy. This experiment confirms the results obtained in the nation-wide survey. Attempts to change opinion in the nation-wide survey seem surprisingly successful in view of the fact that respondents had to put themselves on the defensive in front of the interviewer when changes of opinion were made. Our figures, therefore, are probably conservative.

9. Questions concerned with only a portion of the population and therefore meaningless to many people

To imagine that questions on current issues publicly discussed or receiving wide attention in the press or on the radio are equally meaningful to all groups throughout the country is unrealistic. Obviously there is differential involvement of personal interest, background, and experience. One example of this fact lies in a consideration of how much persons with varying incomes should be taxed. We would expect that a person earning comparatively little would have difficulty projecting himself into the position of a person whose income was measured in terms of five or six figures.

From questions asked by the AIPO in March 1942 the following table was prepared, comparing the opinions of persons in four income groups with respect to their ideas of taxation on persons earning from $1,000 to $100,000 a year.

TABLE 5

	Those Earning Less than $1,000 a Year Say	Those Earning $1,000-$2,000 a Year Say	Those Earning $2,000-$5,000 a Year Say	Those Earning $5,000 a Year and over Say
About those earning $1,000 a year				
Average tax	$8.40	$4.50	$7.25	$11.50
% No answer	10	4	2	3
Total cases	415	562	407	87
About those earning $1,500 a year				
Average tax	$20	$18.50	$24	$39
% No answer	16	12	5	8
Total cases	360	538	369	78
About those earning $2,000 a year				
Average tax	$106	$56	$58	$80
% No answer	16	10	6	7
Total cases	415	562	407	87
About those earning $3,000 a year				
Average tax	$260	$170	$200	$150
% No answer	24	28	9	14
Total cases	360	538	367	78
About those earning $5,000 a year				
Average tax	$520	$470	$470	$490
% No answer	18	13	9	11
Total cases	415	562	407	87
About those earning $10,000 a year				
Average tax	$1,740	$1,480	$1,730	$1,640
% No answer	26	20	13	10
Total cases	360	538	362	78
About those earning $50,000 a year				
Average tax	$12,100	$14,400	$14,400	$16,800
% No answer	21	15	12	11
Total cases	415	562	407	87
About those earning $100,000 a year				
Average tax	$29,000	$31,000	$36,400	$42,300
% No answer	27	23	13	13
Total cases	360	538	367	78

The table shows a steady increase in the percentage of people refusing to state what an income tax should be as the amount to be taxed increases.

As gross income increases, the "no answer" of the lower-income group also increases more rapidly than the "no answer" of the higher-income brackets. It is apparent too, as Gallup has frequently pointed out, that the majority of people do not place income taxes nearly as high as does the Treasury Department.

To study this problem more carefully, 46 people, distributed within various income groups (8 upper, 16 middle, 22 lower) were carefully interviewed by the same interviewers who had done the work on our assignment of 40 cases. These respondents were asked the same questions as persons in the national poll. In addition we tried to find out more exactly how the person estimated the income tax that should be paid by people who were below or above him in the income scale, how sure he was that his figures were more or less right, how concerned he was personally about the income tax problem, and how meaningful the problem was to him.

On the basis of respondents' comments and interviewers' impressions, it was possible to draw up the following table indicating the concern and meaningfulness of the problem to persons in various income groups.

TABLE 6

	Upper	Middle	Lower
Are you concerned about the problem?			
Yes	8	8	8
No	..	8	14
Is problem meaningful?			
Yes	8	4	6
No	..	10	10
Lower income only	..	2	6

It is apparent here that as one goes down the income scale, the whole problem of income taxes is of less concern and meaning to persons in the lower income brackets. Typical comments show the difficulty experienced by people of low income in finding any standards of judgment on which to tax persons with high income:

(Wife of a janitor, when asked how much a person with $100,000 should pay.) "It is hard to say; the government can figure how he is accustomed to living and tax him. He must be paying an awful lot of taxes as is."

(Drugstore clerk, when asked how he estimated his figures.) "If a man can live on $1,000 and pay an income tax, a man earning $50,000 a year can well afford to pay $2,000."

(Truck driver, when asked how much a $50,000-a-year man should pay.) "That guy is taxed already. He is taxed so high I can't figure it out."

(Teletype operator, when asked how he determined income tax.) "If a man earning $5,000 pays so much, then a man earning $50,000 should pay ten times as much and a man earning $100,000 should pay twenty times as much. It's just a matter of arithmetics."

(Laundry worker.) "I don't earn enough to pay an income tax, so I don't know the answer to the question."

Thus the matter of income taxes seems to represent one of those technical questions where the public is unable to have opinions which the expert or even the public itself would regard as sound. Answers to such questions are extremely valuable because of the knowledge they provide of areas of ignorance.

10. *Questions getting only surface rationalizations*

Frequently the true answer to questions that are suspected of being loaded with rationalization can be obtained by follow-up questions comparing other opinions with the opinion already expressed, or by checking behavior. Rationalization is especially likely to occur in those situations where there is some social value placed on a particular answer. In connection with an experiment reported in Chapter 6 the question was asked: "Is your regular job in any way connected with the war effort?" (AIPO) The answer boxes provided were: "Yes, directly," "Yes, indirectly," "No." The 213 persons in this survey who said their work was either directly or indirectly connected with the war were then asked what they did. Analysis of the follow-up question showed:

31%   were in actual defense work,
27%   were doing something that really seemed closely connected with the war,
28%   had a very indirect connection even when their work was very liberally judged from the point of view of its relation to the war,
14%   were clearly rationalizing their positions.

Examples of indirect connections and rationalizations are indicated below.

Examples of Indirect Connection
    Supplying electricity and gas to production
    Selling glass and paint to camps

Dentist examining draftees
Bankers selling bonds
Carpenter on government houses
Railway clerk taking care of correspondence between civilians and
armed forces

Rationalization

(Street Cleaner)—"necessary to health."
(Instructor of Christian education)—"working with youth."
(Jeweler)—"if we don't pay taxes we can't win war."
(Janitor)—"building used for first-aid classes, sugar rationing."
(Manager Department Store)—"serving the public in war time."
(Drug Store Manager)—"selling defense stamps, keeping public
well."
(Manager Lumber Yard)—"buy defense bonds."
(Minister)—"helping to keep up morale of my people."
(Laundry Truck Driver)—"promoting better health by sanitation.
Making possible more time for housewives to spend on OCD
projects."
(Vegetable Peddler)—"helping public out—helping to feed them."
(Clerk in Store selling Orthopedic shoes)—"people are on their feet
more now with defense and all that and need care of their feet."
(Whisky Store Clerk)—"whisky provides more tax than any other
good."
(Service Station Operator)—"the company as a whole has a relation
to the war. It delivers gasoline and parts to Camp ———."
(Teacher of Physical Education)—"keeping up morale of people
through their children."
(Ash Collector)—"help keep city clean."
(Real Estate Broker)—"have to get homes and rentals for defense
people."

11. *Questions getting only stereotyped answers*

An extreme case of rationalization is one where an unusually high
social value is placed on a given answer or where answers altogether
reflect accepted stereotypes. In such instances an individual may hypo-
critically give an answer following an accepted stereotype knowing full
well that he does not believe it, or, what seems more likely in most
instances, the individual may feel that he is answering honestly but may
contradict himself, when brought down to earth by a more specific test
of the stereotype or value in question. A good example is the issue of
freedom of speech.

These figures clearly show that although practically everyone in the
U. S. says he is in favor of freedom of speech, such freedom seems

TABLE 7

AIPO (11/40)		OPOR (7/41)	
Do you believe in freedom of speech?		Do you think that in America anybody should be allowed to speak on any subject he wants to, or do you think there are times when free speech should be prohibited?	
Yes	97%		
No	1		
Don't know	2		
		Allowed at all times	44%
		Prohibit sometimes	53
		No Opinion	3

If "Yes": Do you believe in it to the extent of allowing Fascists and Communists to hold meetings and express their views in this community?

No	72%
Yes	23
No Opinion	5

If "Allow at all times": Do you believe in free speech to the extent of allowing Fascists and Communists to hold meetings and express their views in this community?

No	60%
Yes	37
No Opinion	3

based on the assumption that it is freedom for only certain types of people.

CONCLUSION

We have pointed out here almost a dozen pitfalls that must be avoided if the results obtained in surveys of public opinion are to be reliably interpreted. Many other difficulties remain to be studied. In practice, some, at least, of the sources of misinterpretation can be avoided by careful experimentation with a variety of alternatives and by analysis of results obtained with the use of small populations before larger surveys are undertaken. Sometimes, unfortunately, experience with larger samples is needed before inconsistencies and distortions can be detected.

It should be repeated again that in this study we deliberately stacked the cards to point up the problems that concerned us; the questions taken here from surveys already made by various public opinion investigators were used only for illustration. Difficulties such as those we have brought out are the exception rather than the rule in the work of any careful investigator. The blanket condemnations of public opinion surveys by some critics on the ground that the answers to questions can never really be understood are by no means warranted. Yet our results do sound a clear warning. Investigators must constantly be on the lookout for possible snags likely to be encountered between the time they themselves have a conception of an issue they want to pose to any sample population and the time they report the opinions of that population on the question they thought they were posing.

CHAPTER II

THE WORDING OF QUESTIONS[1]

I T WAS the clear recognition of the importance of wording which resulted in the inauguration of the split-ballot technique by the American Institute of Public Opinion over three years ago and its consistent use ever since. The same method is used often by the *Fortune* poll. The "split-ballot" technique consists of preparing each questionnaire in two alternative forms, each form being submitted to comparable cross-sections of the population. Some of the questions are varied on the two forms to test the effect of wording differences or various ways of presenting issues; other questions are the same on each form and serve as controls.

Because of the absence of any objective criteria of validity, a word must be said about the difficulty of evaluating alternative presentations of issues. It can easily be shown that two different phrasings of an issue yield different response distributions, but there is seldom any way of determining which presentation is the more valid; that is, which provides the more accurate index of the actual state of opinion on the issue. In most cases, evaluations of the relative merits of different presentations of an issue must rest on a priori considerations rather than upon more precise experimental evidence. Elections provide the most convincing means of validation. But conclusions from election predictions cannot be uncritically applied to other types of issues.

Several careful studies in the problem of question wording have already been reported.[2] Indeed, with the wealth of data now available from public opinion polls based on representative samples of the voting population, the study of the wording of questions can begin to take on new dimensions. Poll administrators have faced the problem of wording

[1] By Donald Rugg and Hadley Cantril. This chapter is a revised version of an article by the same authors which appeared in the *Journal of Abnormal and Social Psychology*, 1942, 37, 469-495, and is reprinted here with permission.

[2] See A. B. Blankenship, "Influence of the Question Form on Response in a Public Opinion Poll," *Psychological Record*, 1940, 3, 345-403; S. C. Menefee, "The Effect of Stereotyped Words on Political Judgments," *American Sociological Review*, 1936, 1, 614-621; H. Cantril, "Experiments in the Wording of Questions," *Public Opinion Quarterly*, 1940, 4, 330-332; W. A. Lurie, "The Measurement of Prestige and Prestige Suggestibility," *Journal of Social Psychology*, 1939, 9, 219-225; S. Roslow, W. H. Wulfeck, and P. G. Corby, "Consumer and Opinion Research: Experimental Studies on the Form of the Question," *Journal of Applied Psychology*, 1940, 24, 334-346; P. Studenski, "How Polls Can Mislead," *Harpers*, 1939 (December), 180, 80-83; J. G. Jenkins, *Psychology in Business and Industry*, New York: Wiley, 1935.

as practical men charged with the self-imposed responsibility to report public opinion honestly and faithfully. Hence they have frequently asked themselves, "How is the vote on this issue changed if we vary the wording?" But it must be remembered that public opinion data have in most cases not been gathered by poll administrators with any systematic problem in mind. The result is that data are scattered and often inconclusive in so far as generalization is concerned.

The major task confronting anyone who plunges into the data already accumulated, therefore, is the more or less systematic ordering of the material. The data are brought together here not because they provide any final answers but because they point to problems which must be squarely faced by technicians and because they do add to the material from which social psychology must be built.

RESULTS

The data have been grouped together around the following problems:

A. Effects of Context
>> Contingencies
>> Placement on ballot

B. The alternatives presented
>> Dichotomous vs. multiple choice
>> Order of alternatives
>> Explicit vs. implicit alternatives
>> Free answers

C. Deviations from "objective" wordings
>> Prestige
>> Stereotypes
>> Proposed legal changes
>> Biased wordings
>> Personalization of the question

A.   EFFECTS OF CONTEXT

Contingencies

If one wants to measure some very general attitude, he immediately wonders how he can most accurately pose the issue involved. Suppose one had wanted to measure "interventionism" in the United States before December 7, 1941. Should he simply ask whether the United States ought to declare war, should he poll on some of the numerous specific proposals (e.g. convoys) advanced by interventionist leaders, or should he try to devise some multiple-choice type of question which would attempt to measure graduations of interventionist sentiment? That there exists no single index of "interventionism" is obvious. The amount of interventionist sentiment found is a function of the particular issue used, of the wording of this issue, and of the general context in which it appears. Table 8 illustrates this variability in interventionist sentiment. It is based on the results of five American Institute of Public Opinion and Office of Public Opinion Research surveys, conducted during May, June and September of 1941. Since all the questions were not polled simultaneously, there may be some slight effect of the time element, but not sufficient to obscure the general pattern of differences.

Questions 1 and 3 demonstrate the tendency for replies to pile up on the "about right" alternative, when a middle ground is offered. They also show that when people can identify themselves with the policies of the "United States" rather than those of "President Roosevelt," they are likely to be more interventionist. Since the second question presents the issue of aid to Britain as a challenge, it is not surprising that a very large majority favor continued aid to Britain in this particular context. Whether the fourth question measured *current* interventionist sentiment is doubtful, in as much as it is probable that some of those voting "yes" on this question did not believe a British defeat was at that time inevitable without our help. The question does, however, indicate the strong support of convoys under the condition of a British defeat. The fifth question, in which the alternatives are clearly set against each other, reduces the interventionist vote considerably. The sixth question shows a majority in favor of convoys, although fewer favor them in this context than when a British defeat is predicated upon their absence. Question 7 shows a much larger number of adherents to a policy of direct military intervention than do the related questions 8, 9 and 10—probably due to the fact that the question is a conditional one, and secondarily to the presence of a prestige element. The difference between questions 8 and 9 shows more people in favor of military intervention if they can personally participate in the decision to declare war. Question 10 demonstrates the prejudicial effect of the phrase "send an army."

The data in this table clearly show the danger of interpreting any general opinion on the basis of less than a pattern of questions which place that opinion squarely in a number of contexts and surround it with varying contingencies just as it usually is in everyday life. Figure 1 tells the same story graphically.

Table 8

				% Interventionist Sentiment

1. So far as you, personally, are concerned, do you think the United States has gone too far in helping Britain, or not far enough? (AIPO 6/24/41)   78

Too far	15%	About right	46%
Not far enough	32	No Opinion	7

2. Some people say that if the United States goes on helping England, Germany may start a war against our country. Do you think we should continue to help England, even if we run this risk? (AIPO 5/6/41)   76

Yes 76%   No 21%   No Opinion 3%

3. So far as you, personally, are concerned, do you think President Roosevelt has gone too far in his policies of helping Britain, or not far enough? (AIPO 6/24/41)   74

Too far	20%	About right	57%
Not far enough	17	No Opinion	6

4. If it appears certain to you that Britain will be defeated unless we use part of our navy to protect ships going to Britain, would you favor, or oppose, such convoys? (AIPO 5/6/41)   73

Favor 73%   Oppose 23%   No Opinion 4%

5. Which of these two things do you think is more important for the United States to try to do—(OPOR 5/29/41)   58

To keep out of war ourselves   39% or,
To help England win, even at the risk
   of getting into the war?   58
No choice   3

6. Do you think the United States Navy should be used to convoy (guard) ships carrying war materials to Britain? (AIPO 6/24/41)   56

Yes 56%   No 35%   No Opinion 9%

7. If Roosevelt and our leading military experts say that Britain will be defeated unless we go into the war in the near future, would you favor, or oppose, going into the war within a few days? (AIPO 5/20/41)   51

Favor 51%   Oppose 41%   Don't know 8%

8. If you were asked to vote today on the question of the United States entering the war against Germany and Italy how would you vote—to go into the war now, or to stay out of the war? (AIPO 6/24/41)   22

Go in 22%   Stay out 72%   No Opinion 6%

9. Should the United States enter the war now? (OPOR 9/17/41)   17

Yes 17%   No 76%   No Opinion 7%

10. Should the United States go into the war now and send an army to Europe? (AIPO 9/17/41)   8

Yes 8%   No 88%   No Opinion 4%

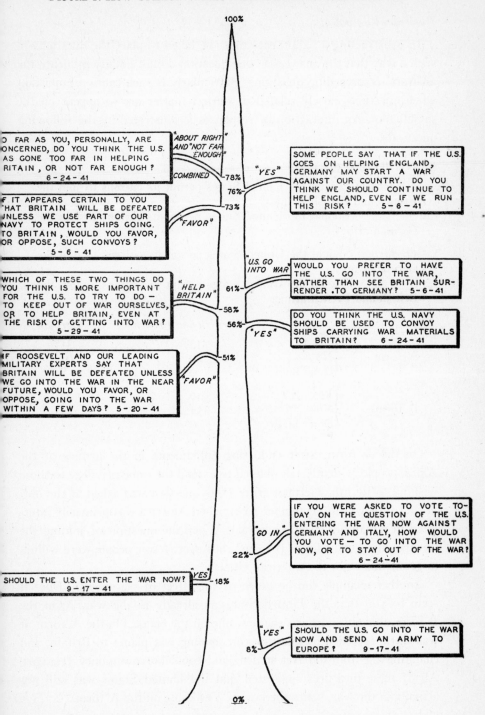

FIGURE 1. How Opinion Varies with Contingencies Involved

Placement on ballot

In constructing a ballot, care must be taken to place the questions in such a way that the answers to one question do not unduly influence the answers to succeeding questions. Particularly is such caution important when questions closely related in subject matter are to appear on the same ballot. An interaction of responses is illustrated by the following questions.

(AIPO 9/1/39)

(*A form:*) Should the United States permit its citizens to join the French and British Armies?
    Should the United States permit its citizens to join the German army?

(*B form:*) Should the United States permit its citizens to join the German army?
    Should the United States permit its citizens to join the British and French armies?

		British and French	German
A form	Yes	45%	31%
	No	46	61
	Don't know	9	8
B form	Yes	40	22
	No	54	74
	Don't know	6	4

On the A form, after endorsing enlistments in the armies of the Allies, people evidently felt obliged to extend the same privilege to those wishing to join the German army (this question was asked at the outbreak of the war in September 1939, when America was primarily interested in remaining strictly neutral). When the question of joining the German army came first (B form), however, fewer people were willing to grant this right to American citizens.

Another example can be given of the effect of placement. "Does it seem to you that the United States is already in the war?" On the B form, this question was the first one on the ballot. On the A form, it was sixth, preceded by questions on sending war planes to Britain, and changing the Johnson Act so England could borrow money from us. All of these measures suggested that the United States was still not actually in the war, hence the lower "Yes" vote on the A form.

(AIPO 1/9/41)	A form	B form
Yes	44%	52%
No	44	40
Undecided	12	8

Of course, one way to minimize the interaction of related questions is to place them as far apart as possible, in the hope that the intervening questions will prevent a carry-over effect. Even with such wide spacing, however, interaction cannot always be prevented, as the next set of questions indicates.

(*A form*—1st question on ballot) At present, men between the ages of 18 and 21 are not drafted. Do you think the law should be changed so that men between the ages of 18 and 21 would be included in the draft, along with those from 21 to 35?

(*A form*—10th question on ballot) At present, men between the ages of 21 and 35 are being drafted. Should the law be changed so that only men between the ages of 18 and 23 would be included in the draft?

(On the *B form*, the same two questions were asked, but the order was reversed; that is, question 1 on the A form was question 10 on the B form, and question 10 on the A form was question 1 on the B form.)

(AIPO 4/25/41)		A form	B form
A-1	Yes	53%	48%
B-10	No	42	46
	No Opinion	5	6
A-10	Yes	25	41
B-1	No	69	51
	No Opinion	6	8

The largest difference occurs on question A-10; B-1, which proposes to restrict the draft age to 18-23. People who had previously voted for inclusive 18-35 age limits on the A form were naturally less inclined to restrict it to 18-23 than were those who answered the question on the 18-23 limit first without having made any previous commitments. The obvious implications in this case is that questions as overlapping as those should not be asked on the same ballot.

It should not be concluded, of course, that the placement of a question *invariably* affects the response. Many negative instances could be cited, even of questions closely related in subject matter.

B. THE ALTERNATIVES PRESENTED

Dichotomous vs. *multiple choice*

The *Fortune* Survey has shown a consistent preference for questions of the multiple-choice form, sometimes dubbed the "cafeteria" question, while the AIPO, although by no means neglecting cafeteria questions, has used preponderantly the direct "yes-no" question. Gallup has defended the yes-no question on the ground that this is the usual type of choice with which the man in the street is faced.[3] Admitting the usefulness of the multiple-choice questions in fields where the choice of alternatives is not a dichotomous one, he nevertheless insists that the yes-no question is more accurate where the issue is clear-cut and calls for unqualified acceptance or rejection. Roper, on the other hand, reports that a four-part attitude scale toward the candidate gave a better prediction of the 1940 election results than did the straight yes-or-no question, "For whom do you expect to vote?"[4]

The relative merits of the multiple-choice and yes-no questions obviously cannot be decided categorically. Some comparisons of the two forms will show under what conditions one form is likely to be superior to the other. In May 1941, the AIPO asked the following split-ballot questions with these results:

(*A form*) If you were asked to vote today on the question of the United States entering the war against Germany and Italy, how would you vote—to go into the war, or to stay out of the war?

      Go in 29%   Stay out 66%   No. Op. 5%

(*B form*) Please tell me which of these policies you think the United States should follow at the present time. (Interviewer hands card to respondent containing the following statements.)

A. Go to war at once against Germany and Italy	6%
B. Supply Britain with all war materials we can and also use our navy to convoy ships carrying these materials to Britain	36
C. Supply Britain with all war materials we can, but do *not* use our navy to convoy these materials	46
D. Stop all further aid to Britain	7
Other replies	1
No Opinion	4

[3] G. Gallup, "Question Wording in Public Opinion Polls," *Sociometry*, 1941, 3, 259-268.

[4] E. Roper, "Checks to Increase Polling Accuracy," *Public Opinion Quarterly*, 1941, 5, 87-90.

It is quite apparent that when a more moderate course was offered, fewer people favored a policy of direct military intervention. Where several distinct alternatives existed with regard to intervention, the B form undoubtedly provided a more realistic presentation of the problem. But if an actual war referendum were in the offing the B form would tend to underestimate the percentage of those voting for outright war.

The multiple-choice question is definitely superior in some cases because it provides for the expression of graduation of attitude, sacrificed in the yes-no type of question. There are, however, possible dangers in the use of the cafeteria question and certain cautions which must be exercised in using it. Gallup points out that a multiple-choice question may, by providing several qualified alternatives, enable respondents to avoid expressing an opinion on the main issue; also that in this situation there operates a human tendency to avoid extreme positions in favor of more moderate ones.[5] If, however, an issue does contain several genuine alternatives, there is very good reason to present these alternatives, not to force them into the framework of a yes-no form.

Once it is decided to put a certain issue in the multiple-choice form, care must be taken to choose realistic alternatives, with a minimum of overlapping. Also, objectivity should be sought by balancing the number of alternatives pro and con. An experiment conducted by the AIPO neatly demonstrates how a preponderance of alternatives on one side or the other can bias the results obtained.[6] On the A form of the ballot this question was used:

Please tell me which of these policies you think the United States should follow at the present time:

1. Go to war at once against Germany and Italy.
2. Supply Britain with all war materials we can send and also use our navy to convoy ships carrying these materials to Britain.
3. Supply Britain with all war materials we can, but do not use our navy to convoy these materials.
4. Return to our previous policy of supplying only those materials which Britain can pay cash for and come and get here.
5. Keep completely neutral by limiting our aid to Britain to foodstuffs and medical supplies.
6. Stop all further aid to Britain.

[5] G. Gallup, *loc. cit.*
[6] Since this experiment was based on a sample taken in only a few cities, the results, while valid for the split-ballot comparison, do not represent opinion in the country as a whole.

The alternatives offered on the B form were:

1. Go to war at once against Germany and Italy with our full military power.
2. Go to war but send only part of our navy and air force and no men of the U. S. army.
3. Supply Britain with all war materials we can and also use our navy to convoy ships carrying these materials to Britain.
4. Go to war but limit our action at this time to this hemisphere.
5. Supply Britain with all war materials we can, but do not use our navy to convoy these materials.
6. Stop all further aid to Britain.

The A form was made reasonably objective by including two degrees of interventionist position, one "borderline" (no. 3), and three graded alternatives on the isolationist side. Form B, on the other hand, was deliberately overweighted with interventionist alternatives (1, 2, 3, 4). The only statement on the isolationist side was an extreme one (6). The results on these alternate forms are shown in Table 9 below.

TABLE 9

Alternative no.	A Form Per cent in Favor		Type of alternative	B Form Per cent in Favor	Alternative no.
1	9%	} 35%	Interventionist	12%	1
			Interventionist	9	2
2	26		Interventionist	22	3
			Interventionist	4	4
3	23		Borderline	36	5
4	13	} 24%	Isolationist		
5	7		Isolationist		7%
6	4		Isolationist	7	6
	18		No Opinion	10	

The next three comparisons offer a modified multiple-choice question versus a straight yes-no.

(AIPO 5/3/40)

(*A form*) During the next four years do you think business should be regulated to a greater extent by the Federal Government?

Yes 28%   No 55%   Don't know 17%

(*B form*) During the next four years, do you think there should be more regulation or less regulation of business, by the Federal Government, than at present?

More 23%   About the same 16%   Less 46%   No Op. 15%

(AIPO 5/3/40)

(*A form*) Do you think labor unions should be regulated to a greater extent by the Federal Government?

   Yes 62%   No 20%   Don't know 18%

(*B form*) During the next four years, do you think there should be more regulation or less regulation of labor unions, by the Federal Government, than at present?

 More 53% About the same 12% Less 16% No Op. 19%

(NORC 9/42)

(*A form*) After the war, do you think the Federal Government should regulate Gas and Electric Companies more or less than it did before the war started (say 1938)?

  More 40% Same 23% Less 16% Depends 2%
        Don't know 19%

(*B form*) After the war, do you think the Federal Government should regulate Gas and Electric Companies more, less or about the same as it did before the war started (say 1938)?

  More 23% Same 54% Less 8% Depends 2%
        Don't know 13%

On the B forms of the first two examples, the "about the same" alternative, although not included in the phrasing of the question, appears as an answer box on the ballot, so that people expressing this opinion can be properly recorded by the interviewer. The A forms make no provision for such an alternative. Logically, people who hold this position should fall into the "No" category on the A forms, but from the results it appears that some of them also select the "Yes" column. The B form seems preferable, then, in that it provides for an additional graduation of opinion.

Another instance of the effect of restricting choices is illustrated in the following questions on the Dies Committee.

(AIPO 2/16/39)

(*A form*) Do you think the Dies Committee has done a good job or a poor job so far?

  Good job 48%   Poor job 21%   No Op. 31%

(*B form*) How good a job do you think the Dies Committee has done so far? (The following answer boxes were provided for classifying the respondents' answers)

  Excellent 10%   Good 24% Fair 31%
  Poor   7%   Very bad 5% No Op. 23%

The "Fair" category, not provided on the A form, receives the largest percentage of responses on the B form.

A question on the NLRB was presented in a similar manner except that on the A form a "fair" answer box was provided, although this alternative was not stated in the question. This expedient yielded comparable results with the B form; that is, "excellent" plus "good" answers on the B form approximately equaled the "good" on the A form; the "fair" percentages were the same on both forms, and the "poor" and "very bad" on the B approximated the "poor" on the A form.

Where a genuine intermediate step exists, as it does in these questions, distortion inevitably results when answers are forced into a dichotomy. Whether a three- or a five-step scale should be used depends on the nature of the issue and the purposes of the inquiry.

In using a trichotomy of two extreme steps plus a middle ground, the problem arises as to whether the middle position ought to be stated in the question, or whether it ought to be provided only in the answer boxes. Where opinion is well crystallized, it probably makes little difference which procedure is followed. Notice the following example.

(AIPO 12/13/39)

(*A form*) Do you think liquor regulations here are too strict, not strict enough, or about right?

    Too strict 6%   Not strict enough 45%   About right 40%
                         No Opinion 9%

(*B form*) Do you think liquor regulations here are too strict or not strict enough?

      Too strict 7%   Not strict enough 47%   About right 37%
                       No Opinion 9%

On any issue where opinion is not so well structured, the insertion of the "about right" alternative in the question itself would draw more people to this position than if it were not thus directly suggested. Under these conditions, it is debatable as to which form should be used. Providing a middle ground position may allow people to avoid the issue; on the other hand, if there is a genuine middle alternative, it is desirable to make it clear that it exists rather than partially ruling it out by not including it in the question.

Order of alternatives

In devising an objective type of question, one is confronted with the problem of the placement of alternatives. For example, should the question read, "Do you think the United States will go into the war in

Europe or do you think we will stay out of the war?" or should it be phrased, "Do you think the United States will stay out of the war in Europe or do you think we will go into the war?" On the surface, it would not appear that a minor variation of this sort should make much difference in the results. Yet there is evidence to show that when one of these alternatives is mentioned second it receives a few more votes than when it comes first. The differences, while not great, appear consistently on repeated polls of the question.

Similarly, on the question:

"Which of these two statements do you think is closer to the truth?
1. England is now fighting mainly to keep her power and wealth.
2. England is now fighting mainly to preserve democracy against the spread of dictatorship,"

interchanging the position of the two alternatives shows that when either of the alternatives is mentioned second, it polls correspondingly more votes than when it is first. It appears that when the question is a fairly complicated one, there is a tendency for the respondent to select the last, more easily remembered, alternative.

The positive evidence for the influence of position comes chiefly from the examples cited above. In a number of other cases, interchanging the position of the alternatives failed to produce significant differences.

Although we cannot draw any hard and fast conclusions regarding the effect of position, certain safeguards ought to be observed. It has been shown previously that suggestibility is likely to be greatest in areas where opinion is relatively uncrystallized. When polling on issues in such areas, therefore, it is particularly advisable to use split-questions on which the position of the alternatives is interchanged. Similarly, on complicated questions, where the factor of recency may operate in favor of the second alternative, it is wise to provide a check in the form of a split-question.

Explicit vs. *implicit alternatives*

A frequent problem in the formation of dichotomous questions is whether or not to write out both alternatives or to state only one, letting the respondent gather the second alternative by inference. There are so far insufficient data from which to generalize. In some instances it appears to make little difference whether or not both alternatives are explicitly stated; in other instances where people are likely to be suggestible, a significant difference may be obtained. The following three questions illustrate the problem and typical results. In the first instance, a difference is obtained on a question which has concerned comparatively few people; in the second and third instances, the issues have long confronted and involved nearly everyone.

(AIPO 8/26/41)

(*A form*) Do you think workers should have the right to elect a representative on the Board of Directors of the company they work for?

Yes 61%   No 23%   No Opinion 16%

(*B form*) Do you think workers should have the right to elect a representative on the Board of Directors of the company they work for, or should all the directors be elected by the owners of the company?

Workers should have right to elect   53%
All directors elected by owners   31
No Opinion   16

(AIPO 2/14/41)

(*A form*) Should the United States stop giving aid to Britain?

Yes 10%   No 87%   No Opinion 3%

(*B form*) Should the United States stop giving aid to Britain, or should we continue to help the British?

Stop helping 7%   Continue 89%   No Opinion 4%

(AIPO 11/10/42)

(*A form*) If the question of prohibition came up again, would you vote to make the whole country dry?

Yes 23%   No 68%   Undecided 9%

(*B form*) If the question of national prohibition should come up again, would you vote wet, or dry?

Wet 65%   Dry 28%   No Opinion 7%

An experiment in the wording of questions was done by NORC involving the use of three comparable sample populations. Comparisons of the A and B forms below show that the blunt statement concerning the need to hate our enemies (A form) gets less attention than the same idea when juxtaposed with its opposite (B form). The differences between the B and C forms illustrate again the importance of context, the C form placing the problem more directly in the setting of a challenge that we can win the war.

(NORC 9/42)

(*A form*) Do you think it is necessary to hate our enemies in order to win the war?

Hate necessary 24%   Hate not necessary 72%   Don't know 4%

(*B form*) Do you think it is necessary to hate our enemies in order to win the war, or do you think we can win the war without hating our enemies?

Hate necessary 31%   Hate not necessary 64%   Qualified 1%
                        Don't know 4%

(*C form*) Do you think we can win the war without hating our enemies, or do you think it is necessary to hate our enemies in order to win the war?

Hate necessary 37%   Hate not necessary 57%   Don't know 6%

In the same experiment NORC found a startling difference on the following two questions, showing clearly that people felt we should begin to think about peace as of September 1942, but not if such thinking would hamper the war effort.

(NORC 9/42)

(*A form*) Do you think we ought to start thinking now about the kind of peace we want after the war?

Yes 81%   No 15%   Don't know 4%

(*B form*) Which of these seems better to you—for us to win the war first and then think about the peace, or to start thinking now about the kind of peace we want after the war?

Win war first 55%   Plan Peace now 41%   Don't know 4%

Free answers

We have so far considered the relative merits of the multiple-choice and dichotomous questions. One other type remains—the free answer, where no definite alternatives are set by the question, and the respondent simply answers the question in his own words. For example, he may be asked (if a preceding question has established the fact that he thinks the United States will eventually enter the war) : "About how soon do you think we will be in the war?" Replies to this question gave the following distribution:

(AIPO 4/8/41)

2 months or less	12%
3 months	8
4 to 6 months	22
Later estimates	31
No Opinion	27

A comparable group was confronted with the dichotomous question: "Do you think we will be in the war within two months?" The answers were: Yes—25 per cent; No—46 per cent; Don't know—29 per cent.

This split provides another illustration of suggestion. When opinion tends to be vague and unstructured on a difficult question like this, and when a definite answer is suggested, as in the second form, different results are produced than when the free-answer situation prevails.

The importance of the degree of crystallization of opinion for the wording of questions is nicely illustrated by another free answer *vs.* stated alternatives split (AIPO 6/29/39). On one form of the ballot, people were asked, "Which European leader, now alive, do you like least?" On the other form, the same question was asked, but respondents where then shown a card containing the names of prominent European leaders. The use of the card had no significant effect, except that it reduced by 9 per cent the amount of no opinion. Perhaps the chief reason for this absence of differences was that dislikes were clearly focused—mostly around Hitler, who was in a class by himself. His partner and closest rival, Mussolini, got about 9 per cent of the votes to Hitler's more than 70 per cent.

On the other hand, the use of a card on the question, "Which European political leader, now alive, do you like best?" produced very significant differences by comparison with the free answer situation. People found it much more difficult to answer the question without the aid of a list of names from which to choose (36 per cent no opinion without the cards, 15 per cent with it). At the time, Chamberlain was the most popular leader under both conditions, but in the free-answer situations he was mentioned by only 24 per cent, as compared with 51 per cent when his name appeared on a card. Anthony Eden, second choice in the free-answer list, was completely displaced by Daladier when his name appeared on the card.

C. Deviation from "Objective" Wording

Prestige

All persons constructing ballots are cautioned not to warp answers by using symbols of prestige. Stagner has been particularly critical of the polls for their use of prestige names.[7]

Before we consider the problem of just how much difference prestige makes, the validity of the basic assumption that the use of prestige names is necessarily bad should be examined. For the academically inclined person taught to evaluate proposals purely on their intrinsic merit, the introduction of an extraneous standard of judgment, such as a prestige

[7] R. Stagner, "A Comparison of the Gallup and Fortune Polls Regarding American Intervention Policy," *Sociometry*, 1941, 3, 239-258.

name, is prejudicial and therefore bad technique. The public as a whole, however, unfortunate though the fact may be, does not react to issues in a detached scientific manner. Reaction to symbols, stereotypes, and prestige associations is part and parcel of the process of popular judgment. In many cases, then, an issue cannot be realistically divorced from the names of its sponsors or supporters, since it is presented to the public with a prestige context, as "the President's proposal," "Colonel Lindbergh's statement," "or Hitler's aim," and it is in such a context that people respond to it.

This consideration, of course, does not mean that any issue must be presented, willy-nilly, with the name of its most prominent supporter attached to it. For one thing, many people may be unaware of its sponsorship, in which case the presence of such a name could be considered unfairly biasing. But on an issue such as the Lend-Lease Bill, whose sponsorship was certainly no secret, there seems no good reason to avoid referring to it as "the President's Lend-Lease Bill."

Instead of placing an indiscriminate ban on the use of prestige names, it is better to determine whether any given issue can be more fairly and realistically presented with or without the attachment of a prominent supporter's name. When in doubt, the best procedure is to use a split ballot, with the name on one form and not on the other. Results of several such splits will be given and considered in relation to the whole problem of prestige.

The largest prestige effect resulting from the use of President Roosevelt's name occurred on the following questions.

(AIPO 6/24/41)

(*A form*) So far as you, personally, are concerned, do you think President Roosevelt has gone too far in his policies of helping Britain, or not far enough?

Too far	20%
About right	57
Not far enough	17
No Opinion	6

(*B form*) So far as you, personally, are concerned, do you think the the United States has gone too far in helping Britain, or not far enough?

Too far	15%
About right	46
Not far enough	32
No Opinion	7

Here the largest difference is in the "not far enough" column, which is sharply decreased when the President's name is used. At the same time, more people endorse the "about right" position, and more are also inclined to think Roosevelt has gone too far than when the question is stated in terms of the "United States." On a subsequent repetition of this split, these differences were greatly reduced, although the same pattern was evident. It may be, of course, that people differentiate between President Roosevelt's *policies*, and what the "United States" has actually done in the way of helping Britain, so that this split does not necessarily constitute merely a test of prestige.

In only one other case did the use of the President's name significantly change the results obtained.

(OPOR 7/10/41)

(*A form*) It has been said recently that in order to keep the Germans out of North and South America we must prevent them from capturing the islands off the west coast of Africa. Do you think we should try to keep the Germans out of the islands off the west coast of Africa?

(*B form*) President Roosevelt said recently that in order to keep the Germans out of North and South America we must prevent them from capturing the islands off the west coast of Africa. Do you think we should try to keep the Germans out of the islands off the west coast of Africa?

	With Roosevelt's name	Without Roosevelt's name
Yes	56%	50%
No	24	21
No Opinion	20	29

The prestige effect of the President's name is both positive and negative: both the "Yes" and "No" percentages are increased, although the increase in the "No" percentage is not statistically significant.

On a number of other questions, on which split-ballot results were available—dealing with such issues as the passage of the Lend-Lease Bill, the adequacy of the national defense effort, conscription of the National Guard for military training, fighting to protect Canada against attack, etc.—there was in no single case a significant difference due to the prestige effect of using President Roosevelt's name. We are left with only the one clear-cut example of Roosevelt's prestige, viz., the question of keeping the Germans out of the islands off the coast of Africa, a question upon which opinion was relatively unformed.

On the evidence from rather limited data, it appears that isolationist leaders had negative prestige, as indicated by the results of the following two questions.

(AIPO) 8/9/40)

(*A form*) Lindbergh says that if Germany wins the war in Europe, the United States should try to have friendly trade and diplomatic relations with Germany. Do you agree or disagree?

(*B form*) It has been suggested that if Germany wins the war in Europe, the United States should try to have friendly trade and diplomatic relations with Germany. Do you agree or disagree?

	With Lindbergh	*Without Lindbergh*
Agree	46%	57%
Disagree	41	25
Don't know	13	18

(OPOR 7/10/41)

(*A form*) Senator Wheeler says that the power of the United States should be put behind a peace movement to end the war now. Do you agree, or disagree with Senator Wheeler's statement?

(*B form*) It has been said recently that the power of the United States should be put behind a peace movement to end the war now. Do you agree, or disagree?

	With Wheeler	*Without Wheeler*
Agree	38%	43%
Disagree	50	48
No Opinion	12	9

Lindbergh's name both crystallizes opinion in the unfavorable direction and also shifts those who would otherwise approve of the policy to an attitude of disapproval. The effect of introducing Wheeler's name, though not so clear-cut, gives evidence again of negative prestige.

Prestige can, of course, be achieved in other ways than with the use of headline names. For example, on the first question below, the prestige effect of the phrase "health clinics" is evident, while on the second, the fact that a bill has been introduced in Congress produces a more favorable response.

(AIPO 12/22/39)

(*A form*) Would you like to see government health clinics furnish birth control information to married people who want it?

(*B form*) Would you like to see the government furnish birth control information to married people who want it?

	"Govt. health clinics"	*"The government"*
Yes	71%	64%
No	18	25
No Opinion	11	11

(AIPO 5/26/39)

(*A form*) A bill has been introduced in Congress to prohibit the advertising of liquor and beer. Do you favor this bill?

(*B form*) Do you think liquor advertising should be prohibited?

	A form	*B form*
Yes	40%	35%
No	49	56
No Opinion	11	9

Stereotypes

Various investigators have shown how the acceptance value of a proposition is changed if it is attached to emotionally toned stereotypes. In Chapter 1 the stereotyped nature of answers to a general question on freedom of speech was noted. Further corroborating examples from the polls can be cited.

The following questions show that when the phrases "go to war," and "training for war," are associated with any issue, it becomes less acceptable.

(AIPO 9/22/39)

(*A form*) If Canada is actually invaded by any European power, do you think the United States should use its army and navy to aid Canada?

(*B form*) If Canada is actually invaded by any European power, do you think the United States should go to war to defend Canada?

	A form	*B form*
Yes	71%	64%
No	23	29
Don't know	6	7

(AIPO 3/23/38)

(*A form*) Should military training be part of the duties of those who attend CCC camps?

(*B form*) Do you think part of the duties of those who attend CCC camps should be training for war?

	A form	B form
Yes	70%	59%
No	23	35
No Opinion	7	6

And in the last week of October 1941, when 24 per cent of the population answered "Yes" to the question, "Should the United States enter the war now?" only 17 per cent of a comparable population voted "Yes" on the question, "Should the United States declare war on Germany now?" A declaration of war seemed more dangerous and final.

Proposed legal changes

The suggestion that a law must be changed in order to carry out a specified policy immediately creates a certain amount of opposition on the part of many people who would otherwise be in favor of the adoption of such a policy. In the two following comparisons, policies are presented for approval or disapproval with the indication on one form that a change of existing laws is involved, but without any such indication on the other.

(AIPO 9/19/39)

(*A form*) Do you think Congress should change the Neutrality Law so that England and France can buy war supplies here?

(*B form*) Do you think England and France should be allowed to buy war supplies in this country?

	A form	B form
Yes	53%	61%
No	33	31
No Opinion	14	8

(AIPO 4/19/39)

(*A form*) We are prevented by law from lending money to foreign countries whose war debts are not paid up-to-date. Do you think we should change this law so that we might lend money to England and France, if there is another war in Europe?

(*B form*) In case Germany and Italy go to war against England and France, should we lend money to England and France to buy airplanes and other war materials in this country?

	A form	B form
Yes	20%	29%
No	75	65
No Opinion	5	6

The next set of questions shows that the proposal of "adding a law to the Constitution" is viewed with less alarm than the suggestion that "the Constitution be changed" to achieve the same purpose.

(AIPO 11/30/39)

(*A form*) Would you favor adding a law to the Constitution to prevent any President of the United States from serving a third term?

(*B form*) Would you favor changing the Constitution to prevent any President of the United States from serving a third term?

	A form	B form
Yes	36%	26%
No	50	65
No Opinion	14	9

Biased wordings

It is almost meaningless to ask whether or not opinion can be affected by biased wordings in the questions. It all depends on the issue involved. The primary use of biased wordings is to provide a method for the determination of the stability of opinion.

An example of the operation of suggestion is seen in the following two questions, asked in October 1939 by AIPO. At this time the public was undecided concerning the likelihood of U. S. involvement in the war.

(*A form*) Do you think the United States will go into the war before it is over?

Yes 41%   No 33%   Don't know 26%

(*B form*) Do you think the United States will succeed in staying out of the war?

Yes 44%   No 30%   Don't know 26%

But differences of opinion by no means always appear when wordings are deliberately forced. For example, in July 1941 OPOR wanted to test the stability of U. S. opinion with respect to aid to Britain after the entrance of Russia into the war. The following questions show that here wording made no difference.

(*A form*) Some people say that since Germany is now fighting Russia, as well as Britain, it is not as necessary for this country to help Britain. Do you agree, or disagree with this?

Agree 20%   Disagree 72%   No Opinion 8%

(*B form*) Some people say that since Germany will probably defeat Russia within a few weeks and then turn her full strength against Britain, it is more important than ever that we help Britain. Do you agree, or disagree with this?

Agree 71%   Disagree 19%   No Opinion 10%

Elmo Roper, director of the *Fortune* Survey,[8] has reported two experiments on the problem of question wording. In the first of these, several issues related to the war were each presented in three forms: first, as straight unloaded questions ("Do you think Hitler wants to dominate the United States?"); second, with an interventionist bias ("Hitler will never be satisfied until he dominates the United States because it is the richest country in the world"—agree or disagree); and third, with a noninterventionist bias ("Hitler is only interested in making Germany a powerful nation in Europe, and talk about his wanting to dominate this country is just British propaganda"—agree or disagree). One group received the set of unbiased questions, while a comparable group received the "interventionist" set, and a third group the "noninterventionist" set.

The most important finding here was that on issues where people were uncertain, it was possible to produce sizable effects by biasing the issue with an interventionist or noninterventionist argument, but where opinion was well crystallized, biasing statements had relatively little effect on the results. The two following questions from Roper's study illustrate this point.

Unbiased Wording	*Interventionist Wording*	*Noninterventionist Wording*
Do you think that Hitler wants to dominate the U.S.?	Hitler will never be satisfied until he dominates the U.S. because it is the richest country in the world	Hitler is only interested in making Germany a powerful nation in Europe, and talk about his wanting to dominate this country is just British propaganda.
Yes 69% No 23 Don't know 8	Agree 68% Disagree 23 Don't know 9	Disagree 68% Agree 21 Don't know 11
Do you think we would be able to keep our democratic form of government if Hitler dominates the rest of the world?	If Hitler wins, we won't be able to keep our democratic form of government long because we will be one nation against the rest of the world.	This country was built up mainly by people who came here to get freedom, and we will keep our democratic form of government even if Hitler does dominate the rest of the world.
No 40% Yes 44 Don't know 16	Agree 47% Disagree 37 Don't know 16	Disagree 27% Agree 60 Don't know 13

As a second part of the experiment each of these three groups was given some identical questions. The supposition was that the group

[8] *Fortune* Survey, Vol. 23, No. 4 (April 1941), p. 102; Vol. 23, No. 6 (June 1941), p. 70.

which had been subjected to the series of questions biased in the interventionist direction might return more interventionist answers on this identical set that did the other groups (who received noninterventionist and neutrally worded questions). Such, however, did not prove to be the case. The replies of all three groups on these identical questions were essentially similar, indicating that the arguments to which they had been subjected had little or no carry-over effect.

A second similar experiment was conducted, using several labor issues, these being stated neutrally, with a prounion bias, and with an antiunion bias. The questions dealt with the desirability of permitting labor in defense industries to strike for such things as working conditions, hours, wages, closed shop, and jurisdictional disputes. The prounion arguments were found to be ineffective, except on the question dealing with working conditions. The antiunion phrasings, however, had a very definite biasing influence, in that they elicited a significantly greater percentage of antiunion responses than did the neutral or prounion statements. The effect is illustrated below by an example taken from Roper's data. There was, furthermore, a carry-over effect in this antiunion group when, as in the previous experiment, the three groups were presented with a set of identical questions dealing with strikes in nondefense industries. The antiunion group returned a larger proportion of antiunion responses on these identical questions than did the neutral and prounion groups. The latter groups were not significantly different on either the biased or identical questions.

Unloaded	*Prounion*	*Antiunion*
Do you think that the government should or should not forbid labor in defense industries the right to strike about working conditions?	Because every man is entitled to safe and healthy working conditions, labor (in defense industries) should be allowed to strike for them.	Because working conditions in this country are the best in the world, labor (in defense industries) should not be allowed to strike about them.
Should 59%	Disagree 45%	Agree 74%
Should not 29	Agree 45	Disagree 17
Don't know 12	Don't know 10	Don't know 9

Personalization of the question

"Personalization" in this context refers, not to the use of the so-called "subjective" type of question, "Do you think, etc.?" but to a form of question which requires the respondent to say whether or not he himself would carry out a specified course of action. The polls afford but few illustrations of such personalized questions, but those which have been asked show interesting results.

On three repetitions of the following split, the "Go in" percentage on the B form ran from 7 to 12 per cent higher than on the A form, clearly significant differences in each case.

(*A form*) Do you think the United States should declare war on Germany and send our army and navy abroad to fight?

(*B form*) If the question of the United States going to war against Germany and Italy came up for a national vote within the next two or three weeks, would you vote to go into the war, or to stay out of the war?

Returns from a similar comparison which has been repeated in split form seven times has averaged 4.5 per cent more in favor of entering the war if people are asked to vote. (*A form*: "Should the United States enter the war now?" vs. *B. form*: "If you were asked to vote today on the question of the United States entering the war against Germany and Italy, how would you vote—to go into the war, or to stay out of the war?")

In one sense, the use of the B form is not realistic, since there exists at present no constitutional provision for a popular referendum on the declaration of war. Yet the results do reveal the effect of phrasing the issue in terms of personal participation. People are less resistant to a policy of military intervention if they feel that they will have a direct part in determining that policy.

Another example of the operation of personalization is afforded by the following two questions:

(AIPO 3/6/40)

(*A form*) In the census which the government is taking this spring, every adult in the country will be asked how much money he or she makes. Do you think people should object to giving the census taker this information about themselves?

Yes 30%   No 64%   No Opinion 6%

(*B form*) In the census which the government is taking this spring, every adult in the country will be asked how much money he or she makes. Will you have any objections to giving a census taker this information about yourself?

Yes 22%   No 77%   No Opinion 1%

The protest vote is greater on the A form, which allows the respondent to register an objection without appearing to be personally uncooperative. In trying to estimate the actual degree of opposition in obtaining the information, it would probably be more accurate to use the indirect, i.e. A form of the question.

A final instance of the effect of personalization is provided by these split questions on the expansion of our army, navy, and air force, asked in May 1940, by AIPO.

(*A form*) Should the United States do any of the following at this time?

   (a) Increase our army further, even if it means more taxes?
      Yes 88%   No 9%   No Opinion 3%

   (b) Increase our navy further, even if it means more taxes?
      Yes 83%   No 12%   No Opinion 5%

   (c) Increase our air force further, even if it means more taxes?
      Yes 90%   No 6%   No Opinion 4%

(*B form*) Should the United States do any of the following at this time?

   (a) Increase our army further, even if you have to pay a special tax?
      Yes 79%   No 14%   No Opinion 7%

   (b) Increase our navy further, even if you have to pay a special tax?
      Yes 78%   No 15%   No Opinion 7%

   (c) Increase our air forces further, even if you have to pay a special tax?
      Yes 86%   No 10%   No Opinion 4%

Although opinion is overwhelmingly in favor of expansion in either case, it will be seen that personalization ("even if you have to pay a special tax") decreases to a small extent the amount of approval.

The few data we have been able to marshal show that a definite effect can be produced by personalizing the issue. In the absence of validating criteria, however, it cannot be said that the personalized form is superior or inferior to the unpersonalized. Obviously, not all types of issues are suited to personalization. Where one does have a choice between personalized and nonpersonalized forms, it is simply a matter of deciding which form presents the issue more realistically and which is more appropriate to the particular purposes of the investigation.

INTERPRETATION

From the foregoing considerations, certain conclusions may be drawn.

1. The extent to which the wording of questions affects the answers obtained depends almost entirely on the degree to which the respondent's mental context is solidly structured. Where people have standards of

judgment resulting in stable frames of reference, the same answer is likely to be obtained irrespective of the way questions are asked. On the other hand, where people lack reliable standards of judgment and consistent frames of reference, they are highly suggestible to the implications of phrases, statements, innuendoes or symbols of any kind that may serve as clues to help them make up their minds.[9]

2. Questions which elicit responses concerning the acceptance of established norms or values, often fail to indicate the true opinion of individuals unless such questions are followed by others which concretize the issues involved or place them on some behavorial level.

Similarly questions which bluntly state some deviation from an established norm or value are less likely to receive favorable replies than questions which imply the same deviation but state it by implication.

3. A few suggestions for the construction of ballots emerge from this review.

a. Since any single opinion datum is meaningful only in so far as it is related to a larger personal and social context, it is essential that responses to many single questions asked by the polls be compared with responses to other questions which place the same issue in different contingencies.

b. No claim can be made that the dichotomous, the multiple-choice, or the free-answer type of question is consistently superior. It is suggested, however, that in general wherever a new and somewhat complicated problem is to be posed or wherever a question concerns an issue about which people have thought little or perhaps care little, the free-answer type of question should be used on at least one form of the ballot to discover (1) to what extent people are aware of the problem posed and (2) in what way they themselves cut the issues. On another form of ballot, a dichotomous or cafeteria question may be used for comparison. After the free answers have been analyzed, more meaningful questions with stated alternatives can be devised.

The chief advantage of the multiple-choice question is that it allows for a more accurate placement of opinion than the dichotomous question in all those instances where the issue may not be clear-cut. The chief danger of the cafeteria question is that the presentation of various alternatives, whether verbally or on printed cards, frequently irritates or confuses respondents to such an extent that the answers they finally give, although they can be classified and percentaged, may have little reliability. There is also the well-known tendency to choose a middle

---

[9] Cf. H. Cantril, *The Psychology of Social Movements*, N.Y.: Wiley, 1941, Chapter 3.

way. The dichotomous question, which has the enormous advantage of simplicity, is recommended wherever its use will not obscure alternatives or force issues. To the general public it is also a more familiar method of presentation than the use of several alternatives.

   c. The split-ballot technique should be used wherever possible in order to test the stability and consistency of opinion by noting the effect of (1) variation between free and prescribed responses, (2) variation of alternative answers presented, (3) variation of contingency surrounding the issue, (4) bias by an introductory statement or deliberately forced wording, (5) prestige introduced by a word, name or phrase, (6) explicit rather than implicit presentation of alternatives, (7) stated deviation from currently accepted practice, (8) variation of the context provided by other questions on the ballot, or (9) personalization of the issue.

CHAPTER III

THE MEASUREMENT OF INTENSITY[1]

URING the summer before our entry into the war an astute political observer returned from a trip through the middle west and remarked: "The public opinion polls show that the country is 70 per cent in favor of the Allies, but I can tell them that this sentiment doesn't go a half inch deep." To interpret poll results adequately it is necessary to know whether an expressed attitude represents a superficially held view which may be discarded the next moment or whether it reflects a cherished conviction which will change only under unusual pressure.

The problem of the depth of opinion, or the intensity of belief, is perhaps one of the most basic questions in the measurement of public opinion. For if we are able to measure the intensity of opinion as well as its direction, we shall know a great deal more about the individuals whose opinions we are studying. We shall know, for one thing, something of the permanence of opinion, its crystallization, the extent to which it is structured, and the degree to which an individual may be expected to be suggestible. If we can determine the intensity of opinion, we should be able to predict much more accurately than we might otherwise what action opinion may lead to, for example, whether or not an individual with a given opinion holds that opinion strongly enough to take the trouble to go out and vote for it or fight for it. If such an opinion is held rigidly enough to be called a prejudice, we should be able to predict the success of those who want to proselyte this opinion. On the other hand, if opinion is strongly held but if all channels of action to which the opinion is directed are blocked, then we can predict frustration to arise either in the individual or group more rapidly than it would if the opinion were only mildly held. If we can break opinion down by intensity, then we should be able to divide any given population accordingly into more and more precisely defined groups. For these reasons, among others, measurement of the intensity of opinion assumes enormous significance.

ANALYSIS OF THE DEVICES USED BY THE AMERICAN INSTITUTE OF PUBLIC OPINION

From time to time the American Institute of Public Opinion has attempted to measure the intensity dimension of opinion. The Institute has

[1] By Daniel Katz.

used three devices: (1) rating by the interviewer of the strength of the respondent's feelings as judged by the respondent's tone of voice, comments and general attitude, (2) the self-rating of the respondent as to whether he felt strongly or mildly about the question and (3) the self-rating of the respondent on a graphic thermometer. The thermometer is an adaptation, suggested by OPOR, of the graphic rating scale which consists of a line with reference points. The usual graphic scale when put to the test was not understood by the man on the street. Hence it had to be popularized as a thermometer.

Comparison of self-rating and interviewer's rating. The evaluation of these devices by the AIPO has been limited to the spread they give in the distribution of responses.[2] There is a consistent, though not always pronounced, tendency for the respondent to give himself a more extreme rating than the interviewer would give him. This is probably a function of two factors: (1) the interviewer on the basis of inadequate information, does not like to make an extreme judgment about the intensity of a person's reaction; (2) the self-rating device uses the words *mildly* and *strongly*, and many respondents may have shied away from such an effeminate and namby-pamby word as *mildly*.

AIPO's data were further analyzed by OPOR. A number of split ballots were compared where the A form of the ballot carried the interviewer's rating and the B form of the ballot carried the self-rating of the respondent. Breakdowns were made on these ballots to see how well the intensity devices classified respondents into groups which reacted differentially on the related questions.

Table 10 gives an example of the results and shows that both of the intensity devices work well in that they produce differences in the expected directions between the attitudes of the strong and mild supporters of the President, when this opinion is related to other questions. There is no conclusive evidence here that either device is more effective than the other; both self- and interviewer's ratings are effective in differentiating intensity groups.

The thermometer as a measure of the intensity of voting intention. The graphic rating scale was applied to the measurement of public opinion on a nation-wide scale for the first time in the 1940 presidential election. The idea of a line with numbers representing degrees of intensity was not immediately clear to many respondents. When the scale was presented as a thermometer, however, with five statements attached to

[2] The analysis was made by Paul Perry of the AIPO.

various positions, the average respondent experienced little difficulty in pointing to the place which expressed his degree of interest in voting in the coming election.

TABLE 10

Comparison of Interviewers' Ratings on Intensity with Self-Ratings on Consistent Differentiation of Attitudes toward Foreign Policy* (AIPO 4/19/39)

	RATINGS OF APPROVAL ON ROOSEVELT'S MESSAGE TO THE DICTATORS				
	Strong Approval	Mild Approval	No Opinion	Mild Disapproval	Strong Disapproval
Is President preventing war or making war more likely?			INTERVIEWERS' RATINGS		
Preventing	68	45	21	16	8
More likely	4	11	12	34	53
No difference	22	32	38	36	33
No opinion	6	12	29	14	6
Total	100	100	100	100	100
Do you approve of the President's foreign policy?			SELF-RATINGS		
Approve	80	63	16	22	7
Disapprove	7	16	19	54	76
No opinion	13	21	65	24	17
Total	100	100	100	100	100
Should we help England at risk of getting into war?			INTERVIEWERS' RATINGS		
Yes	44	34	15	16	14
No	51	61	68	81	85
No opinion	5	5	17	3	1
Total	100	100	100	100	100
Should we do everything to help England except go to war?			SELF-RATINGS		
Yes	79	73	54	63	45
No	18	22	30	34	51
No opinion	3	5	16	3	4
Total	100	100	100	100	100

* The figures in this table are percentages of the intensity groups falling into the response categories listed on the left. Thus the first figure in the first column means that 68 per cent of the strong supporters of Roosevelt's message think that the President is preventing a war.

FIGURE 2. VOTING THERMOMETER

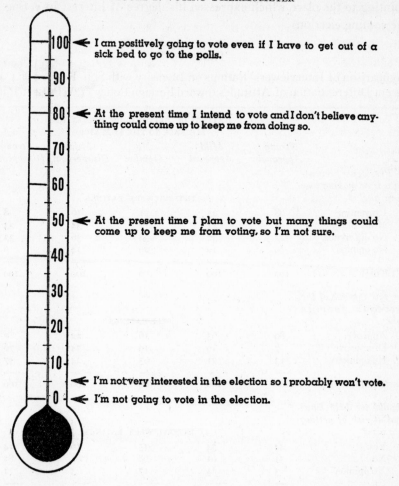

Both Willkie and Roosevelt voters clustered at the top of the scale. The descriptive statements gave a multimodal curve since respondents tended to point to the positions marked by the statements. Only the extreme statement at the 100-degree point and the moderate statement at the 50-degree point, however, had real pulling power; the answers bunched largely around the 100- and 80-degree points, with a small mode at 50 degrees. Hence in classifying Willkie and Roosevelt supporters into groups on the basis of intensity of voting intention, the following divisions were made: weak supporters, under 75; moderate supporters, 75-84 degrees; strong supporters, 85-94 degrees; and very strong supporters, 95 degrees and over. These divisions showed greater intensity of voting intention among the Willkie supporters than among the Roosevelt supporters.

On the same ballot with the thermometer two questions appeared which furnished a test of its discriminating power. One question asked: "Regardless of how you, yourself, plan to vote, which presidential candidate do you think will win?" In using this question of the voter's expectation, it was assumed that those who were most enthusiastic about their candidate would be more enthusiastic about his chances of winning. The second test question consisted of four statements concerning each candidate, statements which varied in the amount of commendation or condemnation of his ability and fitness. They were similar to the ones used by the *Fortune* Survey in its preelection polling.

Table 11 shows the ability of the thermometer to differentiate consistently between the degrees of support of Roosevelt and Willkie. Only 47 per cent of the *weak* Willkie supporters, for example, thought he would win the election, whereas 71 per cent of his *very strong* supporters expected him to win. The classification of Roosevelt supporters does not show as good a differentiation. Ninety-two per cent of his *very strong* supporters expected his election, and 84 per cent of his *weak* supporters thought he would win. The better differentiation for the Willkie supporters as compared with the Roosevelt is to be expected. It took less intensity of feeling for a Roosevelt man to see victory for his candidate than it did for a Willkie supporter.

As another test of the thermometer we can compare the classes of supporters of the two candidates on their selection of statements concerning their candidate's qualifications. The statements from which they were asked to choose concerning Mr. Roosevelt follow:

A. In times like these it is absolutely essential to have a man like Roosevelt for President.
B. There may be some reasons against having Roosevelt as President for another four years but on the whole it is the best thing to do.
C. While Roosevelt has done some good things, the country would be better off under Willkie for the next four years.
D. The reelection of Mr. Roosevelt for another four years would be a very bad thing for the country.

The statements from which they were asked to choose concerning Mr. Willkie follow:

A. Willkie is just the man the country needs for President during the next four years.

TABLE II

The Relation between Intensity of Voting Intention (As Measured by the Thermometer) and Opinions about the Outcome of the Election and about the Candidates.* (AIPO 9/3/40)

	WILLKIE SUPPORTERS				ROOSEVELT SUPPORTERS			
	Very Strong	Strong	Moderate	Weak	Very Strong	Strong	Moderate	Weak
Which candidate will win?								
Willkie	71	55	58	47	3	4	4	5
Roosevelt	14	25	23	29	92	92	89	83
Other	1	1	1	1	0	0	0	0
Undecided	14	19	18	23	5	4	7	12
Total	100	100	100	100	100	100	100	100
A. Willkie just the man	47	36	30	28	0	0	1	0
B. Better than Roosevelt	44	58	57	52	1	0	0	0
C. Not the right experience	2	2	4	4	55	68	69	70
D. Willkie's election a bad thing	0	0	0	1	34	25	24	19
Don't know	7	4	9	15	10	7	6	11
Total	100	100	100	100	100	100	100	100
A. Roosevelt essential	0	1	1	0	62	55	47	40
B. On the whole Roosevelt better	2	1	2	5	31	44	49	56
C. Roosevelt good but Willkie better	41	48	52	52	0	0	1	0
D. Roosevelt's election a bad thing	51	45	38	31	1	1	0	0
Don't know	6	5	7	12	6	0	3	4
Total	100	100	100	100	100	100	100	100

* The figures in the table are percentages of the different intensity groups falling into the response categories listed on the left. Thus the figure in the first row of the first column means that 71 per cent of the very strong Willkie supporters thought he would be elected.

B. Even though Willkie hasn't as much political and international experience as he needs, he still would make a better President than Roosevelt.

C. Willkie is probably an honest and capable business man, but he hasn't had the right experience to be President in times like these.

D. The election of a man like Mr. Willkie at any time would be a very bad thing for the country.

On statement A, that it is absolutely essential in times like these to have a man like Roosevelt, the classes of Roosevelt supporters as determined by the thermometer behaved consistently. Sixty-three per cent of the *very strong* supporters endorsed it, 55 per cent of the *strong* supporters, 47 per cent of the *moderate* supporters, and 40 per cent of the *weak* supporters. On the statement which viewed with alarm the election of Mr. Willkie (D), the differentiation among Roosevelt adherents was less clear but still noticeable. For the four groups ranging from *very strong* to *weak* support for Roosevelt, the percentages endorsing this statement were 34, 25, 24, and 19. The Willkie supporters as classified by the thermometer also reacted consistently (Table 11).

MEASURING INTENSITY OF OPINION BY GRADED SCALE[3]

In March 1941 a sample population was asked the question: "Which of these two things do you think is more important for the United States to try to do: To keep out of war ourselves, or to help England win, even at the risk of getting into the war?" After this question had been answered, respondents were given the following three statements with the instruction to indicate which one best expressed how strongly they felt about the opinion they had just expressed.

I am not at all strongly convinced on this matter.
I guess it is the best thing to do.
I am absolutely convinced that this is what ought to be done.

The three intensity steps gave a better spread for the isolationists than for the interventionists. One-fifth of the isolationists selected the weak intensity statement, about one-third the moderate statement, and almost one-half the strong statement. Only 8 per cent of the interventionists selected the weak statement, 28 per cent the moderate, and 64 per cent the strong. Such a distribution suggests the validity of the intensity scale. Among the isolationists were not only the bitter haters of Euro-

[3] This experiment was conducted by W. K. Salstrom. The construction of the scale was done by the Thurstone method but the statements for the scale were selected to avoid specific reference to particular issues in line with the precedent of Beyle's generalized scales.

pean involvement but also the lukewarm supporters of the status quo. The validity of the intensity device was also indicated by the sex breakdowns, which showed women taking the moderate position on the scale more frequently than men. Polling experience in general is that women do not take so decided a stand on political questions as men.

When the groups of varying degrees of intensity of belief are compared on related questions, the importance of the intensity device is apparent (Table 12). For example, on the question of whether the respondent was willing to fight, or have a member of the family fight, we see a progressive increase in percentages, with the strong isolationists showing 28 per cent willing, the moderate isolationists 35, the weak isolationists 39, the weak interventionists 60, the moderate interventionists 64, and the strong interventionists 82. Although most of the related questions do not show so perfect a progression between the groups, they do indicate the same general tendency. On the whole, however, the intensity device gives two degrees of attitudinal strength on both sides of the issue instead of the three degrees which are possible. Since in most

TABLE 12

Relationship of Intensity of Opinions and Alternatives "Keep Out" or "Help England at Risk of War" to other War Questions (Graded Scale)*

	KEEP OUT			HELP ENGLAND		
	Strong	*Moderate*	*Weak*	*Weak*	*Moderate*	*Strong*
If Nazis win, would we have to do as they wanted us to?	15	22	24	42	45	53
If Germany wins, will we have to pay for strong defense and be poorer than we are now?	50	59	55	70	77	79
If Germany defeats England, will she start a war with U. S. in the next ten years?	28	36	36	67	68	78
If England falls, will Germany control our trade and foreign markets?	31	34	34	66	64	77
Willing to fight or have family member fight?	28	35	39	60	64	82
If Germany wins, will you be as free to do what you want as you are now?	58	46	48	28	27	22
Should U. S. go to war only if invaded?	54	49	48	15	22	12
Was it a mistake for U. S. to enter last war?	73	58	62	35	31	23

* Each figure represents the percentage of a given intensity group who answered "Yes" to questions listed on the left.

instances there is little difference between the weak and moderate groups, the scale might conceivably work as well if the weak statement were omitted.

This experiment demonstrates that simplified forms of intensity devices can be effectively used on public opinion polls. The scale of three intensity statements gave added information to the simple division of approval-disapproval.

An Experiment to Compare the Effectiveness of Various Intensity Devices in the Same Test Situation

The data already considered show the usefulness of a number of devices. However, with the one exception of interviewer's ratings and self-ratings, the available data do not permit a direct comparison of these devices in the same test situation. The present experiment, therefore, was devised to test the effectiveness of a number of techniques for measuring intensity under the same controlled conditions.

Procedure. A ballot was constructed specifically for the purpose of comparing the discriminating power of intensity devices on related questions. In all, seven intensity devices were used: four of these were carefully controlled to give comparable test results. The four devices receiving major consideration were:

(1) *A verbal self-rating of strength of feeling.* (How strongly do you feel about this question? __Very strongly; __Fairly strongly; __Don't care)

(2) *A thermometer or a self-rating on a graphic numerical scale.* (See Fig. 3.)

(3) *A four-step logical scale setting forth the main alternatives on the issue.*

(4) *A verbal self-rating on certainty or sureness of the correctness of one's opinion.* (How sure are you that your opinion is right? __Not sure; __Fairly sure; __Very sure)

Three additional intensity devices were appended to questions on the ballot, but due to the limitation of a single experiment it was not possible to arrange comparable test situations for them. They were appended in this fashion because their addition involved little added expense and could conceivably give some data on their usefulness. These three supplementary devices were:

(5) *The interviewer's rating of the strength of the respondent's attitude.*

(6) *The respondent's self-rating of his degree of personal involvement.* (How much does this question mean to you personally?

___Means very little to me personally; ___Means something to me personally; ___Means a great deal to me personally.)

(7) *The length of time the respondent has been of his opinion.* (When did you make up your mind about this question? ___Just now when you were being asked; ___Within the past few days; ___Within the past few months; ___Have thought this way for a long time.)

FIGURE 3. OPINION THER-
MOMETER

How strongly do you feel on this question?

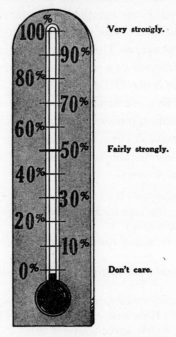

In this experiment the criterion of the efficacy of these devices for measuring intensity was the extent to which they predicted a respondent's answers to related questions.

To make possible a direct comparison of the four major devices, all four were used on the same questions. This necessitated four different ballot forms. In the questions they contained, the ballot forms were identical; they differed only in the order in which the four intensity devices were appended to key questions. Thus on Form A the first key question was followed by the verbal self-rating of strength of feeling, on

Form B this question was followed by the thermometer, on Form C this question appeared as a four-step attitude scale, and on Form D it was followed by the verbal self-rating on sureness of opinion. Similarly, on Form A the second key question was followed by the thermometer, on Form B by the verbal self-rating of strength of feeling, on Form C by the verbal self-rating on sureness of opinion, and on Form D it appeared as a four-step attitude scale. In brief, the four intensity devices were rotated on four key questions, so that direct comparisons of them could be made on the basis of answers to four different key questions.

Four ballots were used. Interviewers were instructed to rotate ballot forms, that is, to use Form A on the first respondent, Form B on the second respondent, Form C on the third respondent, Form D on the fourth respondent, Form A again on the fifth respondent, and so on. The rotation of intensity devices on ballot forms and the rotation of the ballot forms on respondents made it impossible for any selective error to prejudice the results in favor of a particular intensity device. Different results obtained from the different intensity devices could not possibly be attributed to artifactual selection of subjects. Even the effect of the order in which the intensity devices appeared on the ballot was controlled, so that each device had the same advantage or disadvantage in appearing as often in one position as every other device. The double rotation of subjects and intensity devices made possible four series of comparisons on the basis of much smaller groups than if one key question had been employed.

In addition to the four key questions the ballot contained two questions on topics related to each key question, that is, a total of eight questions which could be used as test questions. The ballot also contained the usual items to give background information on respondents such as age, sex, religion, schooling, nationality, economic status and political affiliation.

The field study was undertaken in the metropolitan area of New York and its environs, namely in the boroughs of Manhattan, Queens, Brooklyn, the Bronx, and the city of Newark during the week of February 9-15, 1942. The interviewing staff consisted of twenty experienced interviewers from commercial and research polling organizations.

The major part of the study was conducted through assignment to specific rental areas. The purpose of the assignment to definite areas was not to guard against selective sampling, since selective errors were already ruled out by the design of the experiment, but to obtain a maximum of ballots from the lower income groups. This purpose was further emphasized by instructions to the interviewers to confine themselves to the *average*, the *poor plus*, and the *poor* groups, and to avoid the average plus and the wealthy, on the one hand, and the destitute and relief groups on the other. The emphasis upon low-income groups was to ensure the workability of the intensity devices upon a national cross-section of the population. It is possible to use subtle techniques upon better educated respondents who are trained to make fine verbal discriminations. If devices are to be practical for polling purposes, they must be applicable to people who have never gone beyond grade school.

Because of the high proportion of foreign-born in the metropolitan area among the lower income groups, interviewers were instructed to hold the foreign-born to a maximum of 10 per cent of all respondents. In all, 1,918 interviews were completed within the week, or about 480 for each ballot form.

Results. The four key questions supposed to furnish the bases for the comparison of intensity devices concerned these issues: (1) attitude toward Soviet Russia, (2) the nationalization of industry, (3) satisfaction with the government's conduct of the war, and (4) willingness to discuss peace terms with the German army. Actually only the first two issues proved wholly satisfactory for the purposes of the experiment. The question of satisfaction with the government's conduct of the war proved to be inadequate and the problem of peace discussion gave none of the consistent graduation of intensity required for a comparison of intensity devices.

The failure of the latter two issues to function as usable discriminators of intensity is itself significant. For the average man in the street in February 1942, both his opinion toward the government's conduct of the war and toward the policy to pursue in the event the German army overthrew Hitler were questions on which he had little basis for judgment. His opinions were thus vague and uncrystallized with the result that probably no discrimination between various degrees of intensity would have been possible on any type of scale or intensity device. On the other hand, opinion toward Russia and toward the socialization of industry are relatively old issues for which there are familiar symbols and toward which there are well solidified attitudes.

The test of the intensity measures, in each case, was the extent to which the intensity groups reacted differentially to the test questions. Thus, in the first set of comparisons, those who were *very suspicious* of Russia should have been most in favor of sending fewer supplies, the *fairly suspicious* group next, the *neutral or no opinion* group in the middle, and the *fairly trustful* and *very trustful* groups least in favor of reducing the flow of supplies. The extent to which each intensity device showed such a progressive increase or decrease of percentages, and the extent to which the opinions of the *mild* and *strong* intensity groups were clearly differentiated, were the criteria for the ratings of predictive ability contained in Table 13.

A summary of the predictive performance of the four intensity devices on the two usable key questions is contained in Table 13.

On the basis of these comparisons, the *sureness of rating* and the *thermometer* stood out clearly as the most effective devices. The sureness rating seemed to work better on questions that are still to be decided than on reactions to an accomplished fact.

TABLE 13. PREDICTIVE PERFORMANCE OF INTENSITY DEVICES*

FIRST SET OF COMPARISONS

Intensity question: If Russia should defeat Germany, which of these things do you think Russia would then try to do?
    (1) Try to spread communism all through Europe.
    (2) Work with Britain and the United States to let the countries of Europe choose their own form of government.

Predictive Ability of Intensity Devices

Test questions	Sureness Rating	Ther-mometer	Self-rating or Strength of feeling	Attitude Scale
Send fewer supplies to Russia?	Very good	Good	Fair	Very good
Which gov't—German or Russian —has done more for its people?	Good	Fair	Poor	Poor
Would you like more or less New Deal?	Fair	Good	Poor	Poor

SECOND SET OF COMPARISONS

Intensity question: Should our government take over and run all industries important for carrying on the war?

Predictive Ability of Intensity Devices

Test questions	Sureness Rating	Ther-mometer	Self-rating on Strength	Attitude Scale
Limitation of incomes to $10,000 a year?	Very good	Good	Poor	Very good
Would you like more or less New Deal?	Fair	Fair	Fair	Poor

* The data upon which this summary is based are contained in Appendix 6.

The thermometer device seems to have the greatest usefulness on all types of questions since it does not have to be pretested and changed for different issues. For the public opinion polls it is thus a relatively safe instrument; there is less risk involved in its application, and less expense.

The attitude scale does not seem by comparison so practical an instrument as self-ratings of sureness or self-ratings on a graphic scale. Unless the attitude scale is extensively pretested on every new question, it may neglect significant alternatives or it may not distinguish sharply between the important positions which people actually take on a particular issue.

The direct inquiry on *personal involvement* as a measure was included here to see if it would work empirically in predicting responses to related questions. Results were negative, no doubt due to the fact that personal involvement is at best a vague concept. Previous attempts to develop effort and sacrifice scales have also not proved helpful since specific sacrifices represent such very different degrees of hardship for different people.

While the *age of an opinion* gave some positive indications of usefulness as a measure of intensity, this device did not prove nearly so useful as the thermometer or the rating on sureness. The device is, however, worthy of further investigation, especially where the time intervals employed and the areas of inquiry are systematically varied.

The *interviewer's rating* is a more promising device than the particular personal involvement and time devices employed in this experiment. If interviewers are informed about the error of central tendency (the avoidance of extreme judgments) and are given some training in rating intensity, it is possible that their ratings may prove the most effective intensity device. Evidence from this study is, however, inconclusive, since the interviewer had the benefit of the information obtained through the other devices before making his rating.

It should be pointed out that it seems unlikely that we shall ever have an instrument for measuring intensity that will work equally well for all types of questions. More research is needed to single out the device that will work best for a given type of situation. Where opinion on an issue is well crystallized, where no stigma attaches to the expression of opinion pro or con any intensity device may work well. There may be, on the other hand, situations where interviewers will be able to report more accurately on intensity than the respondents with their self-rating devices. More objective or more indirect instruments may function better than self-rating devices on questions where the individual has little insight or is reluctant to reveal his attitude.

SUMMARY

1. A knowledge of the intensity of an opinion as well as its direction is necessary for both accurate understanding and prediction.

2. The intensity of opinion can be measured. In spite of the theoretical difficulties in conceptualizing the dimension of intensity, in actual practice the various instruments devised to gauge intensity all seem to be tapping essentially the same dimension.

3. The best methods to gauge intensity of opinion found in these studies are (a) individual rating on sureness of opinion, and (b) self-rating on a graphic, thermometer device.

4. Other devices that have proved their usefulness in measuring intensity are: self-rating on the strength of conviction; interviewer's rating of strength of feeling; and an attitude scale if it is carefully constructed with reference to the particular problem at hand.

5. Devices that were tested but found inadequate for the measurement of intensity were: self-rating on personal involvement and the age of an opinion.

CHAPTER IV

THE USE AND VALUE OF A BATTERY OF QUESTIONS[1]

U NLESS observers are generally agreed that opinions have become clearly focused, it is not easy to frame a single question which will separate people into two or three major clusters of opinion. Just before a presidential election, a straightforward question will be enough to separate the overwhelming majority of voters into a few camps. But most issues with which opinion surveys are concerned are by no means as traditional, as clearly bounded, or as immediately important to individuals as those separating presidential candidates.

When we are interested in gauging opinion on problems that have not yet become obviously clear cut and that may have enormously varied significance for different people, it is frequently helpful to use a battery of several questions so the breadth and intensity of opinion can be understood. A single dichotomous or multiple-choice question may artificialize or somewhat distort the groupings of opinion that actually exist in the population, while a free-answer or open-ended question on a very general issue may bring such diversified answers and leave so much responsibility for judgment to the person doing the coding that it becomes difficult to make any final quantitative statement and therefore almost impossible to get any trends of opinion.

From the beginning of World War II in September 1939, the Office of Public Opinion Research has been interested in tracing trends of opinion. At least eighteen months before the U. S. entry into the war the terms "interventionist" and "noninterventionist," or "interventionist" and "isolationist" had become widely used and descriptive of two camps of opinion concerning U. S. policy toward the European conflict. This article illustrates several methods for gauging the percentage of people who in March 1941 could be classified as "interventionist" or "noninterventionist." It touches, furthermore, upon another point which we were interested in studying—some of the characteristics of certain groups that emerge when a battery of questions is used.

METHOD

In this survey we repeated the single determining question frequently used before by OPOR, one found to be highly satisfactory and on which we had a trend together with considerable information concerning

[1] By Frederick Mosteller and Hadley Cantril.

characteristics of people who answered the different alternatives. The question read: "Which of these two things do you think is more important for the United States to do—Keep out of war ourselves, or help England win even at the risk of getting into the war?"[2] This question, on this ballot, was also equipped with the following device to measure intensity: "Which one of these three statements best expresses how strongly you feel that it is more important to try to (keep out of war than to help England) (help England than to keep out of war)? a. I am not at all strongly convinced on this matter; b. I guess it is the best thing to do; c. I am absolutely convinced that this is what ought to be done."

Thus we obtained six possible classifications on the basis of the intensity scale: three interventionist and three noninterventionist categories.

The same survey also contained eight questions designed to get at interventionist or noninterventionist opinion in different ways. A given answer to each question was assumed to indicate (1) an interventionist, (2) a noninterventionist point of view, or (3) no opinion.

1. Would you be willing to fight or have any man of military age in your family fight overseas if the United States gets involved in the war in Europe?

(1) Yes   (2) No   (3) No Opinion

2. Do you think it was a mistake for the United States to enter the last war?

(1) No   (2) Yes   (3) No Opinion

3. Do you think the United States should go to war only after it has actually been invaded, or do you think that there are times when we should fight before we are invaded?

(1) Sometimes fight before invasion (2) Fight only if invaded (3) No Opinion

4. Do you think that, if England falls, Germany will soon be in control of all our trade and foreign markets?

(1) Yes   (2) No   (3) No Opinion

5. If Germany and Italy defeat England in the present war, do you think Germany and Italy would start a war against the United States within the next ten years?

(1) Yes   (2) No   (3) No Opinion

6. Do you think that, if Germany wins the war, we will have to keep up and pay for such a strong national defense that people in this country will be poorer than they are now?

(1) Yes   (2) No   (3) No Opinion

7. Do you think that, if the Nazis win the war, we would eventually have to do pretty much as they wanted us to, like the Poles?

(1) Yes   (2) No   (3) No Opinion

8. If Germany defeats England in the present war, do you think you will be as free to do what you want to as you are now?

(1) No   (2) Yes   (3) No Opinion

---

[2] On this particular survey the "no opinion" or "no choice" answer box was excluded, since the interviewer was asked to discontinue the interview if the respondent had no opinion one way or another. In general, the no opinion vote on this question, around this time, was about 4 per cent.

RESULTS

A. COMPARISON OF FOUR METHODS FOR CALCULATING INTERVENTIONIST AND NONINTERVENTIONIST OPINION

The survey was designed so that the four methods described below could be compared in estimating the number of people who might reliably be classified as interventionist or noninterventionist.

1. *Answer to control question.* Because of our past experience with the determining question and our knowledge that it gave meaningful results, the straight percentage on this question we believed reliable enough to give us one method of differentiating opinion. The results here are:

FIGURE 4

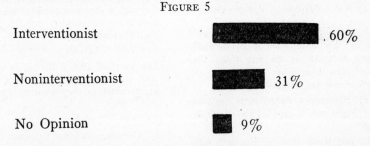

To help England win even
at the risk of getting
into the war.   68%

To keep out of war
ourselves.   32%

2. *Method of averages.* Another practical method of estimating opinion on this general issue is to take the average of the proportions appearing in a particular category on all of the questions. When this is done for the battery of eight questions, we obtain the following percentages:

FIGURE 5

Interventionist   .60%

Noninterventionist   31%

No Opinion   9%

3. *Arbitrary definition.* A third method is to define respondents arbitrarily as interventionist or noninterventionist, in terms of the number of questions they answered in a certain category. In our particular case on this survey we defined interventionists as those who answered four or more questions in an interventionist manner, noninterventionist as those who answered four or more questions in the noninterventionist category. However, persons who answered four questions in each of these two categories were excluded from the categories and arbitrarily

were included among those not earlier defined in the "no opinion" category. The results are:

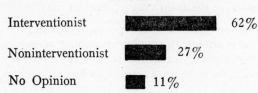

FIGURE 6

Interventionist 62%

Noninterventionist 27%

No Opinion 11%

4. *Index based on battery of questions.* A fourth method described in detail elsewhere,[3] involves the probability that a person in a particular category, such as interventionist, will answer some particular question in the same way a person in another category, say noninterventionist, does. We need to know the probability that a person in the Kth category will answer question J in the Ith category. Since these $P_{IJ/K}$ are not generally known, a practical solution must be supplied. Using this solution we obtain the following proportions based on the data contained in Table 14:

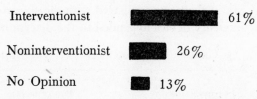

FIGURE 7

Interventionist 61%

Noninterventionist 26%

No Opinion 13%

In the particular problem we faced—that of determining the proportion of the American population who at that time were interventionist or noninterventionist—the solutions obtained from the use of the four methods did not differ significantly.

TABLE 14. NUMBER OF INTERVENTIONIST RESPONSES

		8	7	6	5	4	3	2	1	0	Total
Number	8									59	59
of	7								111	34	145
Isola-	6							121	59	19	200
tionist	5						137	78	27	8	250
Responses	4					180	86	35	17	10	328
	3				214	100	45	16	8	6	389
	2			294	137	63	20	10	4	5	533
	1		342	118	59	34	16	5	2	4	580
	0	343	111	48	13	9	3	4	1	0	532
	Total	343	453	460	423	386	307	270	229	145	3016

[3] Cf. Frederick Mosteller and Philip J. McCarthy, "A Method of Estimating Population Proportions from Responses to Several Questions," *Public Opinion Quarterly,* September 1942, 452-458.

B. INTENSITY SCALE COMPARED TO RESULTS OF QUESTION BATTERY

From Table 14 above the following groupings may be defined:

1. *Strong Interventionist:* 8 interventionist responses.
2. *Medium Interventionist:* 6 or 7 interventionist responses.
3. *Mild Interventionist:* 5 or 4 interventionist responses (with the exception of those with 4 interventionist and 4 noninterventionist responses).
4. *Mild Noninterventionist:* 4 or 5 noninterventionist responses (with the same exception as in 3 above).
5. *Medium Noninterventionist:* 6 noninterventionist responses.
6. *Strong Noninterventionist:* 7 or 8 noninterventionist responses.
7. *Balanced:* 4 interventionist and 4 noninterventionist responses or those with three of each type of response.
8. *Bewildered:* The remainder, that is, those with 3 or less responses in both the interventionist and noninterventionist categories with the exception of those with exactly 3 of each who are already included under the "Balanced" category.

This classification then yields eight mutually exclusive groups. In Table 15 the first six of them are compared with the six groups obtained by the use of the intensity device appended to the determining question.

TABLE 15. GROUPS BASED ON BATTERY QUESTIONS

Groups based on Intensity		INTERVENTIONIST				ISOLATIONIST		
		Strong	Medium	Mild	Mild	Medium	Strong	Total
Inter-	C	260	571	60	76	18	11	996
vention-	B	52	200	164	68	21	8	513
ist	A	17	42	47	21	4	3	134
Iso-	A	1	22	38	44	28	34	167
lation-	B	4	33	55	81	49	37	259
ist	C	4	31	60	116	78	109	398
Total		338	899	424	406	198	202	2467

The product moment correlation coefficient for Table 15 is .63, indicating a fairly high relationship between the results from the eight questions and those from the single determining question spread out by the intensity device used.

Table 15, incidentally, shows that there is only a very slight difference between the distribution of the A and B intensity categories on both the interventionist and noninterventionist when compared to the groupings obtained from the battery of eight questions. If we assume that the categories based on the eight questions are reliable, then we are forced to conclude that categories A and B as determined by the intensity device represent essentially the same type of person. Thus, the intensity device was really only efficient in distinguishing four different categories: strong and weak interventionist, and strong and weak noninterventionist.[4]

C.   Balanced and Bewildered Groups

We have defined the "Balanced" group as those respondents who gave an equal number of interventionist and noninterventionist responses and who had no more than two "no opinion" answers, whereas the "Bewildered" group consists of persons who had no more than three interventionist or noninterventionist responses. The balanced group, on the one hand, had positive but conflicting opinions on the same general issue; the bewildered group, on the other hand, had essentially no consistent opinion at all. The discovery of the persons whom we have labeled "Balanced" or "Bewildered" was possible, of course, only by use of a battery of questions.

Table 16 compares these two groups by education, age, and sex. It shows, as one might expect, that the balanced group is composed of

TABLE 16

	Balanced	*Bewildered*
EDUCATION		
College graduate	33	1
College nongraduate	29	0
High School graduate	58	8
High School nongraduate	40	10
Grade School graduate	34	10
Grade School nongraduate	26	32
	220	61
AGE		
Under 30	62	8
30-49	102	30
50 and Over	59	30
	223	68
SEX		
Men	152	30
Women	73	38
	225	68

[4] Cf. Chapter 3, The Measurement of Intensity, pp. 57-59.

those who, because of training or experience, have more standards of judgment upon which to base opinions; who have in addition, therefore, well-developed specific opinions—which, however, are for them unrelated to the more inclusive frames of reference of interventionism or noninterventionism. The bewildered group differs significantly in that its members lack opinions because of an absence of interest, experience, or training and a consequent failure to have personal standards of judgment upon which opinion may be anchored.

Summary Interpretation

1. The use of a battery of questions in a survey to gauge opinion on a broad issue indicates a technique to discover more accurately the consistency and breadth of opinion. The use of such a method should be of especial value when one confronts the problem of determining to what extent opinion is meaningful, has become crystallized around a major issue at different points of time.

2. If an intensity device is used in combination with a battery of questions, the relationship between two opinion dimensions—breadth and intensity—can be studied. If a cluster of related questions is answered consistently and with strong conviction, then it is almost certain that ego-involvement is the uniting bond.

3. The use of a battery of questions makes it possible to isolate from the total sample those persons who have equivocal answers but whose equivocal answers may spring from quite different mental contexts.

4. The general opinion of the proper course for this country to follow in the spring of 1941 with respect to the war is shown by this study to have been meaningfully divided by the popular descriptive phrases used at the time—interventionist and noninterventionist. Approximately the same proportions of the population were found in these groups by the different methods used to measure them. This fact, together with the high correlation between the intensity measure and the consistency found on the battery of questions, indicates that, for the overwhelming majority of people, opinion on the general role the United States should play was a fairly closed, tightly organized system. Specific opinions seem clearly to be based on frames of references consistently referred to.

This conclusion is, of course, not surprising in view of the personal involvement most people felt with the developing war situation. Furthermore, modern methods of communication made it possible for most people to engender and sustain an interest in the war itself and to gather considerable information about it. This widespread interest combined with knowledge, when absorbed into personal values previously held, gave people standards of judgment from which they derived a frame of reference. If this had not been the case—if frames of reference had not been relatively firmly rooted—it is unlikely that all the various methods employed here would have yielded essentially the same results.

PART II

PROBLEMS CONNECTED WITH INTERVIEWING

CHAPTER V

SECRET VS. *NONSECRET BALLOTS*[1]

WHEN surveys are made using the method of direct interviews, one question immediately arises. To what extent do respondents cover up or distort their real opinions because of the face-to-face situation in which interviewing takes place? The interviewers are, in almost every instance, strangers to the respondents. When strangers ask them for their opinions, there is a possibility that respondents may be suspicious, embarrassed, nervous, inarticulate, irritated, hostile, or patronizing. Evidence reported in Chapter 8 indicates that the greater the difference between the status of the interviewer and the respondent, the more likely is he not to report his true opinions.

In order to get some idea of how much opinions were distorted by the personal equation involved in the usual interviewing situation, two comparable populations were asked the same set of questions: one population filled out a "secret ballot"; the other population was interviewed in the usual way with answers given orally to interviewers. This method has previously been used by AIPO in predicting election returns, the chief result being a marked decrease in the number of "undecided" votes recorded on the secret as compared to the nonsecret ballots.[2] Crossley, who reports the use of a secret ballot in predicting the outcome of the 1940 presidential campaign, cautions that some distortion of the sample is introduced by the elimination of people unable to read or write easily, since they tend to refuse the ballot.[3]

METHOD

In the present study, the secret-ballot technique was applied to ten questions selected because of their controversial nature. Six hundred and twelve cases were obtained, 300 by the method of the secret ballot and 312 by the technique of the conventional interview. The ballot forms were identical except for the heading "SECRET BALLOT" printed in heavy type at the head of half the blanks. The interviewers tried to obtain a fairly homogeneous population in general and concentrated on the lower middle socio-economic status. Urban subjects were used

[1] By William Turnbull.
[2] L. E. Benson, "Studies in Secret Ballot Technique," *Public Opinion Quarterly*, 1941, 79-82.
[3] A. M. Crossley, "Methods Tested During the 1940 Campaign," *Public Opinion Quarterly*, 1941, 83-86.

exclusively; 303 from Brooklyn, 199 from Trenton, New Jersey, and 110 from Philadelphia.[4] As the house-to-house polling method was employed, matching of population samples was obtained by using the secret ballot at every other house. Approximately the same percentage of refusals was obtained with each form.

The interviewers carried a padlocked ballot-box with "SECRET BALLOT" printed ostentatiously on one side. When the secret ballot form was to be used, the box was prominently exhibited, the printing being made obvious to the respondent, who was assured that he would be allowed to fold his own ballot and drop it into the box himself. He was then given the ballot and asked to mark it privately. When the respondent was to be interviewed, the box was set down inconspicuously near the door, and was ostensibly just a container for used ballot forms.

RESULTS

Vital statistics. The distributions of sex, color, income, and religious and political affiliation, as reported by the two groups, show close inter-group correspondence. Age as reported by the secret-ballot group and as estimated by the interviewer in the case of the interviewed group, shows equal similarity of distribution between groups. These facts suggest that the samples were effectively equated by the methods described.

On the question of educational achievement a significant difference between the two groups is found, 13 per cent *more* of the interviewed group stating that they had had *no* schooling, and 11 per cent *more* of the secret ballot group stating that they had had some education at the high-school level.[5]

It is likely that the group personally interviewed reported the facts more accurately, since there is a consistent bias in the direction of higher education on most surveys. The most probable explanation for this state of affairs is that there was a desire on the part of both groups to exaggerate their educational attainments. The interviewed group realized, however, that exaggeration would be apparent to the interviewer. In the case of the secret ballot group, this restraining factor was absent.

Opinions on ten controversial issues. In considering the opinion per-

---

[4] While it is realized that a larger number of cases and more widely representative sampling would be desirable, an experiment performed on such a scale would be extremely expensive. It was felt that the sample used provided the best opportunity for close matching of groups, within the limits of the available funds. Many elaborations of this experiment—involving variations of respondents and interviewers—will suggest themselves. The present study at least opens up the general problem.

[5] In the comparisons made in this study, a difference of 10.5 per cent is significant at the .99 level and a 7 per cent difference at the .90 level.

centages given below, it must be remembered that they are based on small samples which are *not* meant to be representative of the national population.

(1) The largest group difference is found on the question: *Do you think the English will try to get us to do most of the fighting for them in this war, or do you think they will do their fair share of the fighting?* The percentage answers were:

FIGURE 8

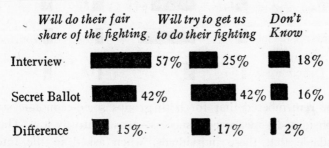

	Will do their fair share of the fighting	Will try to get us to do their fighting	Don't Know
Interview	57%	25%	18%
Secret Ballot	42%	42%	16%
Difference	15%	17%	2%

While the socially approved opinion is one of confidence in the English, apparently there is a considerable undercurrent of mistrust which people do not care to express openly. Most of the difference obtained with this question was found in the answers from 303 cases in the Brooklyn, New York, area where there is a heavy concentration of Irish.

(2) *Do you think the Jews have too much power and influence in this country?*

FIGURE 9

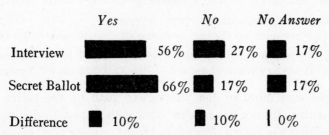

	Yes	No	No Answer
Interview	56%	27%	17%
Secret Ballot	66%	17%	17%
Difference	10%	10%	0%

Again mistrust of an out-group is not readily vocalized. It is interesting to note that here, too, most of the difference was found between the two Brooklyn samples. One of the two interviewers in this area, although a Gentile, was of rather Jewish appearance; after the survey he reported that several of the interviewed group, before they answered his question, asked him if he were Jewish. The factor of the interviewer's appearance, then, presumably induced greater reluctance, on the part of this group, to express disapproval of the Jewish people.[6]

(3) To the question: *Do you think success is dependent mostly on luck, ability, or on pull?* the answers were:

FIGURE 10

	Luck	Ability	Pull	Don't Know
Interview	■14%	■■■ 64%	■ 8%	■14%
Secret Ballot	■ 9%	■■■ 75%	■ 7%	■ 9%
Difference	▌5%	▌11%	▌1%	▌5%

It must be remembered that for both groups socio-economic status— usually considered a measure of success—was relatively low. Thus it is understandable that these individuals, when asked in the interview situation, tend to attribute success to luck or pull, or to give no opinion; the secret-ballot group, on the other hand, more readily concedes the importance of ability.

(4) Several *other differences* are found which, while not significant at the .99 level, are at least suggestive.

	% Difference on Secret Ballot
Do you feel that you personally are doing something that is important in helping to win the war?	9% fewer "Yes"
The way things are going right now, does it seem to you that we are winning the war or losing it?	9% more "Don't know"
In general, do you approve of the way Roosevelt is handling his job as President today?	{ 8% fewer "Approve" { 6% more "No opinion"

Eight per cent more of the interviewed than of the secret group replied that they did not have a clear idea with respect to the question: *Do you feel that you have a clear idea of what this war is all about—that is, what we are fighting for?* If this is not a chance difference, its explanation perhaps lies in the mechanics of the ballot construction. It is possible that although the interviewed subjects felt they had a general idea of what the war was about, they hesitated to say so, fearing that

[6] Except for these two differences between the Brooklyn sample and others, the results from the three urban centers were similar.

they would then be called upon to explain this idea in detail. As this question was the second asked, following one in which the respondent was required to estimate the probable duration of the war, the subjects were not yet accustomed to the "Yes—No" form of most of the answers. The secret ballot group, with the ballot before them, were able to see that further elucidation would not be required of them, and so more readily marked the "Yes."

(5) Apart from the "vital statistics" questions (age, sex, etc.) already discussed, the questions which revealed essentially *no differences* between the answers of the two groups were:

About how much longer do you think the war will last?

If Hitler offered peace now to all countries on the basis of not going farther, but of leaving matters as they are now, would you favor or oppose such a peace?

Which of these two things do you think the United States should try to do when the war is over: stay out of world affairs as much as we can, or take an active part in world affairs?

Conclusions

1. The methods of the interview and the secret ballot do produce marked differences in answers under certain conditions.

2. These differences cast some doubt on the validity of the results obtained by the interview method when the subject feels that his answer, if known, would affect his prestige.

3. The discrepancy is probably great enough to warrant the use of the secret ballot whenever questions which have acquired high social prestige are involved, particularly when the questions are of a highly controversial nature, and of deep personal or social significance.

4. The explanations of the differences obtained in this study are, of course, entirely "ex post facto," and the differences elicited in this investigation can be assumed to be reliable only when the particular constellation of determinants found in this study is present. Had the matched samples been of different socio-economic level, sex ratio, geographical and rural-urban distribution, race proportion, religious denomination, educational achievement, etc., differences of entirely different magnitude might have been found. Further experimentation will be necessary to discover the influence of such determinants on the differences obtained.

What bearing has this study upon polling practice? It has been pointed out that the differences obtained are a function of the determinants operative; with national samples, stratified on the usual variables, the pattern of results might be altered considerably. It is possible that the results reported here exaggerate the discrepancies which usually obtain between "privately" and "publicly" expressed opinions, even on emotionally charged questions such as those used. That smaller differences may be expected when less delicate topics are involved is shown by the previous studies on elections, and by the fact that the more factual questions in this experiment revealed smaller discrepancies.

CHAPTER VI

"TRAINED" VS. "UNTRAINED" INTERVIEWERS[1]

THE purpose of this study was to compare the work of interviewers who had undergone a supervised training period with those who had had no such training. Interviewers from the staffs of two nationally known polling organizations were used in the experiment. One of these organizations, the American Institute of Public Opinion, until recently has secured and supervised the work of most of its interviewers only by mail.[2] Although its interviewers receive, at the start, a manual containing detailed instructions as to correct interviewing procedures, they are not given personal training or supervision by a member of the staff. The other agency, the National Opinion Research Center, likewise provides an instruction booklet for interviewers, but, in addition, its interviewers are personally instructed by a member of the staff and obtain trial interviews under his observation before doing any regular interviewing on their own. The object of the experiment was to determine whether the quality of work turned in by personally trained interviewers is noticeably superior to that done by interviewers whose only training has been by mail, and whom we are here arbitrarily calling "untrained."[3]

PROCEDURE

Selection of interviewers. There were about 60 NORC interviewers who had received the prescribed training. Of these we were finally able to use 55. A corresponding list of AIPO interviewers was drawn up, matched on the basis of geographical location. Wherever possible, AIPO interviewers who were in the same cities as the NORC interviewers were chosen; where such a choice was not possible, interviewers in cities of a comparable size were used. Due to the large size of the AIPO staff, there were often several interviewers available in a given locality. An effort was made to get a fairly random sample of the AIPO interviewers

[1] By Donald Rugg.

[2] Strictly speaking, these interviewers are not AIPO interviewers, but are on the list of Public Opinion Surveys, Inc., the agency which handles the interviewing on American Institute surveys. For convenience, however, the designation "AIPO" will hereafter be applied to these interviewers.

[3] The writer is indebted to the American Institute of Public Opinion and the National Opinion Research Center for making their interviewers and facilities available for this experiment. Special thanks are due Elizabeth Bissell and Samuel Northcross of the AIPO, and Douglas Williams and William Salstrom of the NORC for the time and effort they spent in helping to set up the experiment.

by selecting not more than the proper proportion of the better interviewers (as judged by their previous work) in those cases where a choice was possible.

Questionnaire. The questionnaire was designed to include types of questions most diagnostic of interviewing ability, and known to demand careful interviewing and recording.

PRINCETON UNIVERSITY
OFFICE OF PUBLIC OPINION RESEARCH

1. Do you feel that the information you are getting about the war is true and accurate?

    ☐ Yes ☐ No ☐ Qualified answer ☐ Don't know

    Comment ....

2. Which do you think is our No. 1 enemy in the war—Japan or Germany?

    ☐ Japan ☐ Germany ☐ Both ☐ No opinion

    Why? ....

3. About how much longer do you think the war will last?

    .... ☐ Don t know

4. What will bring the war to an end? ....

5. Which of the following statements comes closest to describing how you feel, on the whole, about the people who live in (Germany) (Japan)?

	German	Japanese
(a) The . . . people will always want to go to war to make themselves as powerful as possible.	☐	☐
(b) The . . . people may not like war, but they have shown that they are too easily led into war by powerful leaders.	☐	☐
(c) The . . . people are like any other people. If they could really choose the leaders they want, they would become good citizens of the world.	☐	☐
Don't know	☐	☐

6. a. Are you employed at the present time?

    ☐ Employed full time   ☐ Student

    ☐ Employed part time   ☐ Housewife

    ☐ Employer   ☐ Retired

         ☐ Unemployed

    If "Employed," either full or part time, or "Employer," ask b and c:

    b. What kind of work do you do? ....

    c. Is your regular job in any way connected with the war effort?

    ☐ Yes, directly   ☐ Yes, indirectly   ☐ No

    If "Yes, directly," or "Yes, indirectly," ask d:

d. How? ....

    If "Yes, indirectly," or "No" on c, ask e:

e. Would you be willing to change your job to one in a defense factory at whatever pay the defense job would give you?

    ☐ Yes   ☐ No   ☐ Already on defense job   ☐Depends

    If "No" or "Depends," ask for MAIN REASON ....

    ....

    If "Housewife," "Unemployed," "Retired," or "Student," on a, ask f:

f. Would you be willing to take a job in a defense industry?

        ☐ Yes   ☐ No   ☐ Depends

    If "No" or "Depends," ask for MAIN REASON ....

    ....

    If "Yes" on e or f, ask g:

g. Would you be willing to take a defense job in another city?

    ☐ Yes   ☐ No   ☐ Depends   ☐ Don't know

7. When the war is over, what do you think should be done to make sure of a lasting peace?

....

....

8. In the past, it has been the policy of draft boards to defer men with dependents. Now they are beginning to draft men with dependents. How do you feel about this new policy?

....

....

9. HAND WHITE CARD TO RESPONDENT. Please tell me in which of these groups the average weekly income of your immediate family belongs. Call by letter.

    ☐ A. Under $10.   ☐ E. Between $30. and $39.99

    ☐ B. Between $10. and $14.99   ☐ F. Between $40. and $59.99

    ☐ C. Between $15. and $19.99   ☐ G. Between $60. and $99.99

    ☐ D. Between $20. and $29.99   ☐ H. $100 and Over

                ☐ Refuses to answer

10. a. Do you remember FOR CERTAIN whether or not you voted in the 1940 presidential election?

    ☐ Yes, voted   ☐ No, didn't vote   ☐ No, too young to vote

    If "Yes," ask:

b. Did you vote for Willkie, Roosevelt, or Thomas?

    ☐ Willkie   ☐ Roosevelt   ☐ Thomas   ☐ Other

11. Are you a member of a church?

    ☐ Yes   Which denomination? ....   ☐ No

12. In what country were your parents born? Father ....

             Mother ....

13. a. What was the name of the last school you attended? ....

....

    b. How far did you go in that school?

      ☐ No schooling   ☐ High school, graduated

      ☐Grammar school, incomplete   ☐ College, incomplete

      ☐ Grammar school, graduated   ☐ College, graduated

      ☐ High school, incomplete   ☐ Other ....

☐ Wealthy ☐ Av. ☐ OR—WPA   ☐ Car   ☐ Man   ☐ Wh.

☐ Av.+   ☐ P.   ☐ OR—Home Relief ☐ No car ☐ Woman ☐ Cl.

SPECIFIC OCCUPATION .... ESTIMATE AGE ....

Is your name in the telephone book (or your family's name)? ☐ Yes   ☐ No

Place of interview: ☐ Home   ☐ Office   ☐ Street   ☐ Other ....

Date of interview ....

Interviewer's initials .... City ....

HAVE YOU CHECKED ANSWERS ON EACH QUESTION
AND ALL VITAL INFORMATION?

Question 1 (war information true and accurate?) was chosen because previous experience had shown that it would yield a relatively large proportion of qualified answers.

Examination of the comments would reveal whether or not the answers had been misclassified; that is, whether instead of being recorded as qualified answers, they should have been marked "Yes" or "No," or vice versa. Question 2 (Japan or Germany our No. 1 enemy? followed by a "why" line) was primarily a test of the interviewers' ability to get good reasons for the opinions expressed. The interviewers were instructed to press for definite estimates on Question 3 (how much longer will the war last?) and their work was judged accordingly. Question 4 (what will bring the war to an end?) was also a test of ability to follow instructions. The interviewers were told that the purpose of the question was to find out which side the respondent thought would win the war. Because the question is indirect, answers such as "a peace treaty," or "a stalemate" are often obtained. In such a case, the interviewer was to ask the respondent which side he thought would win.

Question 5 (statements describing the German and Japanese people—a multiple-choice question) was one which had been used previously by the NORC but which was new to the AIPO interviewers, while question 6 (occupation status, nature of work, willingness to work in a defense job) was familiar to the AIPO staff but new to the NORC interviewers. This gave interviewers of each staff a chance to try their hand at a new type of question. In addition, question 6 required a careful "follow-through" to make sure that the right parts of the questions were being asked of the right people. Question 7 (post-war peace solutions) was in the free-answer form and provided a check on the interviewers' ability to elicit relevant and significant answers. Question 8 (draft men with dependents?) was what might be termed a "free-discussion" question. The question itself merely sets the general subject of discussion. The interviewers were instructed to enter into a free discussion with the respondents, covering such points as: if the respondent is opposed to drafting men with dependents, why is he opposed? Are there any conditions under which he would favor drafting these men? A similar probing of the reasons and conditions of those in favor of drafting was asked for.

Question 9 (weekly family income) had a twofold purpose: (1) it provided a check on the interviewer's economic ratings; (2) the number of persons who refused to answer this question served as an index of the interviewer's success, or lack of success, in breaking down the respondents' resistance to giving this personal type of information. The rest of the questions deal with background information. It is obviously important that the interviewer fill these out completely and accurately. Mistakes and omissions were charged against his record.

Assignment of interviews. Each interviewer had a quota of 10 questionnaires to obtain. He was given a specific economic assignment; that is, he was instructed to interview so many people at each economic level. The economic distribution assigned approximated the estimated income distribution in each locality. The assignments, therefore, varied between localities.

Comparable assignments, however, were given to each *pair* of interviewers (working in the same or similar localities). To accomplish this end, it was necessary to equate the AIPO and NORC systems of economic ratings, since the two organizations use different economic status categories. Although every effort was made to make the assignments for each pair of interviewers equivalent, it is not certain that strict comparability was always achieved. The two systems of classification are set up in different terms and use different criteria; hence it is difficult to translate one into the other. The implications of such discrepancies as may have existed will be discussed later.

The interviewers were further instructed to divide their interviews, at each economic level, as evenly as possible between men and women. They were also told to select half their respondents over 40 years of age, half under 40, and to get a good age spread in each of these broad categories.

In addition to obtaining his quota of ten ballots, each interviewer was asked to fill out an interviewer's ballot, on which he recorded his own opinions and background information about himself, and a supplementary report, which contained his reactions to and criticisms of the questionnaire and his experiences and problems encountered in interviewing.

Rating of returned questionnaires. Ninety-six sets of ballots were finally returned (48 from each organization). These ballots were rated independently by four members of the staff of the Office of Public Opinion Research. The ballots were rated in pairs, in accordance with the method of assignment, and each rater determined whether the work of the AIPO interviewer was better, worse, or equal to the work of the corresponding NORC interviewer. In addition, each interviewer was given a grade ranging A (high) to D— (low). The points considered in arriving at the final grade were the following:

1. *Question 1:* Did the interviewer classify the responses to this question correctly, as judged by the comments? Did he get a good proportion of comments, and did they sound authentic and verbatim?
2. *Question 2:* Did the interviewer get *whys* from all his respondents? Were they full and revealing, or short and stereotyped?
3. *Question 3:* Did the interviewer succeed in getting definite estimates in most cases, or did he have a large proportion of "Don't knows" and indefinite answers?
4. *Question 4:* Did the interviewer get the required information, i.e. which side the respondent thought would win the war?
5. *Question 5:* Were there any omissions or indications that the interviewer did not ask the question or record the answers properly?
6. *Question 6:* Did the interviewer "follow through" properly on this question, asking the appropriate parts of the right people? Did he get complete information?
7. *Question 7:* Judged on the completeness and quality of answers.
8. *Question 8:* Did the interviewer, on this free-discussion question, cover the points which he was instructed to cover in the instructions?
9. *Question 9:* (Family income). How many "refuses to answer"? How many ballots not checked at all?
10. *Question 10:* Checked for omissions.
11. *Question 11:* Checked for omissions. Penalty for giving "Protestant" as an answer, since interviewers were told to give the specific Protestant sect of which the respondent was a member.
12. *Question 12:* Checked for omissions.
13. *Question 13:* Checked for omissions and to see whether name of last school attended corresponded with the answer box checked.

14. *Economic assignment:* Did the interviewer fulfill his economic assignment as directed?
15. *Economic ratings:* Did the evidence from the family-income figure and from the person's occupation indicate that he has been given the correct economic rating?
16. *Occupation:* Did the interviewer get *specific* information on occupation? Such answers as "housewife," "student," "clerk," "works at Ford plant," were penalized.
17. *Other background information:* Information on car, sex, age, telephone, color, and place of interview was checked for completeness.
18. *Sex distribution:* Were the interviews distributed between men and women as directed?
19. *Age distribution:* Did the interviewer distribute his interviews among people of different ages as instructed?
20. *Interviewer's ballot:* Rated for completeness and quality.
21. *Costs:* The interviewers were given fairly wide leeway on this count, but excessive cost was cause for reducing the grade, and low costs, provided they were not associated with sloppy interviewing, were a favorable factor.
22. *Supplementary report:* Rated on the quality of comments and criticisms.

RESULTS

Over-all ratings. The results of the rating by pairs, for each of the four raters, are given in Table 17. This table shows in how many cases the AIPO interviewer was judged to be better than the NORC interviewer with whom he was paired, and vice versa.

TABLE 17. RATERS

	FM	FW	DR	FC	Consensus*
AIPO Better	24	24	18	17	19
NORC Better	22	24	25	27	22
Tie	2		5	4	7
	48	48	48	48	48

* The consensus ratings were derived in the following way: In addition to making a paired comparison of each set of interviewers, the raters gave each interviewer a letter grade from A to D— (pluses and minuses were used). These letter grades were converted to numbers (A = 1; A— = 2, etc. to D— = 11). Each interviewer's numerical grades were then summed to give a total grade score. Where the difference between the AIPO and NORC interviewer's score was 3 or more, the interviewer with the lower score was judged to be better by this "consensus" rating. Where the difference in scores was 2 or less, it was considered a tie. The selection of a difference of 3 as a critical point was not as arbitrary as it might seem, for in nearly all cases where there was a difference of 3 or more in the total score, a majority of raters had made their paired comparison judgments in the expected direction. Where the paired comparison judgments were evenly split, but a difference of 3 or more in the score was present, it was an indication that those who chose the interviewers with the lower score had given them a wider margin over their rivals than did the two raters who chose the interviewers with the higher total score.

Agreement among raters. The next table shows the degree of agreement among the four raters. It indicates in how many cases all four raters agreed that one member of the pair of interviewers was better, in how many cases only three members agreed, etc.

TABLE 18

	AIPO Better	NORC Better	Tie	Total
All four raters agreed	9	15		24
Three of four raters agreed	8	4	1	13
Only two raters agreed	2*	3†	6	11
	19	22	7	48

* In these two cases, the AIPO interviewers were given the edge because two raters chose them, a third rater the NORC, and the fourth judged it a tie.

† In one of these cases, the NORC interviewer was chosen for the reason above. In the other two cases, two raters chose the NORC interviewer, two the AIPO. However, the two who chose the NORC interviewers gave them a wider margin than did the two who chose the AIPO, with the result that there was a difference of 3 or more in the total grade scores.

Average grades. Table 19 shows the average grade given the AIPO and NORC interviewers by each rater. $(4 = B; 5 = B—; 6 = C+)$

TABLE 19. RATERS

	FM	FW	DR	FC	Average
Average AIPO grade	6.2	5.6	4.7	6.4	5.7
Average NORC grade	6.1	5.5	4.3	6.1	5.5

From these over-all comparisons the following conclusions emerge. (1) There was no marked difference, in general, between the judged quality of the work turned in by the AIPO and NORC staffs. (2) Despite the fact that the two staffs were almost on a par, the NORC interviewers had a slight but consistent edge over the AIPO. This conclusion is indicated by the consensus ratings; by the fact that, in the cases in which the NORC interviewers were judged superior, there was more clear-cut agreement among the raters; and finally, by the higher average grade of the NORC interviewers, even by the two raters who did not give the NORC a majority of the paired comparison judgments.

To determine whether this very slight but indicated superiority of the NORC staff was a reflection of personal training *per se*, or whether it was attributable to extraneous uncontrolled factors, the two staffs were examined with reference to their composition (that is, the data available concerning the socio-economic characteristics of the interviewers) and to the comparability of the cross-sections which they interviewed.

Composition of the two staffs. The chief difference in the personnel of the two staffs was in the ratio of men to women. In the AIPO staff this ratio was 7/9, while the NORC staff had only 1 man to every 7 women. It was impossible, in setting up the experiment, to overcome this sex differential, because the NORC staff, as a whole, contained an overwhelming majority of women, whereas a majority of all AIPO interviewers were men. The educational background of the two staffs was strictly comparable, as were their political affiliations (in terms of voting preference in 1940). The NORC interviewers, however, had on the average a slightly higher economic status than the AIPO—indicated by the family income figures and by a much larger proportion of Episcopalians (15 compared to 4 of the AIPOs) in the NORC group. There was a slightly wider age spread in the AIPO group. In general, then, the AIPO interviewers represented a somewhat more heterogeneous group in terms of sex, age, and economic status.

As a check on the influence of the sex disparity, average grades were computed for men and women separately in each staff. The results are given in Table 20.

TABLE 20

	AIPO Men	AIPO Women	NORC Men*	NORC Women
Average grade (average of all four raters' grades)	6.1	5.4	5.6	5.5

* Since there are only six cases in this category, the figure cannot be regarded as very reliable.

An examination of this table makes it clear that the small difference in average grade between the two staffs was a result of the lower grade (higher numerical score) given the AIPO men interviewers. If the AIPO grades are weighted in accordance with the NORC sex ratio, the resulting over-all average figure is identical with that obtained for the NORC staff as a whole (5.5).

The inference from these figures is that *the over-all difference in grades between the two staffs is primarily a reflection of the disparity in the ratio of men to women interviewers.* The women on the two staffs did equally well; it was the men who pulled the AIPO average down. In view of this fact, it is impossible to conclude that "training" as such was responsible for the slight superiority of the NORC staff.

Cross-sections interviewed by the two staffs. The average socio-economic status of the respondents interviewed by the NORC was much higher than that of the AIPO respondents. The median weekly family income of the AIPO respondents was $30.78, of the NORC respondents, $42.67. Fifty-one per cent of the AIPO respondents were high school graduates or better, as compared with 57 per cent of the NORC group. Forty-eight per cent of the AIPO group had telephones, 45 per cent cars, as compared with 61 and 64 per cent, respectively, of the NORC group.

TABLE 21

	Economic Assignment on this Ballot	Usual Economic Assignment	Median Family Income on this Ballot
AIPO		(Approximate)	
Wealthy	} 15%	15%	Over $100
Average plus			92.50
Average	31	35	44.50
Poor	44	43	18.66
On Relief	10	7	11.94
NORC			
A	10	4–8	Over $100
B	30	20–25	72.56
C	32	45–50	39.22
D	18	} 20–25	18.80
On Relief	10		11.36

The reasons for this discrepancy are complicated by the fact that different systems of economic classifications are used by the two organizations. Examination of Table 21, however, will reveal some of the reasons for the noncomparability of the two cross-sections. The AIPO economic distribution on this ballot (on which the attempt was not made to get a complete national sample) was approximately the same as that regularly assigned on national cross-sections. The NORC assignment, on the other hand, was higher than that normally obtained. Even had the NORC distribution on this ballot been the same as that used on national cross-sections, it still would have been considerably higher than the AIPO distribution. This is shown by the median family income figures for each economic group. The AIPO "Poor" group is practically identical with the NORC "D" group in terms of median family income. Yet the AIPO customarily assigns over 40 per cent "Poor" interviews, while the NORC had a quota of about 20 per cent "D" interviews.[4] Similarly, the NORC assigns 45-50 per cent "C" interviews, whereas the AIPO has only 35 per cent of its cases in the "Average" category.

Judged by the objective criteria that are available (such as percentage of telephone ownership), it appears that the AIPO economic cross-section more closely approximated the actual distribution of income in the population as a whole. The upward bias of the NORC cross-section was probably due to a combination of two factors. (1) The criteria for the classification of economic status were not clearly enough defined to permit the interviewers to place respondents correctly in the economic scale. The "D" group which is presumed to constitute only 20 per cent of the population should not have the same median income figure as the "Poor" group, which is estimated to comprise nearly half the population. (2) The interviewers were getting respondents who are too "high" for the categories in which they are placed. The solution of this problem (which, to a lesser or greater extent, is present in all subjective schemes of economic status classification) lies in the substitution of objective indices of economic level (such as rent or actual income) upon which to base the economic cross-section.[5]

This discrepancy in the cross-sections obtained by the two staffs should not have had any material influence on the ratings. Inasmuch as the criteria used in grading were fairly independent of the type of respondent, the fact that the general level of the NORC respondents was higher than that of the AIPO respondents should not have made much difference. The only possible effect of this bias might have been that the NORC respondents, being better educated and more well-to-do in general, were more articulate and returned a smaller percentage of "Don't knows" on the free-answer and "why" questions. This circumstance might have predisposed the raters in their favor, but certainly such an effect would have been very slight.

Comparison of performance on individual criteria. Despite the absence of any clear-cut difference in the over-all performance of the two staffs, some insight into their comparative strengths and weaknesses is afforded by an examination of comparative performance on each of the criteria used in determining the final grade. Since a uniform rating scale was not employed by all four raters, it is impossible to present a consen-

[4] This NORC quota has since been adjusted.
[5] The NORC is now substituting more objective indices of economic status for the old ABCD system.

sus rating for each criterion. However, an objective check was possible on many of these points in terms of an actual tabulation of omissions and inaccuracies. These were supplemented by the writer's subjective evaluations on points which did not lend themselves to objective treatment.

The performance of the *NORC* interviewers was superior on these points:

Question 6 (occupation status, nature of work, willingness to take a defense job)
Despite the fact that this question was familiar to the AIPO interviewers, they handled it less well than did the NORC interviewers. On 82 ballots (out of a total of 478) they failed to get all the required information, while only 59 of the 479 NORC ballots were incomplete.

Question 8 (draft men with dependents?)
The work of 31 of the NORC interviewers on this question was rated "good" by the writer, whereas only 19 AIPO interviewers received a "good" rating. The superiority of the former was a result of their following more closely the instructions they were given about the handling of this free-discussion question.

Completeness of occupation and other background information.
The AIPO interviewers were guilty of a few more omissions here than the NORC.

Sex distribution.
43 NORC interviewers got the proper sex distribution;
30 AIPO interviewers were satisfactory on this count.

Age distribution.
30 NORC interviewers, 22 AIPO, got a good age distribution.

Supplementary report. The average rating of the quality of the NORC reports was higher than that for the AIPO.

The performance of the *AIPO* interviewers was superior on these points:

Question 1 (Information about the war true and accurate?)
The distribution of replies to this question obtained by the two staffs is indicated in the following table:

	AIPO	NORC
Yes	159	220
No	131	122
Qualified answer	150	97
Don't know	35	37
No answer	3	3
	478*	479*

	AIPO	NORC
Got comment	274	184
Didn't get comment	153	270
Comment indicates that answer was misclassified	51	25
	478*	479*

* These figures do not total 480 (the assigned number) because 3 interviewers returned only 9 ballots instead of 10.

The pattern of replies obtained by the two staffs differs rather markedly. AIPO interviewers got a significantly higher proportion of qualified answers, with a correspondingly lower "Yes" percentage. They also got many more comments than did the NORC interviewers. Although it appears that they were guilty of misclassifying more answers than the NORC, this difference is not necessarily significant, since the NORC interviewers obtained fewer comments and hence there were fewer opportunities to judge the adequacy of their classifications.

The "qualified answer" box, frequently used on the regular AIPO questionnaires, was relatively new to the NORC interviewers. This practice factor may account for the difference in replies, in that the AIPO interviewers may have been more "qualified-answer conscious" and less inclined to force qualifications into a yes-no dichotomy.

The AIPO interviewers were clearly superior in eliciting and/or recording spontaneous comments made by the respondents. This is an important ability, since it provides a good indication of the extent to which respondents are interested and actively participating in the interview.

Question 7 (post-war peace solutions)

On this question, the performance of the AIPO interviewers was slightly superior. They got 25 less "Don't know" responses, and the quality of answers they got was judged to be a bit better.

Question 9 (weekly family income)

Fifty-six NORC respondents refused to give their family income, as compared with only 19 of those interviewed by the AIPO. Since the NORC interviewers were not accustomed to getting this type of information, and the AIPO were, the factor of practice is probably responsible for at least part of this difference.

The work of the two staffs did not differ appreciably on these points:

Question 2   (Japan or Germany our No. 1 enemy?)
Question 3   (how much longer will the war last?)
Question 4   (what will bring the war to an end?)
Question 5   (statements describing German and Japanese people)
Question 10 (vote in 1940)
Question 11 (religious affiliation)
Question 12 (parents' nationality)
Question 13 (education)
Fulfillment of economic assignment
Quality of interviewers' ballots
Costs

Sex differences. In view of the difference previously found between men and women in average grades, it was thought that the above differences on individual criteria might also be primarily a result of sex differences. However, an analysis of the results by sex did not show a consistent pattern, and would not permit the conclusion that the work of the AIPO women interviewers was entirely comparable with that of the NORC women. Hence weighting to correct for the disparity in the sex ratios would not have, in the case of these separate criteria, ironed out the differences between the two staffs.

Summary of differences. The NORC interviewers seem to have been somewhat more meticulous and careful in their work. They followed instructions more faithfully and took pains to fill out the required information more carefully. Although completeness and accuracy are stressed in the written instructions to interviewers put out by both organizations, it is likely that the supervised training period undergone by the NORC staff served to inculcate these objectives more effectively.

The AIPO staff, on the other hand, showed greater facility in obtaining spontaneous comments and in overcoming resistance to answering personal questions. Part of this superiority must be ascribed to the factor of practice, since the AIPO interviewers had had more experience with these types of questions, but it is conceivable that the slightly greater socio-economic heterogeneity of the AIPO staff may have made it easier for them to contact and draw out all types of people more effectively.

Summary and Conclusions

1. A technique has been presented for the measurement of interviewer performance in terms of some of the more important criteria of public opinion poll work. This technique was applied to a comparison of the performance of "trained" and "untrained" poll interviewers.

2. In terms of over-all quality of work, as judged by four raters working independently, there was no significant difference between the quality of work turned in by the trained and the untrained interviewers. The small difference which was in evidence was found to be a reflection of a disparity in the sex composition of the two staffs, hence not to be ascribed to the factor of training.

3. Despite the absence of an over-all difference in the quality of work, NORC interviewers were found to be slightly more meticulous in following instructions and getting complete data, while the AIPO interviewers were superior in the matter of eliciting spontaneous comments and securing personal information. These strengths and weaknesses of the two staffs counterbalanced one another in the end.

4. Although this experiment does not indicate that trained interviewers are superior to untrained ones, it does *not* necessarily follow that personal training and supervision of interviewers is of insufficient value to justify the expense involved. The head of the NORC staff stated, in submitting the list of interviewers who were to participate in the experiment, that he did not consider all of them to be really well trained. It is quite probable that a more intensively trained staff would have turned in work of a quality definitely superior to that of untrained interviewers. It

is obvious that, although reasonably adequate work can be obtained from interviewers who are hired and supervised by mail, personal training and supervision of interviewers will keep the quality of personnel and work at a much higher level. AIPO, recognizing this fact, has inaugurated a policy of sending representatives to the field to give their interviewers more intensive, personally supervised training.

CHAPTER VII

THE RELIABILITY OF INTERVIEWERS' RATINGS[1]

IN THE past, checks have been supplied for the reliability of questions used on public opinion polls. In such experiments split-ballot techniques have been applied. Thus it is possible to keep the following factors relatively constant: wording of the question, make-up of cross-section, and time of interview. Such checks, however, do little to answer those critics of public opinion polling methods who point out the paucity of information available concerning the reliability and the validity of the controls used by polling agencies. It is the purpose of this paper to indicate possible techniques for estimating such statistics and to supply the results of the use of these techniques in field experiments.

We shall define a *control* as any socio-economic characteristic which may be used in constructing or in checking the adequacy of a public opinion sample. We shall restrict the term *variable control* to those controls on which errors of classification will appear. Thus *variable controls* will include such characteristics as economic status, religion, possession of car or telephone, occupation, age, or education. Controls which are not variable controls might include sex, geography, or city size. That it is possible to find errors in classification even in these characteristics is clear, but we shall not concern ourselves with such exceptional cases.

We shall consider *reliability* of controls from two points of view: (1) the consistency with which the *same* observers classify the same individuals; (2) the consistency with which *different* observers classify the same individuals. A measure of this reliability might be the correlation coefficient, a contingency coefficient, or the percentage of identical classifications.

By *validity* of a control we shall mean a measure of the ability of observers to classify what they are supposed to classify. Results of studies given here on the subject of validity will be unsatisfactory for numerous reasons. It is to be hoped, however, that others will apply the obvious, but expensive, techniques to get improved measures.

SAME INTERVIEWERS USED ON A PANEL

In studying the case where the same interviewer reclassifies an individual the following technique was used:

(1) A small sample was set up according to the stratifications usually

[1] By Frederick Mosteller.

employed by the Office of Public Opinion Research. These are city size, state, economic status, and sex. The interviewer was asked to obtain the name and address of each respondent if possible.

(2) After a period of three weeks the same interviewers were supplied with the names and addresses of their respondents and asked to reinterview them, incidentally collecting the vital statistics on these respondents again.

The accompanying table indicates the result when the same interviewers reclassify individuals according to economic status.

TABLE 22. ECONOMIC STATUS

| | | Classification at Second Interview | | | | | |
		W	Av.+	Av.	P	OR	Total
Classification at	W	8	1				9
First Interview	Av.+	2	39	23			64
	Av.		13	111	10		134
	P			10	56	1	67
	OR		1	1	1	1	4
	Total	10	54	145	67	2	278

$r = .79$, Identical Classifications 77%.

In Table 22 and in the succeeding tables in this chapter, r is a product moment correlation coefficient.

In Table 23 the estimates of age of respondent given by the interviewer on the two occasions are tabulated by ten-year intervals.

TABLE 23. ESTIMATES OF AGE

| | | Second Interview | | | | | | | |
		20-9	30-9	40-9	50-9	60-9	70-9	80-9	Total
First	20-9	29							29
Interview	30-9	1	68	3		1			73
	40-9		4	54	2				60
	50-9		1	7	47	3			58
	60-9				3	39	1		43
	70-9					3	8		11
	80-9							3	3
	Total	30	73	64	52	46	9	3	277

$r = .97$, Classifications in same Ten-Year Interval 90%.

It will be interesting to compare the results of Table 23 with those obtained when different interviewers are used on successive interviews, since many interviewers merely ask the age of respondent. The decrease in reliability when we have different interviewers, therefore, may be due in large part to differences in relations between interviewer and respondent rather than to differences in actual ability of interviewers to estimate age. On the other hand, the high reliability observed cannot be said to be due to any ability on the part of the interviewers.

TABLE 24. INFORMATION ABOUT OWNERSHIP OF CARS

		Second Interview		
		Car	No Car	Total
First	Car	167	3	170
Interview	No car	6	80	86
	Total	173	83	256

Identical Classifications 96.5%.

It may be of some interest to compare these results with the responses of the same individuals to the same opinion question.

TABLE 25

Do you think Roosevelt is doing a good job, only a fair job, or a bad job in running the country?

		Second Interview			
		Good job	Fair job	Bad job	Total
First	Good job	131	28		159
Interview	Fair job	13	75	7	95
	Bad job		13	19	32
	Total	144	116	26	286

Identical Responses 79%.

We put no interpretation on this table; it is offered only as one example of the reliability of an opinion question where opinion may be said to have attained about as high a degree of crystallization as can be expected on the type of question usually studied in public opinion polls. This table does give us a chance to compare the reliability of our controls with the reliability of one of our most stable opinion questions.

DIFFERENT INTERVIEWERS CLASSIFYING THE SAME INDIVIDUALS

In this second study where we compared results of different interviewers interviewing the same people, the following technique was used to check the reliability of information on voting, economic status, age, and car and telephone information.

(1) Interviewers were assigned as usual according to stratifications usually employed by the Office of Public Opinion Research: city size, state, economic status, and sex. The interviewer was asked to obtain the name and address of his respondents if possible. Thus a panel was formed.

(2) In cities over 100,000 new interviewers were sent out to report on the paneled respondents. Thus both interviewers supplied the usual information on the same respondents with, of course, a lapse of time (about two months).

(3) Tables were set up and correlation coefficients and percentages of identical classifications were computed to compare the classifications made on these individuals by the different interviewers.

It must be remembered that the first interviewer was working under an assignment on economic status. In other words, the first interviewer had to get a certain number of persons in each of the categories Wealthy, Average Plus, Average, Poor, and On Relief. The second interviewer was doing what might be called "free interviewing" since he had no such restriction on his economic classification. Although theoretically, of course, the first interviewer had as much leeway as the second, since he could pick his respondents as he pleased, it is clear that when working on an assignment under the pressure of time, an interviewer may be tempted to classify a nearly borderline individual in a category which will best suit his assignment.

The accompanying table indicates the manner in which the two different sets of interviewers classified the same respondents according to economic status.

TABLE 26. ECONOMIC STATUS

		Classification by Second Interviewer				
		W	Av.+	Av.	P	OR	Total
Classification	W	3	3	4			10
by first	Av.+	4	20	21			45
Interviewer	Av.	2	24	74	5		105
	P	1	2	57	59	6	125
	OR			8	9	9	26
•	Total	10	49	164	73	15	311

$r = .63$, Identical Classifications 54%.

In Table 27 the estimates of age of respondent as given by the two interviewers are tabulated by ten-year intervals.

TABLE 27. ESTIMATES OF AGE

		Second Interview								
		Under 20	20-9	30-9	40-9	50-9	60-9	70-9	80-9	Total
First	20-9	I	41	II	7					60
Interview	30-9		4	65	II	2	2			84
	40-9	I		14	46	6				67
	50-9			I	7	25	4			37
	60-9					9	22	2		33
	70-9							4		4
	80-9							I	2	3
	Total	2	45	91	71	42	28	7	2	288

$r = .91$, Classifications in same Ten-Year Interval, 71%.

We repeat that the high correlation found in Table 27 is not due principally to consistency in observation by different interviewers, but rather to the consistency of the respondent in stating his own age.

Table 28 and Table 29 represent information gathered by the interviewers on possession of car and telephone.

TABLE 28. INFORMATION ABOUT OWNERSHIP OF CAR

		Second Interview		
		Car	No Car	Total
First	Car	158	23	181
Interview	No Car	18	89	107
	Total	176	112	288

Identical Classifications 86%.

TABLE 29. INFORMATION ABOUT TELEPHONE

		Second Interview		
		Telephone	No Telephone	Total
First	Tel.	161	17	178
Interview	No Tel.	24	105	129
	Total	185	122	307

Identical Classifications 87%

Table 30 supplies the result of asking the same question about voting. In this case, it must be remembered the reliability is just a measure of the consistency of the respondent in answering the same question, if we assume that the interviewer reports that response without error.

TABLE 30. RESPONSE TO VOTING QUESTION

		Second Interview			
		Didn't Vote	Voted Willkie	Voted Roosevelt	Total
First	Didn't vote	44	6	6	56
Interview	Voted Willkie	2	86	10	98
	Voted Roosevelt	6	8	118	132
	Total	52	100	134	286

Identical Responses 87%.

If we consider the tables on car, telephone, and voting as comparisons of the respondents' consistency in answering the same question, it appears that respondents in big cities answer these purely factual questions in exactly the same manner in about 87 per cent of the cases. This percentage is certainly higher than the percentage of times different interviewers classify identically the same individual on economic status. One reason we have a lower reliability in the case of economic status is that such classifications are less clean-cut than, say, "voted for Roosevelt." When we used the same interviewer on both interviews, however, we obtained a higher reliability.

Another panel study made by OPOR was conducted in Chicago, and was composed of native whites. The first interviewers had quotas on economic status composed only of Wealthy, Average Plus, and Average, while the second interviewers were allowed to classify freely.

The results on economic status are shown in Table 31.

TABLE 31. ECONOMIC STATUS

		Second Interview				
		Wealthy	Average Plus	Average	Poor	Total
First	Wealthy	11	7	1	0	19
Interview	Average Plus	13	11	9	0	33
	Average	8	24	59	5	96
	Total	32	42	69	5	148

Identical Classifications 55%

Due to the truncation of the economic distribution, there seems to have been no improvement in ability to classify respondents identically on both interviews. This result certainly supports the hypothesis that errors in classification are due to the fineness of the categories rather than the number of categories used.

Without supplying the data we will give herewith the percentages of identical classifications in the vital information of the Chicago poll corresponding to Tables 27-30:

1. In the same 10-year age bracket, 74%,
2. Identical car information, 89%,
3. Identical telephone information, 90%,
4. Identical voting information, 90%.

Although we have slightly higher percentages of identical classifications throughout the vital information of the Chicago poll, as compared with the poll in cities over 100,000 mentioned earlier, the differences cannot be said to be significantly higher at even the .10 level. If these differences are reliable, however, it is impossible to say whether they are due to restriction of the sample, more careful selection of interviewers, or the shorter time lag between interviews (ten days in the Chicago interview as compared with two months in the first poll mentioned).

VALIDITY OF CONTROLS

One way of measuring the validity of information supplied by the polls on economic status is to choose a group of people, study their economic characteristics, and have them classified by experts. Then one could correlate the results given by the interviewers with the opinions of experts. For the present paper, however, the expense of this method made it impractical.

A less satisfactory procedure is to ask the respondents to which average weekly income group they belong and correlate these responses with the interviewers' classification. The result of such a procedure is shown in Table 32.

TABLE 32

Please tell me in which of these groups the average weekly income of your immediate family belongs

		Over $60.	$40. $60.	$30. $40.	$20. $30.	$15. $20.	Under $15.	Total
Classification	W	195	17	5	1		1	219
by	A+	580	276	61	37	16	7	977
Interviewer	A	326	936	815	487	145	82	2791
	P+	30	106	284	416	211	105	1152
	P	30	124	331	732	705	745	2667
	OAA & OR	3	6	19	75	180	625	908
	Total	1164	1465	1515	1748	1257	1565	8714

$$r = .73.$$

Naturally, this method has several drawbacks. The interviewers' estimate of the respondent's economic status is probably not independent of the statement about income given by the respondent. There are, of course, errors due to lack of veracity on the part of the respondent.

If we restrict ourselves to cities over 100,000 we get the result given in Table 33.

TABLE 33. CITIES OVER 100,000

Question: same as on Table 32

		Over $60.	$40. $60.	$30. $40.	$20. $30.	$15. $20.	Under $15.	Total
Classification	W	32	1	2				35
by	A+	80	19	3				102
Interviewer	A	46	123	73	25	6	3	276
	P+	4	21	61	64	19	4	173
	P	2	4	25	66	81	54	232
	OAA & OR	1	2	4	13	36	69	125
	Total	165	170	168	168	142	130	943

$r = .81.$

It will be noted that the correlation is significantly increased as a result of holding the population density more nearly constant.

With respondents on farms and in towns of less than 2,500, we find a correlation of .72 between the same variables. If cash income has less importance in determining socio-economic status on farms and in small communities, such a drop in correlation is readily explained. On the other hand, the difference may be due to a generally higher level of interviewer ability in large cities.

Respondents' own ratings. It may be of interest to compare the respondent's own classification of his income group with that of the interviewer (Table 34).

TABLE 34

What income group in our country do you feel you are a member of?

		Upper	Upper Middle	Middle	Lower Middle	Lower	Total
Classification	W	18	19	30	3		70
by	A+	18	103	173	24	12	322
Interviewer	A	4	56	546	190	78	874
	P+	1	16	253	193	118	581
	P	1	6	164	225	358	754
	OAA & OR			45	62	248	355
	Total	42	202	1211	697	814	2966

$r = .60.$

We find a considerably lower correlation between the respondent's subjective classification of his income group and the interviewer's classification, as shown in Table 34, than in that between the respondent's objective classification of his income status and the interviewer's classification of economic status as indicated in Table 33. This difference is principally due to the well-known tendency of the higher income groups to classify themselves in somewhat lower brackets than they are, and of the poor to overestimate their income level.

The most likely reason for this tendency is the difference in standards of judgment used by the upper and lower income groups. Upper income people seem to compare themselves with an even higher income group, while the poor see all around them people even worse off than they are.

The correlation between the interviewer's classification and the respondent's subjective classification of himself is slightly higher than the correlation between the respondent's subjective and objective classifications of himself. These correlations are respectively .60 and .58.

Summary

1. When the *same* interviewers reinterview the same respondents, the reliability of their ratings on controls is high. A correlation of .79 was obtained between ratings on income, .97 between ratings on age.

2. When *different* interviewers interview the same respondents, the reliability of their ratings is also found to be high. A correlation of .63 is obtained between ratings of different interviewers on income, .91 between ratings on age.

3. Further studies on the problem of validity of ratings are needed. They have not been done by OPOR because of the expense involved. The study reported here is not regarded as highly satisfactory, although it does provide certain evidence that interviewers' ratings on economic status as judged by reported income is high (r of .73). A higher correlation was found in urban than in rural areas.

4. The interviewers' classifications of respondents' incomes correlates more highly with the respondents' reported incomes (.73) than does either (a) the respondents' subjective classification of their income groups with the interviewers' classification (.60) or, (b) the respondents' classification of themselves and the incomes they say they receive (.58).

CHAPTER VIII

INTERVIEWER BIAS AND RAPPORT[1]

COMPARATIVELY little is known of the many factors at play when a survey is in the field and interviewers are meeting the sample population face to face. To what extent do respondents react to the question itself and to what extent to some characteristic of the interviewer or to some extraneous factor in the environment? Do the opinions of interviewers affect the intonations and inflections of his voice, his gestures, and his whole manner when he is asking someone else for his opinion? How much do interviewers force vague and inconclusive answers into the specific categories called for on the questionnaire? Some of these points have been discussed academically and vaguely with interviewers themselves during their training, but little is known about the degree to which they may and do affect poll results.

The studies reported here explore some, but by no means all, of the possible distortions of opinion due to the face-to-face relationship between interviewer and respondent.

1. *Influence of interviewers' opinions*

For some time the American Institute of Public Opinion and the Office of Public Opinion Research have made a practice of surveying the opinions of interviewers at the same time their national surveys are conducted. Each of the approximately 200 interviewers who receives an assignment on a national survey is sent an "Interviewer's Ballot." This ballot, identical with that used on the national survey, is to be filled out by the interviewer himself, expressing his own opinions; and he returns his own ballot with his completed assignment.[2] Hence it has been possible

---

[1] This problem was first examined by William Salstrom when he was a research assistant at OPOR. He is responsible for most of the over-all analysis of interviewer bias and the studies of bias in sections and in different-sized cities. Salstrom is now Associate Director of the National Opinion Research Center of Denver University. The other analyses presented here were made by Daniel Katz, Donald Rugg, Frederick Mosteller, and Frederick Williams.

[2] In interpreting the results shown below, the reader must be warned that there was no objective means of determining whether any particular interviewer filled in his "Interviewer's Ballot" on the questionnaire used in this analysis *before* or *after* completing his interviewing assignment. If many of the interviewers did their interviewing first and had their own opinions formed by the responses of their respondents, the differences shown below may be slightly exaggerated. It is not possible to determine from these data exactly how much effect this factor may have had, but it is doubtful that the accumulated effect would invalidate the results.

to analyze the results found on any particular question for the national population by the opinions of the interviewers themselves.

This analysis—to determine the extent to which interviewers with different opinions reported similar opinions from respondents—was carried out on an AIPO survey made in October 1940. Although only a small number of questions was asked on this survey, over 12,000 interviews were completed on the same questions within a single week. However, approximately one-third of the interviews had to be eliminated on the basis of two counts. An interviewer's entire assignment was excluded (1) if the interviewer failed to return an Interviewer's Ballot or (2) if the interviewer used an assistant to help him with part of the assignment. This second qualification was necessary since the assistants seldom sent in an interviewer's ballot.

This survey was aimed mainly at predicting the forthcoming presidential election, and the ballot included only one nonelection question, as follows:

"Which of these two things do you think is more important for the United States to try to do—
To keep out of war ourselves, or
To help England win, even at the risk of getting into the war?"

On this ballot there was also a category for respondents who could express "No Choice" between the above two alternatives. In the following analysis the respondents who expressed "No Choice" were arbitrarily omitted in order to simplify the presentation.[3]

The ballots for the national sample were divided according to the interviewers' opinions on the above question concerning helping England or keeping strictly out of the war. Then each of these groups was sorted to find what percentage of the respondents in each group chose each of the alternatives. The results are shown in Figure 11.

The 16-per cent difference in results between these two groups has a critical ratio of 13.9. This difference is so great for the size of the sample used that the possibility of this difference occurring by chance is almost incalculably small.

When this same analysis is carried out on certain subgroups of the population, the differences are in the same direction: the "Keep-Out" interviewers consistently get a higher "Keep-Out" vote among their

[3] In future analyses the differences in the amount of "No Opinion" vote obtained by different interviewers should be examined. In fact, a brief analysis indicated that, on this question, about a fourth of the interviewers were responsible for obtaining 80 per cent of the "No Choice" vote.

FIGURE 11. COMPARISON OF INTERVIEWERS' AND RE-
SPONDENTS' OPINIONS

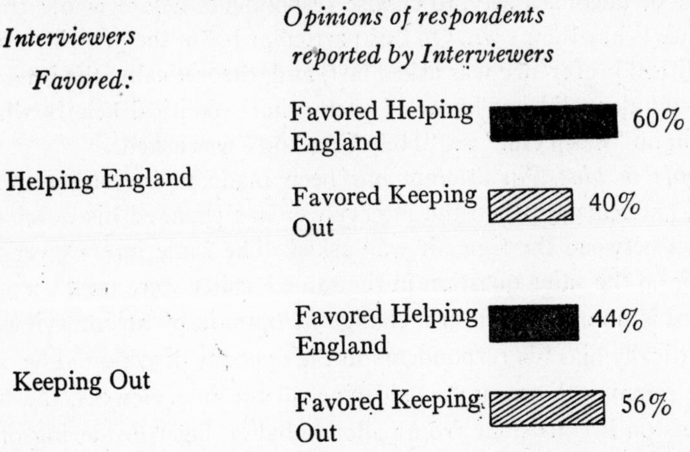

Interviewers
Favored:

*Opinions of respondents
reported by Interviewers*

Helping England

Favored Helping
England   60%

Favored Keeping
Out   40%

Keeping Out

Favored Helping
England   44%

Favored Keeping
Out   56%

respondents than do the "Help-England" interviewers. For instance, when the questionnaires are divided by seven geographical regions of the United States and within each of the regions by the sex and the 1940 political party preference of the respondents, not one of the differences in the resulting twenty-eight cells is in the opposite direction from that found on the totals.

A further analysis of these figures was made in which the interviewer's political preference was related to the respondent's political preference in addition to the relationship between the interviewer's and the respondent's choices on the question "Keep Out" *vs.* "Help England."

TABLE 35. RELATIONSHIP BETWEEN INTERVIEWERS' AND RESPONDENTS' POLITICAL AND WAR ATTITUDES

Interviewer's 1940 Preference	Respondent's 1940 Preference	% "Keep-Out" Obtained by "Keep-Out" Interviewers	% "Keep-Out" Obtained by "Help-England" Interviewers	Diff.	C.R.
Roosevelt	Roosevelt	51.1%	30.9%	20.2%	8.7
Willkie	Willkie	64.0	43.4	20.6	9.1
Roosevelt	Willkie	56.2	49.6	6.6	1.9
Willkie	Roosevelt	47.8	37.7	10.1	4.2

It will be noticed in Table 35 that when interviewers are dealing with respondents whose political preference is the same as their own, they are more likely to obtain answers to the questions in correspondence with their own opinions on the "Keep Out—Help England" question than when they are interviewing respondents of opposite political beliefs. This fact opens the possibility that interviewers have a tendency, consciously or unconsciously, to choose respondents whose whole frame of reference is like their own. On this particular ballot the question concerning political preference was asked last, and, theoretically, the interviewer and respondent did not know of each other's political beliefs when the question on "Keep Out" *vs.* "Help England" was asked.

Trends in bias. An attempt has been made to investigate the bias trends, particularly when the interviewer has changed his opinion on a question between the times it was asked. The same interviewers interviewing on the same question in the same locality were used.

There is no evidence that a change of opinion by an interviewer will automatically bias his respondents in the opposite direction. The over-all picture remains the same: considering all the interviewers, the bias on the question is consistent from ballot to ballot, but considering only the interviewers duplicated on the two ballots and their change or constancy of opinion, the data do not indicate any positive results.

An example of the type of data resulting from this study is the following:

Do you think the government is giving the public as much information as it should about the war?

Interviewers' Responses			Respondents Say:	
1st Ballot	*2nd Ballot*		*1st Ballot*	*2nd Ballot*
		Yes	54%	72%
Yes	Yes	No	37	21
		No Opinion	9	7
		Cases	740	785
		Yes	48%	63%
Yes	No	No	44	28
		No Opinion	8	1
		Cases	110	111
		Yes	48%	68%
No	Yes	No	43	26
		No Opinion	9	6
		Cases	225	213
		Yes	43%	63%
No	No	No	47	27
		No Opinion	10	10
		Cases	206	245

Although this tabulation does indicate a slight tendency on the part of respondents to increase or decrease their "Yes" response relative to changes of opinion by interviewers, the results are well within the sampling error even at the .90 level of significance. It has been observed, furthermore, that this tendency is not consistent from question to question.

Bias on "open-ended" questions. Not so generally known is the effect of interviewer bias on "open-ended" or "free-answer" questions as compared with "closed-end" questions. After extensive investigation OPOR found that when experienced interviewers were used, there was no evidence that open-ended questions produced more bias due to interviewer opinion than did dichotomous questions. This finding is important because of the present tendency on the part of some agencies to employ free-answer questions almost exclusively and because of their great value in exploratory work.

2. Differences when area is held constant

It is reasonable to ask if these differences are really due to interviewer bias, or perhaps due to the concentration of isolationist and interventionist opinion in certain areas. Interviewers chosen in a certain area could, by chance, represent the opinions of the majority of residents in that area.

In order to test this hypothesis the questionnaires were further analyzed by pairing interviewers who worked in the same areas and obtained similar samples, but who held opposite views on the question of "Keep Out" *vs.* "Help England."

It was possible to pick out twenty-two cities and towns in which two interviewers with opposing opinions could be compared. The results of the two groups differed by 9.4 per cent (C.R. = 3.0). Thus it would seem that, even when area is held constant, the "Keep-Out" interviewers get significantly more "Keep-Out" responses than do the "Help-England" interviewers. But when we compare this difference with that obtained when the interviewers were not paired, we find a drop from 16 per cent difference to 9.4 per cent. It would appear that we have accounted for at least part of the obtained difference merely on the basis of place of interview. Such a supposition, however, is not the real answer as the following analysis shows.

3. Differences by size of place

The questionnaires used on the paired-interviewer analysis were divided into three groups according to the size of the place in which the interviewing was done. Another survey, taken about the same time was used for this analysis. The question analyzed was: "Do you think that the United States Navy should be used to convoy (guard) ships carrying war materials to Britain?"

Results are shown in Figure 12.

FIGURE 12. COMPARISON OF INTERVIEWERS' AND RESPONDENTS'
OPINIONS BY SIZE OF TOWN IN WHICH INTERVIEWING OCCURRED

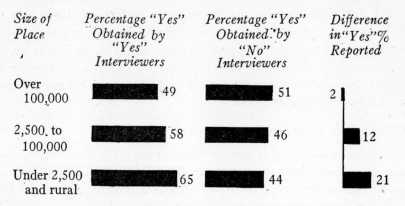

Size of Place	Percentage "Yes" Obtained by "Yes" Interviewers	Percentage "Yes" Obtained by "No" Interviewers	Difference in "Yes"% Reported
Over 100,000	49	51	2
2,500 to 100,000	58	46	12
Under 2,500 and rural	65	44	21

Figure 12 shows that in large cities interviewers' opinions are not effectively correlated with the opinions of their respondents. In fact, a slight negative difference is obtained. In the small towns and rural farm areas, on the contrary, the difference is large.

Several factors may bear on this result. In the first place, an interviewer is probably better known by his respondents in a small town than in a large city. As a result, he may consciously or unconsciously choose respondents who think as he does himself, or, at least, with whom he is acquainted and who may be most likely to share his own views. Or, the respondents may answer in terms of their knowledge of the interviewer's opinions. Secondly, interviewers in larger cities, for the most part, receive larger interviewing assignments, receive assignments more frequently and also stay with the organization longer. Since interviewers are usually instructed to avoid their friends when choosing respondents, interviewers in large cities are less likely to interview persons with whom they have had previous acquaintance.

One suggestion which arises from this analysis is that interviewing in small towns and rural areas should be handled by people who are not local residents, but who may, for example, be sent from large cities in the area.

4. *Difference in socio-economic status of interviewers*

a. *Differences in sex, age, and income.* The differences between opinions on a variety of questions reported by interviewers when interviewers are separated by sex, age, or income are neither consistent nor significant. The considerable data analyzed by OPOR on these variables do not provide us with a solution to the problem: what is the most unbiased type of interviewer? It is likely that the most important variables are not rough indices of this sort but other more subtle variables such as those reported below. ,

b. *Class differences.* The interviewers of most polling organizations are white-collar workers, with the appearance and attitude typical of educated members of the middle class. Does their class membership influence their selection of respondents or the opinions which respondents express to them? The problem here is not so much one of bias as it is degree of rapport between members of different social classes.

In an experiment previously reported, the same assignments were given to nine middle-class interviewers and eleven specially trained working-class interviewers in a low-income area of Pittsburgh, Pennsylvania.[4] The ballot included questions on labor issues, the war, and government ownership of industry. Each interviewing staff was given the same type of sample population to poll, and each staff completed about 600 interviews. The study was made in March 1941.

On the average, the working-class interviewers selected respondents who were higher in socio-economic status than the respondents selected by the middle-class interviewers. In other words, the selection went exactly counter to the theory that a person in a given economic class tends to select people like himself. The main reason for the difference in groups interviewed lay in the inexperience of the working-class interviewers. Five of the nine middle-class interviewers, regularly employed by AIPO, had become accustomed to going very low in the socio-economic scale in order to get a true cross-section of the population. Many of the working-class group, on the other hand, new to the whole interviewing procedure, placed a premium on interviewing middle- and upper-income people because they thought their opinions were worth more than those of the uninformed and the poorly dressed.

In spite of this fact, the opinions reported by the working-class interviewers were consistently more radical than those reported by the middle-class interviewers. The difference was especially marked on labor ques-

[4] Daniel Katz, "Do Interviewers Bias Polls?", *Public Opinion Quarterly*, 1942, 6, 248-268.

tions, particularly for the trade-union members interviewed by the two staffs. An example of this difference is shown in Figure 13, where union-members were asked whether or not they favored a law against sit-down strikes.

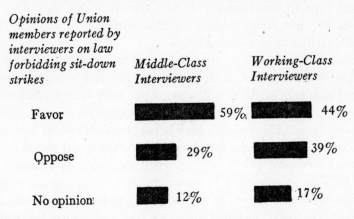

FIGURE 13. COMPARISON OF INTERVIEWS MADE BY MID-
DLE-CLASS AND WORKING-CLASS INTERVIEWERS

Opinions of Union members reported by interviewers on law forbidding sit-down strikes	Middle-Class Interviewers	Working-Class Interviewers
Favor	59%	44%
Oppose	29%	39%
No opinion	12%	17%

On war questions the working-class interviewers reported more isolationist sentiment than did the middle-class interviewers.

These differences in reported opinion parallel the differences in opinion between the two interviewing staffs themselves—the working-class interviewers were somewhat more radical and more isolationist in their views than the middle-class interviewers.

Two facts make it seem likely that the findings of the working-class group are more representative of the true state of opinion in this low-income area of an industrial city than are those of the middle-class interviewers: (1) The opinions reported by the five experienced AIPO interviewers are on most questions more radical than those reported by the four newly trained white-collar interviewers—the more experienced middle-class interviewers swing over in the direction of the findings of the working-class interviewers. (2) the comments reported by the working-class interviewers show that they had better rapport with their respondents than did the middle-class interviewers. Particularly was this true on labor issues. The working-class people interviewed in this experiment—especially the respondents with strong prolabor views—seemed to express themselves more freely to interviewers whom they regarded as members of their own class.

c. *Racial differences.* When interviewing any persons who are members of a minority racial group in a culture, it is of the utmost importance to have interviewers who are either members of the race or who, because of their special linguistic background or an intimate association with the group, are known from previous experience to be able to gain immediate confidence and get complete rapport. Here, again, we are not concerned with bias as such but with a condition affecting the reliability of an expressed opinion.

An experiment done by the National Opinion Research Center in May 1942 neatly contrasts the difference of opinion reported by white and Negro interviewers of Negroes in a large southern city. White and Negro interviewers were given the same assignments. Each interviewing staff completed approximately 500 cases. Figure 14 shows the results.[5]

5. *The Relation of interviewing experience to interview bias*

To determine whether experienced interviewers show less bias than inexperienced ones, the results of twelve questions on two OPOR questionnaires were examined.[6]

[5] These figures are taken from the newspaper *PM*, New York City, September 9, 1942.
[6] The questions were:

Ballot A (July 10, 1941)
Senator Wheeler says that the power of the United States should be put behind a peace movement to end the war now. Do you agree, or disagree, with Senator Wheeler's statement?
Do you approve, or disapprove, of the government's action in taking over the defense of Iceland?
Which of these two things do you think is the more important—That Germany be defeated, or That this country keep out of war?
It has been said recently that in order to keep the Germans out of North and South America, we must prevent them from capturing the islands off the west coast of Africa. Do you think we should try to keep the Germans out of the islands off the west coast of Africa?
Should the United States take steps now to keep Japan from becoming more powerful, even if this means risking a war with Japan?
Do you think that in America anybody should be allowed to speak on any subject any time he wants to, or do you think there are times when free speech should be prohibited?

Ballot B (November 19, 1941)
Do you feel that, in general, the information you are getting about the war situation is true and accurate?
Do you think the government is giving the public as much information as it should about the war?
Should the United States take steps now to keep Japan from becoming more powerful, even if this means we have to go to war against Japan?
Do you believe the British are doing all they possibly can to win the war? If Germany should defeat England and Russia in the present war, do you think Germany would start a war against the United States within the next ten years?
In general, do you approve, or disapprove, of the way Roosevelt is handling his job as President today?

FIGURE 14

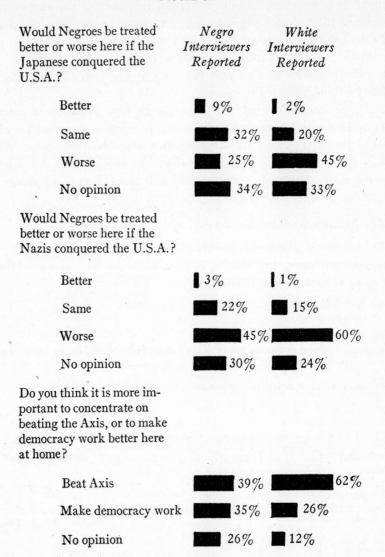

Would Negroes be treated better or worse here if the Japanese conquered the U.S.A.?	Negro Interviewers Reported	White Interviewers Reported
Better	9%	2%
Same	32%	20%
Worse	25%	45%
No opinion	34%	33%

Would Negroes be treated better or worse here if the Nazis conquered the U.S.A.?		
Better	3%	1%
Same	22%	15%
Worse	45%	60%
No opinion	30%	24%

Do you think it is more important to concentrate on beating the Axis, or to make democracy work better here at home?		
Beat Axis	39%	62%
Make democracy work	35%	26%
No opinion	26%	12%

Approximately 200 interviewers worked on each of the two questionnaires. Of these, the fifty interviewers who were most experienced and the fifty who were least experienced were selected in each case. The criterion of experience used was the total number of assignments each interviewer had done. The median number of assignments for the experienced groups was around 50, while for the less experienced in terviewers it was less than 10. On each assignment, interviewers were given an average of fifteen ballots.

The measure of interviewer bias used is the same as that described above on page 108.

Table 36 compares the average bias for the experienced and the less experienced interviewers on the 12 questions used. That longer interviewing experience was not effective in reducing the amount of interviewer bias is evident.

TABLE 36. COMPARISON OF REPORTS OF EXPERIENCED AND LESS EXPERIENCED INTERVIEWERS

Interviewers	Average Bias in Per cent	Average Deviation
Experienced	5.06	1.86
Less Experienced	5.02	2.36

6. Correcting for interviewer bias

What should the investigator do to correct for interviewer bias? Just what adjustment might be made is difficult to determine in advance. If an investigator is using interviewers to gather information on a wide variety of issues—which is the usual case—it becomes highly impracticable to assign interviews in advance even to interviewers whose opinions have been probed. Gallup uses approximately an equal number of Republican and Democratic interviewers, but obviously party affiliation is only one of many sources of bias.

The studies reported here may leave the impression that because of interviewer bias the work of public opinion polls is largely invalidated. But by and large, the over-all difference obtained in a figure on a national poll will not vary significantly from a figure adjusted for interviewer bias. For example, it will be recalled that a difference of 16 per cent was obtained in the answers reported by interviewers who favored helping England at the risk of war and those who thought we should try to keep out of war. However, if we give the "Help-England" and the "Keep-out" interviewers equal weights in the sample, the national percentage for "keep out" increases by only 1.3 per cent, which is not statistically significant.

The results reported above, although of precautionary value and of psychological interest, should not greatly disturb any investigator who uses common sense in setting up his assignment, who can plan controlled investigations when he suspects that lack of rapport may influence expressed opinion, or who realizes the elementary principle that class and racial discrepancies between a "regular" native, white-collar, middle-class interviewer and various other members of the population not fitting into this social niche must be minimized by special supplementary interviewers.

By and large, if an investigator is interested in correcting for interviewer bias (not lack of rapport due to class or racial differences), it appears that he will be playing safe if he selects an equal number of interviewers who reflect the major biases an issue is likely to arouse.[7]

Summary

The studies reported here are essentially exploratory: they point out certain problems affecting the face-to-face interviewing situation and indicate strongly the need for further research before systematic generalizations can be made on the problem of interviewer bias and interviewer rapport. The following conclusions, however, seem tenable.

1. The opinions interviewers report have been found on certain questions to correlate with the opinions of the interviewers themselves.

2. There appears to be an inverse correlation between the degree of relationship between interviewers' and respondents' opinions and the size of the town in which interviewing occurs.

3. Interviewers who are highly experienced show as much bias as less experienced interviewers.

4. Discrepancies between interviewers and respondents on the ground of class or race definitely hamper rapport and create a distortion of true opinion.

5. Although interviewer bias exists, by and large the biases in one direction cancel those in the opposite direction, so that the over-all percentage of opinion is not likely to be significantly wrong. (This conclusion is, of course, not meant to imply that error due to lack of rapport tends to cancel itself out.) If an investigator wants to minimize interviewer bias, he should choose an equal number of interviewers who are biased in different directions.

[7] See Appendix 2 for formulae demonstrating this conclusion.

CHAPTER IX

REFUSALS AS A SOURCE OF BIAS[1]

THE problem of this article is the effect of refusals in distorting the ideal stratified sample of the public opinion polls. Our method will be to compare the characteristics of people interviewed with those who are approached but from whom complete interviews cannot be obtained.

On two surveys made by the Office of Public Opinion Research in March and July 1942, interviewers were given the following instructions: "On this assignment we are asking you to keep a complete record of all people you approach who *for any reason whatsoever* refuse to be interviewed or who discontinue an interview that has been started. In every instance you should try to obtain the answer to the first question on the regular ballot. If you are not able to obtain an answer to the first question, fill in the information about the person on the record form. We want this record regardless of the reason for failure to complete the interview. Prosaic reasons like 'I have to catch the next bus downtown' are just as important as ones like 'I don't talk to anybody about the war.' From our standpoint the most important thing is that you send us *complete information about each person approached.* The refusals and incompleted interviews are just as important as the ballots, and the time you spend on them should, of course, be included in your interviewing bill."

Four hundred and twenty-nine refusals and incompleted interviews were recorded in the March survey, and 476 in the July survey. This represents in both cases 14 per cent of the people approached for interviews. Table 37 shows the distribution of refusals and incompleted interviews, and also of completed interviews by city size, economic status, sex, and color.

We see here that refusals are most frequent among poor people, women, and in large cities. Refusals did not introduce any biases with respect to the representation of each variable in the total sample, since interviewers were assigned a particular number of farmers, poor people, men, Negroes, etc., and told to continue interviewing until they had the required number. However, this compensating procedure does not correct biases on variables such as age and nationality background, which

[1] By John Harding.

TABLE 37. DISTRIBUTION OF INCOMPLETED AND COMPLETED INTERVIEWS BY
CITY SIZE, ECONOMIC STATUS, SEX, AND COLOR

| | MARCH, 1942 | | JULY, 1942 | |
	Incompleted Interviews	Completed Interviews	Incompleted Interviews	Completed Interviews
City Size				
Cities over 500,000	29%	19%	25%	17%
100,000 to 500,000	23	17	19	15
10,000 to 100,000	24	17	16	17
2,500 to 10,000	8	12	12	15
Under 2,500	7	18	17	17
Farms	9	17	11	19
Income				
Wealthy and Average plus	11	14	10	14
Average	30	36	33	37
Poor	54	42	50	42
On Relief	5	8	7	7
Sex				
Men	40	51	47	51
Women	60	49	53	49
Color				
White	94	96	91	90
Negro	6	4	9	10

were not controlled in making up the interviewers' assignments. (Attempting to control more than a few variables adds very greatly to the expense of interviewing.) Table 38 shows the percentage of incompleted and completed interviews that fall into each of these classifications.

It is clear that refusals are more common among older people; the total number of refusals is so small, however, that this difference does not bias the age distribution of the final cross section to any appreciable extent. If complete interviews had been obtained from all the respondents approached, 18 per cent of our cross section would have been under 30, 48 per cent between 30 and 49, and 34 per cent 50 or over—in no age group is the bias greater than 1 per cent.

The interviewers were asked to report in every case the reason for failure to secure a complete interview. The reasons are listed in Table 39.

The general impression one gets from this table is that most refusals result from factors independent of respondents' opinions concerning the specific questions on the ballot. This impression is strengthened by Table 40, which shows that the majority of incompleted interviews are terminated before even the first question has been asked (despite the instructions given to the interviewers).

TABLE 38. DISTRIBUTION OF INCOMPLETED AND COMPLETED INTERVIEWS BY
AGE AND NATIONALITY

	JULY, 1942	
	Incompleted Interviews	Completed Interviews
Age		
Under 30	12%	18%
30-49	45	49
50 and over	43	33
Nationality Background		
United States	70	71
Great Britain and Dominions	4	7
Ireland	4	4
Germany	7	4
Italy	5	2
Occupied countries	7	6
Other	3	6

TABLE 39. REASONS FOR INCOMPLETED INTERVIEWS

	March, 1942	July, 1942
Respondent refuses to talk about anything—too busy, not interested, or suspicious.	76%	60%
Respondent refuses to talk about the war.	6	6
Interview discontinued—respondent can't understand questions, or talks at random.	12	23
Interruptions.	2	3
Respondent is sick.	3	4
Respondent cannot be included in interviewer's assignment—interviewer has approached the wrong person.	1	2
No reason given.	..	2

On both the March and July ballots the first question respondents were asked was whether we should consider Japan or Germany our No. 1 enemy in this war. Table 41 gives the distribution of answers among those people who did give their opinions on this first question but refused to continue the interview—103 on the March ballot and 108 on the July ballot. The distribution of answers in the completed interviews on each ballot is shown for comparison.

TABLE 40. LENGTH OF INTERVIEWS

	March, 1942	July, 1942
Interview terminated before first question has been asked.	61%	46%
Interview terminated after first question.	30	48
Interview terminated after several questions.	9	6

Although there is a striking difference between the incompleted and the completed interviews on the March ballot, this difference is reversed in July. Since interviewers often find that respondents answer questions in a superficial manner on the basis of the headlines in the morning paper, or whatever else happens to be at the top of their minds, it is natural that this tendency should be exaggerated among people who were not much interested in the interview and were about to refuse to continue with it. Thus their answers might be expected to deviate from those of the regular cross section in the direction of greater conformity to the emphases suggested by temporary fluctuations in the course of the war.[2]

An examination of the *New York Times* for the two-week period during which interviewing was done on the March ballot shows that on eleven days the No. 1 story on the front page concerned the war with Japan, on two days it concerned the war with Germany, and on one day it dealt with neither. However, on every day of the two-week period during which interviewing was done on the July ballot, the No. 1 story on the front page of the *Times* concerned the war with Germany. This change in emphasis, which was paralleled in other newspapers and radio treatments of the war, had its effect on the opinions of the regular cross section—there was an increase of 4 per cent in the number who thought Germany was our chief enemy—but this was slight when compared to its effect on the people who did not complete the interview, where the increase was 27 per cent.

TABLE 41

Answers to First Question: Is Japan or Germany our Chief Enemy?

	March, 1942		July, 1942	
	INCOMPLETED INTERVIEWS	COMPLETED INTERVIEWS	INCOMPLETED INTERVIEWS	COMPLETED INTERVIEWS
Japan	34%	29%	23%	30%
Germany	31	47	58	51
Both	35	24	19	19

[2] This explanation and its demonstration were suggested by Louis Barron.

These findings suggest that the opinions of people who refuse to be interviewed are often more superficial and unstable than those of more cooperative respondents. Even the differences found on this question, however, are not large enough to have much practical significance; inclusion of the incomplete interviews in the cross section would on neither the March nor the July ballot change the proportion of any by more than 1 per cent.

Our conclusion from these data is that refusals do not greatly affect the extent to which the sample secured by poll interviewers is a representative cross section of the population. The most important evidence for this conclusion is the small number of refusals and incompleted interviews—about 14 per cent of the number of people approached. This number is too small to make any appreciable difference to the composition of the final cross section with respect to any of the variables we have investigated; and it is probably too small to make much difference with respect even to such intangible factors as "suspiciousness" or "extent of subversive opinions."

It is extremely doubtful that the bias introduced into poll results by the refusal of some people to be interviewed can compare in size with the bias resulting from the tendency of interviewers to select their respondents in an unrandom fashion, or the bias introduced by the divergence of respondents' answers from their true opinions.

PART III

SOME PROBLEMS IN SAMPLING

CHAPTER X

SOME GENERAL PRINCIPLES OF SAMPLING[1]

THE basic principle of modern research is to get the facts. In social and economic research facts of interest often concern a very large group—frequently the total population. But the total population about which we seek information is so large, and the needed facts are so many and change so rapidly, that it becomes very difficult to subject the population to investigation. Because of such obstacles we must have very efficient methods if we are to determine the facts inexpensively, accurately, and quickly. The two methods most widely used today for studying human population are:

1. *The complete census,* in which data on every unit of the total population (person, family, household, dwelling) are collected and classified.

2. *The sample,* in which data for only a small but representative cross-section of the population are collected and classified.
   The census is, of course, the fundamental method of research.

The reasons for not always taking a complete census are:

(a) It is not always possible to get timely and accurate data from the whole of a large group of people. In particular, it is not possible to get these data with a limited budget.

> The 1940 census cost about $50,000,000.
> The unemployment census of 1937 cost $1,986,595.46.

(b) Sometimes something analogous to the indeterminacy principle in physics occurs, where the very act of observing a social phenomenon affects the phenomenon itself. For example, consider the effect of an attempt to find out by complete census how many people listening to their radios at 6:45 P.M. on any particular night know the sponsor of the program. The necessary attendant publicity would mold and perhaps even change the public's listening habits. Another example would be the case where the manufacturer of some commodity such as electric light bulbs would like to test the breaking strength of his product. A complete census would mean breaking every bulb.

[1] By J. Stevens Stock, Bureau of Agricultural Economics, Department of Agriculture. Some of the material is taken from the manuscript of a book being written jointly by Mr. Stock and Lester Frankel of the Census Bureau.
   (*Editor's note:* Mr. Stock's original draft has been somewhat reordered without his assistance since he entered the armed forces shortly after writing the chapter.)

PARTIAL INVESTIGATIONS

The alternative to a census, or complete enumeration is a *partial investigation*.[2] Partial investigations may be divided into two types, depending on whether the data collected have come to hand incidentally or have been specially selected for investigation because of their representative character. We shall refer to the former as the "by-product method" and the latter as the "sampling method."

The by-product method. Severe criticism has been leveled at the use of data which have come to hand incidentally and which may, despite their availability, be hopelessly inadequate to represent the totality which is being studied. For example, very accurate data on the births and deaths in any one hospital could easily be obtained, but they would not serve for the computation of general birth and death rates. Much of the data that are collected and published by governmental bureaus have come into being only incidentally as by-products of the administration of some Federal plan—e.g. the data on occupations collected by the United States Employment Service. Statistics from these sources are often useful in representing a much larger group than that covered by the administration itself. Undoubtedly these by-product data will continue to serve an important need in social and economic research; but generalizations from them should always be made with extreme caution.

The sampling method. The difficulty with the by-product method is that the data may be unrepresentative. The sampling method is designed to overcome this difficulty. When properly used, it guarantees that the data collected are representative of the entire population in which one is interested. This means that in a city where one person in twenty holds a given opinion, a properly selected sample of the people in that city will also show about one person in twenty with that opinion. An investigator making a sampling survey is like the banker in a gambling house. Though the roulette wheel may turn up double zero three times in succession, the banker knows, if his wheel is properly constructed, that in the course of an evening's play all the numbers will come up in approximately equal proportions.

The position of the person doing the sampling, however, is really better than that of the banker; for he is able to spin the wheel as many times as he likes and control it to the extent of ensuring that an equal proportion of red and black numbers will come up, an equal proportion of odd and even numbers, etc. Thus in sampling one may bet on what is

2 Adolph Jensen, "Report on the Representative Method in Statistics," *Bulletin de L'Institut Internationale de Statistique*, 1926, Vol. 22, Part 1, p. 360.

practically a sure thing. Although an adequate sample may be only a small part of the total group under consideration, the odds can be made very high that the results will be, within very restricted limits, the same as those which a complete census would have yielded.

The application of sampling methods has been very general. Engineers work out the strength of certain materials by testing samples of them in the laboratory; the quality of the contents of a grain elevator is determined by a small sample; doctors have found the effectiveness of treatments by investigation of relatively few patients; a doctor determines the blood count of a single patient from a small blood sample. There is hardly a field of human activity in which we do not find sampling methods in practical use.

Scientific use of sampling goes back over a hundred years to the time when it was first realized that a few well-chosen observations may disclose nearly as much information as an exhaustive study. With the advent of straw polls and public opinion surveys in the last twenty years the public, too, has become conscious of the idea of sampling. Very interesting but purely romantic lore has sprung up about the possibility of finding Mr. Average Man and multiplying him by 132 million. It is fortunate that the ever-mounting confidence of the public has been checked from time to time by such calamitous results as the failure of the *Literary Digest* presidential poll in 1936. These failures emphasize the precautions which it is necessary to take in sampling studies. Though the public may expect magic from sampling techniques, these methods are reliable only in the hands of the trained and careful investigator.

SOME TECHNICAL TERMS

1. A *sample* is the mass of units or groups selected for investigation.

2. The *population* or *universe* is the total group under study, which the sample is supposed to represent. Examples of populations are: all the people in the United States; all the families in a certain city; the prices of bread in all grocery stores on a given date.

3. If we expect to get the true reflection of the universe in our sample, the sample is said to be *unbiased* and *representative*. A ten per cent sample of all people in a given town may be representative of that town with regard to the proportion unemployed; it, will be so if we expect to get the same proportion of employed and unemployed in the sample as there are in the entire town.

4. A representative sample which is large enough for generalization about certain characteristics is said to be *adequate*. The adequacy of a

sample depends much more upon the total number of cases included than on the ratio of this number to the total population. Thus if the town from which our ten per cent sample was taken has only one hundred people in it, the sample will be inadequate; while if it has ten thousand people, the sample will probably be very adequate. If the sample is not representative, of course, it cannot be adequate.

5. The contrast between "adequacy" and the "representativeness" of a sample has also been expressed by a distinction between *degree of precision* and *degree of accuracy*.[3] This distinction is fundamental to a proper understanding of sampling procedures. Sampling is precise if the statistical fluctuations, or "random errors" are small. Precision is partially attained by large samples; absolute precision by complete census. Accuracy means the absence of biased, nonstatistical, or "systematic" errors and errors of calculation. It can be obtained only by careful planning and repeated checks. A complete census may be absolutely precise and yet hopelessly inaccurate; conversely, a sample may not be as precise as, yet considerably more accurate than, a complete census.

The Problem of Precision

Much confusion has arisen as to how large a sample should be in any particular case. The reason for this uncertainty is that the precision of any sampling procedure depends on a number of interacting variables, of which the most important are:

1. The variability of the characteristics being measured within the group being studied. For instance, if one wished to study the average height of six-year-old children, a very much smaller sample would be needed than if one were studying the heights of people of all ages.

2. The size of the sampling unit. For instance, a sample of five whole states could not be expected to represent the entire United States as well as an equal number of persons selected at random from all the states. A good way to visualize the effect of a few or many different random selections is to think how much more unpredictable your winnings would be if you matched ten-dollar gold pieces than if you matched the same total amount of money in pennies. Just as you are much more likely to come out even if you give yourself many chances to recoup your losses, so in sampling you are much more likely to balance out errors by allowing many chances for compensating errors. A sample of many small units, each randomly chosen, is almost without exception to be

---

[3] This distinction is credited to W. A. Shewhart of the Bell Telephone Laboratories.

preferred to an equal sample of a few large units, even though they appear to be well chosen.

3. The effectiveness of the stratification (*vide infra*) : that is, the degree to which the sampling method adopted ensures the proper representation of each class of the total group under study. Thus, a sample to measure demographic characteristics should be set up in such a way that each age and sex group is represented in the sample in as nearly correct a proportion as possible.

4. The size of the group under study. This variable has been thought by many to be *the* determining factor in setting the size of a sample. As a matter of fact, for relatively small samples its effect is negligible. An analogy may help to make this clear : to determine what kinds of soup are contained in a barrel and a bowl, it is not necessary to consume a much greater amount from the barrel.

In practical sampling work it is necessary to strike a balance between two factors : the degree of precision one desires in his results, and the amount of time and money one has available. In general, the expense of a sample increases proportionately to the number of cases, while the precision of the sample increases proportionately to the square root of the number of cases. This is the reason for the increasingly widespread use of small samples in public opinion research.[4]

THE PROBLEM OF ACCURACY

As we have just seen, the precision of a sample is something which can be known quite definitely when the size of the sample is specified. The accuracy of the sample is another matter. There are no mathematical procedures for determining in advance the extent of systematic biases, or the degree to which a sample is really representative of a particular pop-

[4] *Editor's note:* For the situation which is typical in opinion surveys—stratified sampling by a number of interviewers working in different areas—Chart 1 in Appendix 4 shows to a good approximation the degree of precision which can be obtained with samples of any size from 50 to 10,000 cases. What we are interested in is the proportion of people with a given opinion. Without a complete census we can never be sure from the evidence of our sample that *exactly* 80 per cent of the people hold a given opinion; but we can be fairly sure (for example) that between 70 and 90 per cent hold that opinion, and very, very sure that between 60 and 100 per cent hold the opinion. *The degree of precision of a sample is represented by the width of the interval within which we can be 99 per cent sure that the true percentage falls.*

The use of Chart 1 may be illustrated by a specific example. If we have a properly selected sample of size 100 from a particular population, and if the proportion of (let us say) Roosevelt supporters in the sample is 50 per cent, we can say that the proportion of Roosevelt supporters in that population is between 38 and 62 per cent—and we will be right 99 times out of 100. If our sample had 1,000 cases instead of 100, we could say that the proportion of Roosevelt supporters in the population was between 46 and 54 per cent —and still be right 99 times out of 100. If we had taken a sample of 10,000 we could say, with 99 per cent confidence, that the population proportion was between 48.7 and 51.3 per cent.

ulation. The best we can do is to check our sample as frequently as possible against some other data—the classic example is election returns. Over a period of time we will become aware of, and perhaps be able to correct, any bias there is in our sampling procedure.

The next paragraphs describe some principles which, if successfully followed, will ensure sampling accuracy. These are ideal procedures, which in practice can only be approximated; though the approximation may often be extremely good. The purpose of all these procedures is to secure a *representative sample*, in order to make it possible to generalize the results of a partial investigation.

Random selection denotes the method of selecting for investigation a number of units according to some mechanical principle or other which is unconnected with the subject and purpose of the inquiry. The selection is usually arranged so that every single unit in the totality has an equal chance of inclusion in the sample.

   (a) In *unrestricted random sampling* units are selected at random from the totality of cases.
   (b) In *restricted* or *stratified sampling* the universe is divided into several strata or subuniverses by some criterion, and units are selected at random within these strata.

Inherent in the representative method is the requirement that there be some randomness in the selection of the sample; this we need in order to be assured by the laws of probability that the results approximate what a census would have shown. It is therefore necessary to take careful precautions that "the method of selecting the sample is entirely unrelated to the data we intend to get from the sample."[5]

For example, the questionnaires for the *Literary Digest* poll were sent to persons whose names appeared in telephone books. The necessary assumption was that the fact of a person's name appearing in the telephone book was entirely unrelated to how that person would vote. Such apparently was not the case in 1936. The difficulty of meeting the specification of randomness can always be overcome if we can specify that the selection shall be made such "that every unit of the population to be represented has an equal chance of being included in the sample."

The practical work in selecting a sample usually centers around two conditions: first, to make certain that the group from which the sample is drawn is in fact the group that it is desired to represent or is itself a representative sample of that group; and second, that every unit has an

[5] More precisely this statement should be: "The probability of inclusion in the sample or exclusion from the sample of any unit of the group to be represented must be uncorrelated with (independent of) any characteristic to be represented by the sample."

equal chance of being included in the sample. Here we shall deal with certain pitfalls in sampling and discuss a few of the ingenious methods which have been proposed for sampling under certain very common conditions.

Some Sources of Sampling Data

Sampling from files. One of the easiest and most common ways of sampling is possible where there exists a complete file of folders, cards, or schedules that represent all the units of the population to be studied. In this case, by selecting every fifth or tenth card or folder, or some other number, or, if the cards or folders are of uniform thickness, by making a selection every so many inches throughout the file, a representative sample may be obtained very easily. If each folder or schedule contains the necessary information, it remains only to tabulate the results. If, on the contrary, the folder merely designates the units for study, it is then necessary to go to these units (they may be families, business houses, blocks in a city, mile-square areas) and procure the information.

If the file lacks certain units of the entire group under study these units must be given their chances of being selected unless we can safely assume that the missing units are exactly similar in all general characteristics to the ones included. For example, in selecting samples from the Real Property Inventory files, where certain data for new houses were not yet in the file, it was necessary to make up a separate file of the new dwelling units from the city engineer's records and sample in the same way from this second file. If certain folders are out of a file, in use for other purposes, it is convenient to designate their positions with blank folders in order to give them their proper chance of being included in the sample.

A danger in sampling from geographical files, as well as in sampling from many other media, so arranged, is *periodicity*. For instance, if there is a predominance of ten houses to a block in any city and we select every 5th, 10th or 20th or any multiple of 10 houses, we might happen to get all corner houses or no corner houses in our sample. Since corner houses are generally higher in value and predominantly contain persons of somewhat higher income class, there would be danger of a serious bias because of having too many or too few occupants of corner houses. In sampling from alphabetical files, however, this danger is not present.

Selecting every nth unit in a file or selecting units every so many inches in a file may be somewhat better than a sampling procedure in which a single folder is selected "at random," a second folder is selected independently of the first, a third folder independently of the first two selections, and so on until the desired number of folders have been chosen.

In an alphabetical file it precludes the possibility of getting a predominance of persons with certain last names and thus, perhaps, overrepresenting a nationality or racial group; since it ensures that every surname in the file will occur in nearly the proper proportion in the sample.

In geographically arranged files, or files which are arranged by some even more pertinent characteristic, the advantage of taking every nth card may be quite significant. It ensures, for instance, that from a geographically arranged file, each part of the locality shall be represented in equal proportions. This, of course, is the effect of stratification. It should be noted here that if the file can be arranged in an order which is related to the data to be determined from the sample, an increase in efficiency will result.[6] Such efficiency may or may not, of course, be worth the added expense of sorting the file in a different order.[7]

In all public opinion surveys, and in the majority of social and economic researches, complete data cannot be obtained from files but must be secured by direct interviews. In this situation the sample may be chosen by the individual interviewers (subject to general instructions from the central office, from lists or records of some kind) and the field worker told the specific names of the people he is to interview, or the specific addresses of the places where he is to go for interviews.

We shall discuss the second method first, outlining each of the many different procedures that may be used by the central office in selecting the sample. At the end of the chapter we shall discuss more briefly the first method (in which the choice of the actual sampling units is left to the interviewer) as it is being applied by most opinion research agencies today.

Sampling from records and lists. The main problem in using this procedure is to get a list which includes the whole of the universe in which one is interested. Telephone books, gas, electricity, and water-meter records, though sometimes convenient sampling media, are subject to grave dangers. It is of utmost importance that they be checked to make sure that the whole universe is present, nothing more and nothing less; that each unit occurs only once; and that the records are up to date.

---

[6] In comparing two samples of the same size, it is customary to compare the statistical errors resulting from each. The sample with the smaller error is said to be more efficient. Thus, when one says a certain sampling technique is more efficient than some other, it simply means that for the same size of sample, the former has a smaller error.

[7] *Editor's note:* A discussion of the relative efficiency of random and stratified sampling will be found in Appendix 3, Note 1: "The Efficiency of Stratified Sampling" and Note 2: "The Effect of Stratification in Practical Polling."

The names in the telephone book seldom represent a general population, except perhaps the population of telephone subscribers. The experience of the *Literary Digest* poll showed that telephone subscribers were predominantly persons of higher than average income levels. Gas and electricity meter records are probably not only less biased in their representation of the general population, but are kept more current than the telephone book. This has been found especially true in certain large cities with public utilities.

In some cities, however, large apartment houses and other multiple dwelling units have only one gas or electric meter. In a small sample the chance of inclusion or exclusion of one large apartment house could cause serious error in the result. This danger may be overcome by listing all single dwelling units in apartment buildings and sampling them separately or by selecting—say—every third unit of every fourth apartment house for a sample of one in twelve. Such a process of sampling in subunits from a sample of larger units is called *subsampling*. It has very general use and is an effective compromise between the expense of sampling many small units and the lack of precision of sampling a few large units. The proper proportions for subsampling may be determined only from considerations of somewhat complicated formulas. In general, however, it should be remembered that the larger the sampling unit, the poorer will be the precision.

Some localities have personal property records or real estate tax records which are complete. Here a difficulty arises from the fact that the owner of the property might not be the resident. In such cases, a subsample of the tenants must be selected from a sample of large property owners, in the same way suggested for apartment houses. The advantage of the tax records is that they cover rural as well as urban localities.

Sampling from city directories. City directories, while more inclusive, present some of the same difficulties for sampling purposes as telephone books. They have a tendency in some cities to overrepresent the upper economic levels. This is not, however, always true, because city directories are not always by-products of any business activity other than that of making available a list of names of the residents of a locality.

In small cities, directories usually have a nearly complete coverage. In large cities the cost of collecting and publishing so many data often makes it impossible either to attain complete coverage of families and households who have low buying power or to keep the book up to date. It is the experience of the writer that in most instances only the address section is useful for sampling and that usually the presence of an address section in a city directory indicates that the coverage is more complete than otherwise. At least it is possible to check the address section with published street guides, maps, and city engineer's records to see that all the streets are included. If certain streets are missing, it is possible to make up block lists of all the houses on these streets in order to supplement the directory.

Some city directories show the race and occupation of each householder, whether or not the householder owns the house, or has a telephone. A preliminary sample may indicate that there is an underrepresentation of one of these characteristics as compared with data available from other sources. In Birmingham, Alabama, for example, a sample of one in twelve households from the address section yielded only a third of the number of Negro households that would have been expected from an examination of 1930 census figures. A comparison of the streets in the directory with those listed earlier by a health census showed that two-thirds of the city's Negro families lived on alleys; the directory did not show alleys. A subsample of one-sixth of the households in one-half of the alleys was then added to the original sample.

The data for most directories are collected several months prior to the actual publication date. In order to bring a directory up to date, it is necessary to consult whatever office issues building permits in the locality, and to make a supplementary list of all residential units built for a period several months prior to publication date. Many city engineers and licensing officials file these permits chronologically. This method is convenient, for then the person making up the list needs merely to copy the addresses from the files, working from the latest back until he finds buildings which are shown in the city directory.

Block and areal sampling. Where complete quasi-universes, such as complete lists of households or buildings, do not exist for a given locality, often there are lists of blocks or other small area subdivisions which can easily be made. Then, instead of sampling households or dwelling units, we may select for complete enumeration—or more preferable for further subsampling—a random sample of these larger area units. Larger units of sampling imply fewer units selected and hence less precision. This disadvantage, however, is often compensated in areal surveys by decrease in time and costs of travel between interviews. The cost of getting the interviewer to his first interview each day and the subsequent cost of travel between each interview sometimes amounts to as much as 50 per cent of the direct cost per schedule—depending, of course, upon the density of sampling units, the transportation facilities in any area, and the number of questions to be asked in each interview. More-over, with fewer sampling units, the universe may be sorted and thereby stratified, thus recovering certain losses in precision. Here again, a judg-ment on the most efficient sampling procedure can be made only after careful study of the comparative costs and precision of various alternate methods.

The proper choice of sampling unit in areal sampling can come only from an examination of the heterogeneity between sampling units. If the people living in a given locality were assigned their place of residence randomly, then any one group of contiguous blocks in a city, or any township in rural areas would make up a representative sample. The social geography of every locality, however, is a mottled affair; there are Negro sections, little Italies, Chinatowns, truck-farming regions. Each of these regions can be properly represented in a stratified sample with a large number of small sampling units. However, if the sampling units are too large and there are too few of them, there can be little pre-cision in the results.

Block or areal sampling nearly always requires a map.[8] In using a map as a sampling medium, it is necessary to assure the proper areal distribu-tion of points selected for sampling. An even distribution of points may be selected by drawing across the map two intersecting sets of equally spaced parallel lines to form a grid. The points of intersection would form the selected points on the map. The directions of the two sets of lines should be chosen so that they will not parallel too many of the streets or roads on the map, for many of the points of intersection thus selected might fall along a single road.

Along with the selection of the points on a map, one must determine what the areal sampling unit is to be and how it will be designated by the points. In order to get a sample in cities, each point on the map may be taken to represent the block in which it falls. A list would then be made of the dwelling units on each block thus sampled, and from this list a subsample selected to yield the desired number of households to be included in the sample. The proper balance of the number of blocks with the subsampling ratio of houses would be determined by a consideration of the heterogeneity between blocks and the cost of travel between households. The cardinal difficulty with this method is that blocks have a chance of being included in the sample proportionate to their area. For this reason, in Philadelphia, such a sampling method gave a bias of too many wealthy households, since there exists a marked relationship

[8] See Appendix 5 for sources of maps.

between the size of the block on which a household is located and the economic level of that household.

This difficulty may be overcome by dividing the larger blocks into a number of smaller areas before selecting the points on the map. Blocks should be divided by imaginary lines drawn between physical objects such as street intersections or culverts shown on the map. In that way the interviewer may know exactly what is and what is not in the sampled area, without going to the trouble of measuring from the scale of the map and on the group the exact dimensions of that part of the block which is to be considered in the sample or to block list for subsampling.

In rural or open country areas, the sample points on the map may be taken to designate the nearest, say, three or four, houses. The objections to this procedure, however, are:

1. It assumes that the population density is practically uniform throughout the area sample. Although this is seldom true for as large an area as a county, nevertheless, if the number of points in each township is chosen proportional to the population of that township, the chance of inclusion of a household in sparsely settled townships can be made nearly the same as that of a household in the more densely settled ones. A better way of overcoming this difficulty is to include not just the nearest houses but all houses within a certain specified radius.

2. If the map is not a detailed one, there is some difficulty in locating on the terrain the exact spot designated by the point on the map. Even more difficult is a determination of what is included within a specified radius of the selected point.

3. Sometimes a point will fall between two parallel roads which are not connected by a nearby crossroad. Thus, the designated nearest houses will be on both roads, near together in a direct line but possibly miles of travel apart.

A convenient way of avoiding many of these difficulties in urban areas is to number all blocks on the map in the city and select every nth block for enumeration or for subsampling of the houses or dwelling units on the selected blocks. In rural areas, road segments between intersections or any physical objects may be numbered, and every nth segment selected for inclusion in the sample. In such cases it must be remembered that every house with an entrance on or served by a private lane leading off the selected road segment must be considered as included on that road segment. Sometimes the road-segment sampling unit may be cut in half by assigning a number to each side of the road and thus considering both sides as separate sampling units. Subsampling, however, is in this case a more effective way of reducing the sample.

This completes our discussion of sampling procedures in which the sample is made up at the central office. This method is the one used by most government agencies making sampling studies—the Bureau of the Census, the Bureau of Agricultural Economics, and the Bureau of Labor Statistics. In most practical situations it is probably the most accurate method possible, since it ensures that the method of selecting units for the sample is random and is consistent throughout the universe being sampled. The sampling is done in one place where rigid controls may be applied, all the clerical work may be checked, and there is in addition a positive check on the interviewers.

The two great disadvantages of this method for opinion research are: (1) it is very expensive, and (2) it does not usually allow respondents to remain anonymous. Opinion surveys are particularly dependent on an inexpensive method of sampling because the information gathered goes out of date so quickly. In most cases also we are content with less precise and accurate results than we perhaps would be in social and economic research. An example of this is the situation in election campaigns; what we really want to know is often simply: Who will win?

The problem of anonymity in interviews is a ticklish one. There is evidence that people do not always give their true opinions even to a stranger who does not know their names or their addresses and has no way of checking up on them again. Perhaps this difficulty could be overcome through use of the "secret ballot technique" described in Chapter 5 of this volume.

CONTROLLED SAMPLING

The most common method of sampling used by opinion research agencies in the United States today is to combine certain controls set by the central office with instructions to interviewers to interview persons of a certain type. Suppose we want to get a national sample of the adult population for a public opinion poll. First we divide the country into various *geographical sections* (New England, the Middle Atlantic states, the South, etc.). Then we divide each section into various layers according to degree of *urbanization*, separating into one category cities over 500,000, into another category cities of 100,000 to 500,000, etc. This much of our sampling is done entirely at the central office, and interviewers are then employed who live in or near the points decided upon in the sample and are assigned the number of interviews in their locality necessary to fill out the sample properly. Up to this point, any selection of the sample by the interviewer is entirely absent—the interviewer is selected because *he* fits into the sample.

The interviewer is then sent an assignment which usually instructs him to select a specified number of people in different *economic status groups*, a specified number of *Negroes*, and a specified number of *farmers*. In judging economic status, interviewers are instructed (either by mail or personal training) in what is meant by a "wealthy" person, what is meant by a person of "average income," etc. Since economic status cannot be uniformly measured by income because of regional differences, occupational variations, and family circumstances, a multiple index of economic status must be used.[9] The number of farmers is specified to interviewers; this is because interviewers in small towns or cities are likely to be used to interview in rural areas, and not all people who live in rural areas can properly be called farmers. So far, then, we have a sample which is controlled on five variables: section of the country, size of town, economic status, color, farm or nonfarm.

It is, furthermore, the custom of most opinion research agencies to request interviewers to get a distribution by *age* and by *sex*. Usually this request takes the form of a blanket instruction to get, say, half the assignment from people "over 40," half from people "under 40"; half men and half women.

This procedure does not mean, of course, that an attempt is made to distribute one variable properly within another and that within a third variable. That is, the interviewer is not expected to get the proper age distribution among white people in the average income group. Not only would such a demand be highly impracticable and costly, but, furthermore, a single interviewer generally has too few cases to work with for any such elaborate procedure.

Some such method as this of controlled sampling is the most inexpensive in operation. But it must be used with caution, since it allows wide latitude to the interviewer's choice, which may be consciously or unconsciously biased even though he is restricted within certain limits. The method assumes both that interviewers have high integrity and that they have been carefully instructed. Hence, each interviewer must be periodically checked by an examination of his ballots, comparing, for example, economic status distribution he reports with the telephone or car ownership, with occupation, or education. The practical value of this method

[9] Cf. Elmo Roper, "Classifying Respondents by Economic Status," *Public Opinion Quarterly*, 1940, 4, 270-273.

has been amply demonstrated by the performance of the American Institute of Public Opinion and the *Fortune* poll in predicting elections.

However, the problem of interviewer bias is perennial. Consider some actual examples of the technique used by certain interviewers in securing a respondent. One interviewer said that she had a panel which was very easy to contact. For instance, her family doctor, his wife, and their maid helped fill her quotas for the following categories: two upper-income persons, one lower; two women, one man; two whites, one Negro; two working people, one nonworker. Of course, she admitted, they all gave almost the same answers. Another interviewer got her interviews by standing in a railroad station, for, said she, "all kinds of people can be found in a station." She was really surprised at the suggestion that such would include only very active groups of people, would most surely not contain a fair representation of housewives with children.

A rural interviewer admitted considerable difficulty making his prescribed quota of small farms. He attained success, he said, by looking for farms that appeared to be small farms and conducting interviews in them; in so doing, he made just about the right number of misjudgments in his selection. Thus, when at the end of the interview he asked the size of the farm and found it a large one, he could check off one farm from the large-farm quota he was required to meet. He admitted, to be sure, that this procedure caused his large-farm quota to be made up of large farms which looked like small farms.

A traveling interviewer reported he interviewed the waitress at each meal to make up his quota of young working women; mailmen and policemen he counted on to fill the quota of working men. Unemployed men he always found sitting in a park.

These illustrations can be multiplied many times. A look at the interviews turned in by each interviewer often shows that, though he meets his quota in each category, each interviewer has a certain set of favorites. It is implicit in the specification of random sampling that the part of the population which is unobserved must be just as representative a sample as the part observed.

Summary

Tremendously expensive is a complete census of any large population. Modern social and economic research relies increasingly on the use of representative samples. If these samples are properly chosen, they furnish a basis for valid inferences about the populations they represent. *Precision* in a sample can always be ensured by taking a sufficiently large number of cases. *Accuracy* can only be secured by the conscientious application of a carefully designed method of selecting units for inclusion in the sample. The fundamental method of selection is *random sampling*. Ideally every unit in the population should have an equal chance of being included in the sample. The most practical and widely used method of selection is *stratified random sampling*. With this method the population is divided into numerous layers or strata, and units are drawn as nearly as possible at random from each layer. The proportionate representation of each layer in the sample is the same as its proportionate representation in the whole population.

A stratified random sample may be entirely selected in the central office, in which case the interviewer's quota will consist of a specific list of names and addresses; or the stratification alone may be determined by the central office, in which case the interviewer's quota will consist of a set number of interviews with each of various *types* of people. With this method the individuals representing each type are selected "at random" by the interviewer. The first method, widely used by government agencies, is more accurate but also more expensive. The second method is relatively inexpensive and accurate enough for most public opinion research. It is used by the vast majority of opinion research agencies today.

CHAPTER XI

HOW REPRESENTATIVE ARE "REPRESENTATIVE SAMPLES"?[1]

P OLL samples are often referred to as accurate miniatures of the national population. Such a statement carries the implication that the elements of the total population are present in the poll sample in the same proportions as they occur in the country as a whole. In this chapter, we will attempt to show to what extent a poll cross-section does reproduce—in miniature—the larger population from which it is drawn by comparing the composition of typical poll samples with census data on the national population. Since any public opinion investigator can easily shift his criteria for selecting samples and since improvements in sampling are constantly being made, the comparisons shown here may soon be out of date. However, the comparisons of today still contain warnings for tomorrow.

To scale down all the elements and characteristics of the population to obtain a perfectly comparable miniature sample would obviously be a superhuman task. Furthermore, practical considerations require that the sample be set up in terms which will make it possible for interviewers to select the proper types of respondents without too much difficulty. In the construction of nation-wide poll samples, consequently, the standard practice is to stratify—that is to make the proportions of the sample the same as the proportions in the population which is being sampled—this with respect to the factors of geographical and rural-urban distribution, color, and economic status.

In addition to these four controls, the factors of age and sex are frequently used in stratification. Other factors, such as religious affiliation, amount of education, nationality background, and occupation, are not usually directly controlled, the assumption being that the process of random selection, facilitated by the control of the previously mentioned factors, will yield a distribution of these uncontrolled variables approximating their distribution in the national population. The validity of this assumption can be tested by comparing the distribution of these variables actually obtained in poll samples with census figures giving their distribution in the total population.[2]

[1] By Donald Rugg.
[2] Of the uncontrolled variables, comparisons will be made only for education and occupation. The available data on religious affiliation are not accurate enough to use,

There are two aspects of a poll sample which may be examined for representativeness. One is the make-up of the sample assigned to interviewers; the other is the sample actually returned. On the returned ballots, however, the percentage distribution on any one of the controlled variables rarely varies from the assigned percentages by more than two or three per cent. The comparisons which follow are in terms of actual returns, rather than of assigned quotas.

These comparisons are made between census figures and two typical poll samples. One of these samples represents the typical *social cross-section* used by the American Institute of Public Opinion, while the other is a representative sample of the National Opinion Research Center.[3] Both these samples are stratified with respect to sectional and rural-urban distribution, color, economic status, and sex, and the age distribution is partially controlled. Comparisons with the census figures will be made (1) for the controlled variables—section, rural-urban, color, sex, economic status; (2) for the partially controlled variable—age; and (3) for two of the uncontrolled variables—education and occupation. The census figures are from the 1940 census and, except in the case of education and occupation,[4] are based on the adult population, 21 years of age and over.

Controlled Variables

A. Sectional Distribution

The only discrepancy of any size which appears in Table 42 is the AIPO figure for the Rocky Mountain section. The reason is that the AIPO arbitrarily assigns a minimum of 25 interviews to a state. Since there are several thinly populated states in this region, such a practice gives it a quota slightly out of line with its actual population proportion. This inflated Rocky Mountain sample does, however, make the figures obtained for this region more reliable than they would be if only 3 per cent of the sample cases were allotted to it. Furthermore, this small amount of inflation has only a very slight, if any, effect on the national figures.

since they are not based on a standardized definition of what constitutes membership in a church. 1940 census figures on nationality background (birthplace of the respondent's parents) are not available at this writing.

[3] The NORC always uses a social cross-section.

[4] Census figures for education are based on persons 25 years of age and over; for occupation, on persons 14 years of age and over. However, it is fairly safe to assume that the *proportions* in each educational and occupational group remain constant enough to permit comparisons with the poll samples, which are based on the adult population.

TABLE 42

Sections	AIPO Sample	NORC Sample	Census Figures
New England	6.4%	7.0%	6.7%
Middle Atlantic (inc. Del., Md., and W.Va.)	23.6		25.1
Middle Atlantic (N.Y., N.J., and Pa. only)	.	21.1	22.2
East Central	17.7		18.7
East North Central		21.5	21.1
West Central	12.6		12.8
West North Central		10.7	10.4
South	25.1		25.5
South Atlantic		12.8	11.9
East South Central		7.6	7.3
West South Central		9.5	9.2
Rocky Mountain	6.8	3.0	3.0
Pacific Coast	7.8	6.8	8.2

B. Rural-urban Distribution, Sex, and Color

On these controlled variables, as shown in Table 43, the sample percentages are very close to the census figures.

It should be noted, with reference to the above variables, that the sectional and rural-urban distributions are automatically controlled in the selection of localities to be interviewed, while sex and color are attributes which can be readily determined by the interviewers. Practically the only way, therefore, in which a sample can be biased with reference to these factors (provided, of course, that it is accurately set up) is by incomplete returns. The available evidence indicates that this source of bias is negligible in most cases.

The factor of economic status is likewise "controlled." The quotas for each economic level are made up from various indirect indices (such as telephone ownership) and then these levels are translated into socio-

TABLE 43

Rural-urban divisions	AIPO Sample	NORC Sample	Census Figures
Urban	63.1%	59.1%	60.3%
Rural-nonfarm	17.3	20.6	19.8
Rural-farm	19.6	20.3	19.9
Color			
White	90.0	91.2	90.2
Negro	10.0	8.8	9.8
Sex			
Men	51.0	50.6	50.0
Women	49.0	49.4	50.0

psychological terms for the interviewers. Thus the latter are told to get so many respondents of status "B," or so many "Average-Plus" people. These levels are not defined in terms of actual income, which is difficult to ascertain, and which is not, in itself, an absolute index of economic status. An income of $5,000 is one thing in New York City, and something quite different in a small midwestern community.[5] The definitions are rather in terms of such things as a person's occupation, the comforts and luxuries which he possesses, etc.—which, in effect, constitute a sliding scale applicable to any community.

Although no census figures are available for comparison, we can be reasonably sure that, providing the interviewers get the assigned quotas and *correctly classify* respondents as to economic status, the economic cross-section will be a representative one. The evidence indicates that, as in the case of other controlled variables, the distribution of returned ballots very closely approximates the assigned distribution. Bias can still enter, nevertheless, because of the failure of the interviewers to classify respondents correctly by income. For example, a person who is actually "poor" may be classified as "average," an "average" person as "average plus," etc.

There is good evidence, indeed, to indicate that such a tendency on the part of interviewers is actually present, and that, as a consequence, poll samples are usually somewhat biased toward the upper economic levels. This evidence comes from an examination of the educational and occupational distributions, which will be discussed below.[6] The upward bias probably results in large part from the reluctance of middle-class interviewers to approach the lowest income groups, who are most likely to be inarticulate and suspicious.

Partially Controlled Variables

C. Age

Although it does not assign definite age quotas, the AIPO instructs its interviewers to get a good age spread. The NORC goes one step further, instructing interviewers to get half their respondents under 40 years of age, half over 40.

A comparison of the AIPO sample with the census data reveals that there are too few in the 20-29 age group, and a few too many in each of the other age groups from 30 to 60. Since the 20-29 group has cur-

---

[5] Cf. E. Roper, "Classifying Respondents by Economic Status," *Public Opinion Quarterly*, 1940, 2, 270-272.

[6] See also Chapters 14 and 15.

TABLE 44

Age Groups	AIPO Sample	NORC Sample	Census Figures
20-29	17.4%	22.3%	23.8%
30-39	24.8	27.4	23.6
40-49	24.0	24.3	20.4
50-59	17.8	} 26.0	15.7
60-69	10.8		10.2
70 and over	5.2		6.3

rently been depleted by the draft, however, and since soldiers are naturally less accessible for interviewing than civilians, this emphasis is easily accounted for. It is likely, then, that the AIPO interviewers are getting a pretty good random age sample of the civilian population. The NORC, on the other hand, gets approximately the correct proportions of the under- and over-40 groups because these are assigned. But within these two broad groupings, there are divergences from the census figures. The NORC sample shows too many in the 30-50 groups, and too few over 50.

The significance of these divergences should not be overemphasized. Unless there is an exceptionally sharp difference of opinion by age on an issue these inaccuracies in the sample will make little or no difference in the over-all percentages.

The AIPO system of a random age assignment appears to be quite satisfactory in terms of national distribution for the civilian population. (If a proportional sample of soldiers were desired, it would be necessary to assign specific quotas, since random selection would not give them proportional representation.) It is possible, of course, that age biases may occur within subsamples of the national sample. The NORC system of partially controlling age, while it probably helps to obviate such subsample biases, does not yield a better distribution for the country as a whole. Furthermore, unless NORC intends to sample the military as well as the civilian population, the under-40/over-40 ratio should be slightly reduced to correct for the depletion of the younger-age categories by the draft.

D. *Education*

When we come to education (Table 45), we find by all odds the most serious bias in the poll samples to date. A small portion of it may be due to a prestige factor, that is, the tendency of people to give inflated estimates of the amount of education they have had (although this propensity presumably could have operated on the census as well). But by far the greatest part is a result of the combination of two factors: (1) the previously mentioned upward bias of the economic distribution—since economic status and education are highly correlated, this economic bias produces a corresponding education bias, and (2) probably most important of all, the tendency on the part of interviewers to select, within each economic category, the more articulate, and hence usually better-educated, respondents.

TABLE 45

School Years Completed	AIPO Sample	NORC Sample	Census
0-8	38.5%	39.0%	60.4%
9-12	34.9	39.3	29.5
Over 12	26.6	21.7	10.1

A partial correction of the education bias can be effected by overcoming the economic bias, either by assigning larger quotas to the lower-income categories, or by replacing the present criteria largely subjective, with more objective ones.[7] Even such precautions will still fail to overcome that portion of the bias which results from the selection of the more articulate respondents. Probably the only way to correct that completely is to employ an entirely different system of sampling, one which does not leave the selection of the respondents to the interviewer, but requires him to interview specific individuals who have been chosen in advance.

To employ a system of this sort, it is necessary to enumerate completely the population of the communities used in the sample. A sample is then drawn from the enumeration. The selection of the sample is based on an intricate stratification process. Since the interviewers are assigned specific individuals, numerous call-backs are often necessary to contact the respondents. A new sample must be constructed for each survey, since reinterviewing the same persons creates an artificial situation. All in all, this system, despite its desirable refinements, is too complicated and costly for general use by polling organizations.

E. *Occupation*

The overrepresentation, in the poll samples, of the groups labeled professional, and proprietors, managers, and officials, and the accom-

[7] NORC is now using a system of economic assignments based on relatively objective criteria.

panying underrepresentation of the worker groups show that a definite occupation bias exists. They point likewise to a corresponding economic status bias, since the two variables are closely related.

TABLE 46

	AIPO Sample	NORC Sample	Census
Professional and semi-professional	11.4%	11.6%	5.6%
Proprietors, managers and officials	13.1	18.7	9.8
Clerical, sales, etc.	16.2	12.8	12.9
Foremen, craftsmen, etc. (skilled workers)	9.5	10.9	14.6
Operatives (semi-skilled)	10.9	11.8	18.4
Service workers	11.5	7.2	6.9
Laborers (unskilled workers)	7.1	5.1	8.8
Farmers and farm labor	20.3	21.9	23.0

The bias is one which probably results in part from the reluctance of the typical middle-class interviewer to approach people in the lowest economic brackets; also from the fact that, when he does contact these people, it is relatively difficult for him to secure rapport with them. An analysis of special refusal forms, on which the interviewer records reasons for refusals together with background data on the persons refusing, substantiates some such theory. Analysis indicates a slightly higher rate of refusal in the lower income and occupation categories.[8]

Although the occupational bias is not of unduly large proportions, it is clearly evident, and indicates the need for some sort of correction. Possible methods of correction have indeed already been outlined.

[8] For a more complete discussion of the effect of refusals on the sample obtained, see Chapter 9.

CHAPTER XII

THE USE OF SMALL SAMPLES[1]

THE problem of making accurate estimates on the basis of small samples which can be rapidly obtained is of interest to any polling agency engaged in practical work. Like many practical problems fringed with restrictions on time, personnel, and cost, one can safely say there is no "best" solution to this problem, even if it is admitted that there are solutions.

The studies reported here check the accuracy of small samples in three different ways: (I) small sample surveys are tested against actual election returns; (II) small sample surveys are tested against regular poll results; and (III) small samples are worked out in the laboratory with various indices and checked against regular poll results.

SMALL SAMPLES TESTED AGAINST ELECTIONS

1. *Predicting the New York state gubernatorial vote.* In this experiment OPOR investigated the voting intentions of a carefully stratified sample of 200 people in New York state. The survey was made by a single interviewer who traveled around the state during the week preceding the 1942 gubernatorial election of November 3.

Interviews were distributed as follows:

New York City	Number of Interviews
Manhattan	24
Brooklyn	34
Bronx	19
Queens	19
Upstate	
Cities over 500,000 (Buffalo)	9
100,000 to 500,000	10
10,000 to 100,000	40
2,500 to 10,000	10
Under 2,500	25
Farms	10
Total	200

[1] A number of persons contributed to this chapter. The one-man poll of New York State was made by John Harding, the survey of an eastern county was made by Carroll Moore, the Canadian plebiscite study was administered by Daniel Katz and Hadley Cantril, the spot checks against regular poll results were made by Hadley Cantril, and

Respondents were selected to provide a good cross-section of the population with respect to color, economic status, and age. Only registered voters were interviewed. The voting intentions of the 200 people in our sample were:

Dewey	115
Bennett	72
Alfange	12
Amter	1
Total	200

Table 47 shows the percentage of the major party vote actually polled in the election by each of the three main candidates. This may be compared with our prediction and with the forecasts of two other surveys made at the same time on a much larger scale. It is clear that the accuracy of the small sample study was not very much less than that of the two extensive surveys.

TABLE 47. PERCENTAGE OF MAJOR PARTY VOTE

	Actual Election	OPOR Small-Sample Prediction	AIPO Prediction	N. Y. Daily News Prediction
Dewey	53%	58%	53%	57%
Bennett	37	36	39	37
Alfange	10	6	8	6
Number of cases	4,112,000	200	2,800	48,000

2. *Predicting a primary race in a single county.* During the first week of August 1942, a special survey was made in an eastern county to test the standing of candidates in the Republican primary. The total population of the county is approximately 100,000. A sample of 233 cases was interviewed. Controls of economic status, age, and sex were used. The primary was held on September 15, 1942.

The survey and election results are compared below.

	Small-Sample Prediction	Actual Election
Candidate A	38.8%	39.4%
Candidate B	61.2	60.6

3. *Predicting a plebiscite in Canada: a method for estimating public sentiment in a foreign country.* This experiment was designed essentially

the laboratory work on small samples was done by Frederick Mosteller and Frederick Williams. The election and plebiscite predictions reported here are filed at OPOR in the form of telegrams sent to the editor before the elections were held. The chapter was prepared by Hadley Cantril.

to test the possibility of gauging public opinion in a foreign country where conditions would make it impracticable to use methods currently employed in this country. The particular limitations foreseen and taken into account in this experiment were: (1) the difficulty of getting a large number of cases, (2) the impossibility of using a formal ballot and a rather formal approach, and (3) the unlikelihood that trained interviewers would be available.

Accordingly (1) the total number of interviews assigned was 200, (2) a casual, conversational approach was used, and (3) entirely untrained people were engaged to do the interviewing and were given only general instructions.

The plebiscite held in Canada on the question of conscription (April 27, 1942) provided an opportunity to check the results of such an experiment.

Two interviewers were employed, neither of whom had had any experience in public-opinion polling. One was sent to the province of Quebec, the other to the province of Ontario. The Quebec observer was an American woman of French extraction, the Ontario observer a graduate student from Princeton. All their reporting was limited to these two provinces. They started interviewing one week before the plebiscite. The two interviewers were given ballot forms and told to memorize the information called for; under no circumstances were they to allow the respondent to see the ballot. After every conversation they were to find some private spot where they could immediately record the necessary information. Each observer was instructed to obtain at least 100 ballots. Other instructions to the interviewers follow:

1. Do not get more than one ballot in one family, one farm, one apartment building. Scatter your ballots widely.
2. Send your completed ballots to OPOR every night by air mail.
3. In addition to the specific cross-section assigned to you, try to secure adequate representation of the various economic groups on a geographical basis. That is, when in a town or city do not concentrate on one area but cover the whole town, spending more time in the large poor areas and less time in the smaller areas of good homes. Remember that the usual error is to give more attention to the upper-income group than is justified by their numerical strength. A rough scale to bear in mind is that the upper-income group is about 15 per cent of the population, the middle-income group about 35 per cent, and the lower-income group about 50 per cent.

    In general, use your own good judgment to supplement your

specific cross-section. Consult local sources on population distribution.

4. There are almost unlimited ways of making contacts with people and starting conversations. It is easy to engage people in converversation in public places such as busses, street cars, stores, bars, amusement places. It is more difficult to sample farmers and housewives. Farmers with road stands can be reached by making small purchases. Other farmhouses can be approached by some assumed errand such as a search for a relative living thereabouts.

5. Be sure to record information from respondent as soon as possible after conversation.

The ballot. The ballot form called for all the information thought necessary to predict public sentiment. It asked not only for the respondent's own vote on the plebiscite but for his estimate of the vote of friends and the local community and his reasons for his own opinion. It called also for his attitude on conscription as well as for the usual background information such as occupation, schooling, income grouping, sex, age, political affiliation, religion. Where some of these data were difficult to secure in informal conversation, the observer was instructed not to probe too much for it. The observer also summarized his impression of each respondent in a brief paragraph.

The cross-section. The cross-sections assigned for Ontario and Quebec were on the simple basis of geographical distribution. The observer was told to obtain proportionally as many ballots from rural areas as these areas constituted of the total population. In the same way cities and towns were grouped into five classes according to size and ballots were to be distributed according to the proportion that a class of town was of the total population. In addition, the observer in Quebec was told to keep her ratio of French Canadians to British Canadians as it was in the total population. This determination was left to her research in Canadian libraries.

A more detailed cross-section was not laid out for two reasons: (1) A small sample such as 100 cases cannot be hedged about with too many restrictions if inexperienced interviewers are to do a job fast. It is better to keep the cross-section as representative as possible on the basis of a few important criteria than to overload the work of the observer with complicated and detailed restrictions. If a few basic criteria are observed such as geographical distribution and, in Quebec, nationality distribution, the sample should not be biased by selective errors. (2) Frequently for work in foreign countries, the cross-sectional information available is limited to basic demographic data.

Cross-Section for Ontario 100 Cases		Cross-Section for Quebec 100 Cases	
Sex ratio		Sex ratio	
2 men to 1 woman	Cases	2 men to 1 woman	Cases
From Toronto	19	From Montreal	28
From Hamilton and Ottawa	8	From Quebec	5
From typical towns under 100,000 and over 20,000 like Windsor, Kitchener, and Brantford	9	From typical towns under 100,000 and over 20,000 like Three Rivers and Sherbrooke	8
From typical towns under 20,000 and over 5,000	15	From typical towns under 20,000 and over 5,000	8
From typical towns under 5,000	9	From typical towns under 5,000	14
From farms and small unincorporated villages	40	From farms and small unincorporated villages	37

Interviewers' approach to respondents. The two interviewers selected used their own ingenuity in starting conversations that would lead up to the conscription issue of the plebiscite. The man who interviewed in Ontario used two approaches, depending upon whether he was working in the city or in the country. In the cities he merely told people that he was a student in an American university, was interested in Canada and the war, and was wondering what people in Canada were thinking about the war in general. Eventually he brought the conversation around to the assignment. In rural areas he frequently told farmers that he thought a relative of his had once lived in that area and he wondered if they had ever known a family by the name of "Hinshaw." No farmer ever knew. But many suggested that an old-timer down the road might know. The young woman who interviewed in Quebec and who spoke French fluently said she had recently come from France, was just traveling around Canada, etc.

Results. Each of the interviewers mailed his results to the Princeton office at the end of each day's interviewing. Results were tabulated and the following percentage predictions made on Monday afternoon, April 27. No reference was made to the results of the Canadian Institute, and the Institute's final figures were not obtained until the data in this experiment were tabulated and telephoned to the Institute.

One hundred and seven cases were obtained in Quebec; 101 in Ontario. The results by province are set forth in Table 48.

To obtain a rough national prediction on the basis of the two provinces, the assumption was made that Quebec was unique because of its cultural background and that all the remainder of Canada would vote the way Ontario voted. The *World Almanac* of 1942 was consulted for population distribution. The rough figure of 11,000,000 for the total population of Canada was taken and 3,140,000 for Quebec. On the basis

TABLE 48. RESULTS BY PROVINCE

| | QUEBEC | | | | ONTARIO | |
	Cases	% of Total Vote	% of Opinion Vote	Cases	% of Total Vote	% of Opinion Vote
For	31	29	32	68	67	88
Against	66	62	68	9	9	12
Not Voting or No Opinion	10	9	—	24	24	—

of these figures the Quebec returns were weighted with 1; the Ontario figures with 2.33. The figures arrived at for the Dominion were, then, those of Table 49.

TABLE 49. PREDICTION FOR DOMINION

	% of Total Vote	% of Opinion Vote
For	55	69
Against	25	31
No Opinion or Nonvoters	20	—

Tables 50 and 51 compare the results of the small sample with the last figures reported by the Canadian Institute of Public Opinion before the plebiscite, and with the actual vote.

TABLE 50. PERCENTAGE OF VOTING POPULATION

| | OPOR Small Sample | | CIPO | | FINAL VOTE | |
	For	Against	For	Against	For	Against
Quebec	32	68	25	75	28	72
Ontario	88	12	87	13	84	16
Dominion of Canada	69	31	68	32	64.5	35.5

TABLE 51. PERCENTAGE ERROR

	OPOR Small Sample	CIPO
Quebec	4	3
Ontario	4	3
Dominion of Canada	4.5	3.5

Summary interpretation. 1. This experiment again seems to indicate the usefulness of a small sample for the prediction of an over-all result.

2. The experiment also indicates that untrained—but able and conscientious—people can do this type of job.

3. Probably the chief reason for the success of the experiment was the instruction to interviewers to keep moving, to cover the area assigned fairly thoroughly from a geographical point of view, bearing in mind—but not having as stated controls—income distribution and, in the case of Quebec, cultural background.

4. The possibility and value of a casual, informal approach are also demonstrated. When reliance is to be placed on so few cases, everything possible should be done to ensure faithful reporting.

5. All of the interviewing was done in one week—indicating that rather extensive coverage combined with the casual, conversation approach is practicable.

Small Samples Tested Against Regular Poll Results

Telegraphic polls. A common use of small samples in public opinion and market research is the "telegraphic poll." Here the investigator has worked out a relatively small sample of two hundred, three hundred, or five hundred cases, and has already instructed certain interviewers carefully distributed throughout the country concerning the number and distribution of cases. Replies are sent to the central office by telegram.

An example of a telegraphic poll is a survey made by OPOR on June 25, 1942, after the British setback in Libya. Twenty interviewers were used. Two hundred people distributed by region and income were asked the question: "Do you think the British are doing all they possibly can to win the war?" OPOR also included this question in a Gallup ballot that went into the field at the same time in the regular way. The comparative results were:

	200 Case Sample	Percentage from Regular AIPO Sample
Yes	56	58
No	41	33
No Opinion	3	9

Another survey of 200 cases obtained by 22 interviewers and stratified by region, city size, economic status, age, and sex was made by OPOR in October 1942. The same question was included in a regular nation-wide ballot of 3,200 cases sent out at the same time. The question, along with the results of the small sample and the larger survey, was:

"President Roosevelt recently made a secret two weeks' tour of the country. Do you think it was best to keep the President's trip a secret or should the newspapers have been allowed to report it from the beginning?" (October 1942)

	200 Case Sample	Regular Sample
Keep it secret	78%	73%
Should have reported	14	16
No opinion	8	11

Spot checks. The use of small samples can be further simplified and the cost of gathering information considerably reduced if one does not include the regional control in the sample. Obviously such small samples are valid on national issues only where one suspects regional differences will be at a minimum. OPOR made two studies of small samples where interviewing was confined entirely to the New Jersey area, and even within that to an area not more than 40 miles from Princeton. The only instructions given to interviewers were to distribute income into the upper, middle, and lower groups on a 1 : 4 : 5 ratio.

The two studies dealt with topics which were of considerable news value at the time and on which public discussion and opinion might be presumed widespread and relatively vigorous. The two questions tested were also inserted in AIPO ballots sent to interviewers within a few days after the local small sample study had been made. The results of these studies are shown below:

Question	Date	Size of Small Sample	Percentage from Small Sample		Percentage from Regular National Sample	
1. Have you heard about the trial of the 8 German spies?	7/13/42	264 cases	Yes No	98 2	Yes No	92 8
If "Yes" (*A form* of ballot) : The Army says the trials should be kept secret for military reasons and will not allow newspapers to report it. Do you agree that the trial should be kept secret, or should newspapers be allowed to report it?		130	Secret Report No Op.	69 27 4	Secret Report No Op.	66 27 7
If "Yes" (*B form* of ballot) : Which of these statements best expresses your opinion as to whether or not the trial should be made public? *a.* The public should be given complete information about the spy trial.						

Question	Date	Size of Small Sample	Percentage from Small Sample		Percentage from Regular National Sample	
b. The decision of whether or not the trial should be made public should be left up to the men in charge of reporting war news for the government.		129	a. b. c. d.	14 9 77 0	a. b. c. d.	12 12 72 4
c. If the Army says the trial should be kept secret for military reasons, I think it should be kept secret.						
d. No opinion.						
2. If President Roosevelt made a radio talk explaining that it would be necessary to ration gasoline to reduce everybody's driving by as much as one-third from what is being driven now in order to save rubber, would you be willing to see this done?	8/23/42	200	Yes No Qualified Answer No Op.	88 8 4 0	Yes No Qualified Answer No Op.	87 8 1 4

Two other small sample studies were made in the greater New York area using only 52 cases. An economic distribution of 12 per cent above average, 20 per cent average, and 68 per cent poor was assigned. The chief interviewer in the New York area furthermore was asked to work out what he regarded as the proper religious distribution for the 52 cases he and two other interviewers were to gather. The questions asked in these studies were, again, questions on which comparatively small regional variation was expected. The same questions were inserted on regular AIPO ballots at approximately the same time the local studies were being made. Here are the results.

Question	Date	Size of Small Sample	Percentage from Small Sample		Percentage from Regular National Sample
1. The way things are going right now, does it seem to you that we are winning the war, or losing it?	1/15/43	52	Winning Losing Neither No Op.	75 2 4 19	76 2 16 6
2. Do you favor or oppose continuing the lease-lend program?	1/15/43	52	Favor Oppose No Op.	88 6 6	82 9 9

In order to test the discrepancies between several small samples taken simultaneously in the same area, seven interviewers were provided with a regular Gallup ballot at the same time the ballot was being used by AIPO interviewers on the regular national sample.[2] Each of the seven interviewers was given the same classification of respondents to interview. The assignment was stratified by income, sex, and age. All interviewers were told to work in Philadelphia. Each interviewer selected her respondents and completed her assignment quite independently of all other interviewers.

Table 52 shows the results on all opinion questions asked of 50 people by each interviewer and compares these results to AIPO's national total. When the observed range of the percentages obtained is compared to the theoretical limits for a sample of 50 cases, we find that out of 84 comparisons, only two deviate beyond the theoretical limits using AIPO's national total as a standard.[3]

Widest variations from AIPO's results are found where they would be most expected: in a question concerning opinion toward standard time *vs.* war time (where rural-urban differences are high), in a question asking about Roosevelt as a fourth-term candidate (where eastern urban populations with large proportions of industrial workers and foreign born boost the Roosevelt vote), and a question asking how large the army should be (where wide variations are found because standards of judgment are lacking on this technical question).

Agreement between interviewers was surprisingly good. The average deviations of each interviewer's results ranged from five to seven per cent.

A question used on a spot check made of 42 workers in the New Jersey area compares favorably to a regular AIPO survey of all those in the regular sample who said they were employed.

		OPOR 42 Case Sample 1-5-43	Regular AIPO Sample 3-24-43
After the war is over do you expect to be able to keep your present job or will you have to look for a new job?	Expect to keep job	84%	79%
	Look for new job	8	13
	Don't know	8	8

[2] This experiment was done by Dr. Donald V. MacKinnon and Dr. Mary Henle of the Department of Psychology, Bryn Mawr University in cooperation with OPOR. The seven interviewers were students in a psychology seminar at Bryn Mawr. None of the interviewers had had any previous experience. Interviewing was done during the second week of March 1943.

[3] A chart for determining theoretical confidence limits is found in Appendix 4, Figure 42.

Another local spot check made where the 50 cases were stratified only by income comes close to a comparable question asked at approximately the same time of a 3,000 case nation-wide sample surveyed by NORC.

OPOR		NORC	
50 Case Sample		3,000 Case Sample	
1-4-43		1-43	
Which of these seems better to you—for us to win the war first and then think about the peace or to start now thinking about the kind of peace we want after the war?		In addition to waging the war, should the Allies start talking and preparing now for the kind of peace we want after the war, or should we think and plan only for winning the war, letting peace plans wait?	
Plan peace now	64%	Prepare now	58%
Win war first	34	Wait	40
Don't know	2	Don't know	2

Two other questions asked by OPOR of nation-wide small samples, stratified by region and income, compare favorably with larger samples.

		400 Case Sample 4-2-43	Regular AIPO Sample 4-6-43
Should the countries fighting the Axis set up an international police force after the war is over to try to keep peace throughout the world?	Yes	79%	75%
	No	13	14
	No Opinion	8	11

985 Case Sample		Regular AIPO Sample	
3-25-43		3-24-43	
Have you heard or read of a new plan announced by the President for social security after the war?		Have you heard or read about the National Resources Board plan for the post-war period?	
Have heard	35%	Yes	34%
Have not heard	65	No	66

Discussion. In spite of the astonishingly parallel results between a small number of cases and the larger national surveys, few investigators would care to risk their scientific or public reputations on results obtained from such tiny samples. So far no serious upsets seem to have occurred in AIPO's use of telegraphic ballots or OPOR's few studies. However, the investigator who uses small samples must keep his fingers crossed, since regional differences, the influence of interest groups, or other peculiar circumstances may very likely arise in certain areas of the country, or within certain layers of the population to invalidate his small sample completely. Also, quite obviously, the telegraphic poll and the spot check allow no possibility of breakdowns or analyses.

TABLE 52

	AIPO National Total	Interviewers							Observed Range	Theoretical Range
		A	B	C	D	E	F	G		
Do you think food rationing is necessary?										
Yes	85%	90%	84%	86%	88%	86%	86%	84%	84-90	69-94
No	11	8	6	6	8	10	10	6		
No Opinion	4	2	10	8	4	4	4	10		
Do you understand how the food rationing point system works?										
Yes	66	60	60	60	66	60	80	68	60-80	47-80
No	34	40	40	40	34	40	20	32		
A bill in Congress calls for the return to Standard Time throughout the nation. If the question were voted on in this state would you vote for returning to Standard Time or staying on War Time?										
Standard	42	14	30	28	30	34	34	30	42-78	39-73
War Time	44	78	62	58	42	54	52	50		
No Opinion	14	8	8	14	28	12	14	20		
There is an argument in Washington as to whether this country should build up our armed forces to 11,000,000 men this year. Do you think we should or should not increase our armed forces to 11,000,000 men this year?										
Should	44	60	78	60	28	56	66	60	28-78	41-74
Should Not	33	16	14	12	38	18	16	16		
No Opinion	23	24	8	28	34	26	18	24		

(Continued on p. 162)

	AIPO National Total	A	B	C	Interviewers D	E	F	G	Observed Range	Theoretical Range
If you could ask any question you wanted to of any of these men which ONE would you like to ask a question of?										
Wickard	18%	6%	6%	4%	4%	6%	6%	10%		
Hershey	12	6	4	8	12	4	8	4		
McNutt	16	16	16	28	6	16	12	8		
Stimson	6	10	8	6	10	14	8	10		
Morgenthau	9	12	12	8	20	16	16	18		
Jeffers	11	2	6	6	2	6	0	4		
No Answer	28	48	48	40	46	38	50	46	38-50	29-63
If the war is over and Roosevelt runs for a fourth term next year, do you think you will vote for him or against him?										
For	37	58	50	58	48	50	60	56	48-60	37-71
Against	50	40	36	30	46	40	26	36		
No Opinion	13	2	14	12	6	10	14	8		
Do you think you (or your husband) will have to file a Federal income tax report by March 15 on the money you made last year (1942)?										
Yes	69	84	76	70	76	80	76	72	70-84	58-88
No	26	14	24	28	24	18	24	28		
Don't Know	3	2	0	2	0	2	0	0		
Do you think you (or your husband) will have to pay a tax?										
Yes	55	66	64	60	66	78	64	68	60-78	49-81
No	39	30	34	36	32	20	30	30		
Don't Know	6	4	2	4	2	2	6	2		

	AIPO National Total	A	B	C	D	E	F	G	Observed Range	Theoretical Range
					Interviewers					
Have you (or your husband) ever filed a Federal income tax report before?										
Yes	56%	70%	54%	66%	72%	62%	50%	52%	50-72	43-76
No	42	28	46	34	26	36	42	46		
Don't Know	2	2	0	0	2	2	8	0		
Have you heard of the Ruml income tax plan?										
Yes	82	72	60	66	70	78	72	82	60-82	53-84
No	18	28	40	34	30	22	28	18		
In politics do you consider yourself a Republican, Democrat, Socialist, or Independent?										
Republican	37	48	34	34	50	38	38	46	34-50	25-59
Democrat	44	30	46	36	34	28	38	28		
Socialist	1	0	0	0	0	0	2	0		
Independent	18	20	18	30	16	34	18	20		
Which party do you want to see win the presidential election next year—the Democrats or the Republicans?										
Republicans	35	20	22	20	22	14	26	16		32-66
Democrats	43	48	56	46	38	44	58	54	38-58	
Other	2	0	6	0	0	0	0	0		
No Opinion	20	32	16	32	40	42	16	30		

Testing Small Samples in the Laboratory

A check on the accuracy of small sample results can be made in the laboratory by constructing small samples on the basis of various indices.

If the results of the usual nation-wide surveys are available, checks on the accuracy of small samples may be made by constructing small samples according to any set of indices desired, separating these samples out of some larger survey and comparing the small sample with the results of the regular survey.

In the small samples generally used in practical polling, only simple controls such as region, city size, and economic status are assigned. Moreover, these controls are usually assigned to interviewers only as general guides to the selection of respondents. The problem of the selection of indices upon which to stratify a small sample obviously bears investigation. The present study reports an attempt to select indices. It also reports a corollary investigation which sought practical verification for the statement that random sampling does not give as accurate results as sampling based on a careful selection of respondents.

In these studies, certain restrictions were made at the beginning concerning the number of ballots a single interviewer would obtain. These restrictions, which are completely arbitrary, represent a compromise between practical and theoretical aspects of the problem. The assumption is that until an interviewer acquires experience with a new ballot or question, his results may not be representative of the persons he has questioned. Consequently, any sampling method depending on sending from one to three ballots (using new questions) to an interviewer may result in returns much more atypical than would be expected from sampling errors. For this reason we shall settle on seven interviews as a minimum for a single interviewer. At the same time in order to maximize the number of places sampled, we shall consider ten as the maximum number of interviews allotted to a single interviewer.

It is clear that under these conditions proportionate sampling by region and city size cannot be very practical. We cannot cover any particular region or city size adequately. Consequently, we use a method suggested by the Latin Square technique employed in agricultural experiments.

An ordinary situation occurs when we have an n x n table. We choose one cell to represent the ith row and jth column (the cell at their intersection); this cell is the only one sampled in either that row or column. In agricultural experiments it is usual to pick a pattern of n cells at random so that each row and column are represented.

In our case we can improve on randomness, since some city sizes represent some regions better than others (and conversely). For example, we would not use cities of 500,000 and over to represent the South and Southwest, where there were no cities of that size recorded in the 1940 census.

We choose the following regions and city sizes for our work:

Region	City Size
1. New England	1. Farm
2. Middle Atlantic	2. Small town
3. East Central	3. 2,500-10,000
4. West Central	4. 10,000-100,000
5. South and Southwest	5. 100,000-500,000
6. Rocky Mountain and Pacific Coast	6. 500,000 and over

Our method of procedure is to take the largest city size and find the region whose population has the largest proportion in that city size. This turns out to be the middle Atlantic states with over 36 per cent represented. Eliminating this region and city size, we consider the next city size, and find the east central to be the best represented of the remaining regions by cities of size 100,000-500,000, etc. A number of other methods could have been used, of course. The pairs chosen were:

City Size	Region
Farm	West Central
Small town	South and Southwest
2,500-10,000	Rocky Mountain and Pacific Coast
10,000-100,000	New England
100,000-500,000	East Central
500,000 and over	Middle Atlantic

We now come to the assignment of cases. For the cell representing the ith row and jth column we obtain the product of the total population of the row and the total of the column divided by the total population of the table. Doing this for each of the six cells used, we get six numbers whose total is taken as 100 per cent. Then the number of people assigned in a cell must be proportional to the number for that cell obtained by the method described. A tabulation of a sample of 200 cases would appear as in Table 53, with economic status, sex, and age stratified within a cell.

Verification. The archives at OPOR contain hundreds of ballots based on many types of cross-section. An OPOR ballot which polled the national population on many phases of opinion toward the war effort, and which was based upon a social sample was selected for study. It was

TABLE 53. SAMPLE OF 200

Section and City Size	Upper Income	Average Income	Poor	On Relief	No. Inter- viewers	Total
New England; 10,000-100,000	2	4	6	2	2	14
Middle Atlantic; 500,000 and Over	8	18	24	4	5	54
East Central; 100,000-500,000	6	12	16	2	3	36
West Central; Farm	2	10	12	4	4	28
South and Southwest; Small Town	4	14	18	4	4	40
Rocky Mt. and Pacific Coast; 2,500-10,000	4	12	10	2	4	28
Totals	26	70	86	18	22	200

Special Notes:

1. Instruct interviewers to get approximately half men and half women at each economic status level.
2. Instruct interviewers to get approximately half over 40 years old, half under.
3. Be sure to weight New York City in middle Atlantic-city category.
4. Be sure to have more than one interviewer in New York City.
5. Be sure to scatter West Central-farm category geographically: same with all categories in so far as practicable.

decided that from this population of 2,543 cases various samples could be compared with the results on the total ballot.

One hundred cases were selected at random from the total ballot. Our index of deviation was taken to be the sum of the absolute values of the deviations of the sampling percentages from the population percentages divided by the number of questions, in this case eleven (Table 54).

Another random sample of 200 cases was selected. The deviation proved to be smaller than was the case when only 100 respondents were selected at random (Table 54). This smaller deviation, however, had approximately the decrease to be expected from random sampling theory due to the increase in number of cases.

In view of the fact, however, that all sampling must be geographically located (in practice, of course, we cannot take a random sample in the United States), another hundred cases were selected at random within the proper sectional and city-size distributions. Little variation was found from the deviation of the 100-case strictly random sample. Such a result was to be expected, since the type of questions used was not so closely related to region or city size as, say, economic status or education. Nevertheless, even these results are strictly academic, to be used only as an indication, since in the field we cannot ask interviewers to "get a random sample of *n* people from your district" and expect the distribu-

TABLE 54. VERIFICATION OF SMALL SAMPLES CONSTRUCTED WITH VARIOUS INDICES

Construction of Sample	Average Deviation
Random	
100 cases	15.5
200 "	9.6
Section and Rural-urban selected (100 cases)	14.3
Selected three variables	
Section, Rural-urban Sex (100 cases)	12.4
" " " Age (100 cases)	12.2
" " " Economic (100 cases)	9.2
" " " Education (100 cases)	12.4
Selected four variables	
Section, Rural-urban Sex Economic (200 cases)	9.3
Section, Rural-urban Sex Economic (100 cases)	12.7
" " " Age Education (100 cases)	14.2, 10.4 (replicated)
" " " Econ. " (100 cases)	11.3
" " " Econ. Age (100 cases)	10.4
" " " Sex, Ed. (100 cases)	9.4
" " " Sex, Age (100 cases)	8.0, 11.5 (replicated)

tion of these people on the usual variables to approximate the true distribution.

The next step was to set up tables showing the number of cases to be apportioned within various categories, when various other indices were held constant (using in all cases the Latin Square setup for region and city-size described here). The indices chosen were sex, age, economic status, and education. Stratification on the basis of each one of these and section and city-size returned least deviation for the sample based on economic status. The six possible combinations of two of these four variables (using the same section and city-size distribution in each case) provided the basis for the construction of six more samples. One additional sample of 200 cases was built up from the variables: section, city-size, sex, and economic status. The comparisons with the actual percentages reported for the whole ballot are shown in Table 54.

In order to avoid giving a false impression of the reliability of the ordering of the average deviations due to the various methods of constructing samples, replication of samples showing the smallest and largest deviations was made. It will be seen that in the replication the magnitudes of the average deviation reversed in these two cases.

If, to obtain our average deviation, we had used the number of categories in the eleven questions instead of the number of questions, we would have found that in samples of both 200 and 100 the average deviation for a single category was about 3 per cent. In fact, in the case of samples of 200 it was 2.6 per cent, for samples of 100 (with four variables stratified) it was 3.0 per cent. Comparing these with the expected average deviation for the dichotomous cases where the split is 50-50 or 90-10 (assuming normal distributions, etc.), we see that in the 50-50 case we should expect a 5 per cent average deviation, in the 90-10 case an average deviation of 3 per cent. Therefore, using this rough measure we may consider our results as somewhat better than those expected for random sampling.

The following tabulation shows the agreement between actual proportion and sample of 100 proportions when we stratify on economic status and sex using the Latin Square method on region and city size. It will be noticed that the agreement is very good over the whole range of questions. Further, from observation alone, it is clear that attitudes most closely related to economic status (and consequently education and information) are those on which the best results are obtained. Examples of these are voting in 1940, the question concerning our chief enemy, and the question concerning trustworthiness of people.

Which do you think is our No. 1 enemy in the war—Japan or Germany?	Sample	Actual
Japan	26%	28%
Germany	50	47
Both	22	23
No Opinion	2	2

Do you think we are now doing all we can to defeat Japan and Germany, or could we be doing more?	Sample	Actual
Doing all we can	49	46
Could be doing more	40	48
No Opinion	11	6

Which of these two things do you think the U. S. should do:	Sample	Actual
Send army abroad	42	55
Keep at home	34	28
Other	12	11
No Opinion	12	6

Which do you think has the smartest military leaders at present?	Sample	Actual
Germany	26%	21%
Russia	11	12
U. S.	50	52
No Opinion	13	15

Which do you think has the strongest navy at present?	Sample	Actual
Japan	17	17
England	21	15
U. S.	50	50
No Opinion	12	19

If Hitler offered peace now, would you favor or oppose accepting?	Sample	Actual
Favor	15	8
Oppose	80	88
No Opinion	5	4

Do you think the British are doing all they possibly can to win the war?	Sample	Actual
Yes	46	51
No	44	38
No Opinion	10	11

	Sample	Actual
Do you think most people can be trusted?		
Yes	70%	66%
No	26	25
No Opinion	4	6
Qualified Answer	0	3
Do you think success is dependent mostly on		
Luck	19	12
Ability	65	70
Pull	27	22
No Opinion	3	5
(Some people gave two responses)		

	Sample	Actual
Do you approve or disapprove of the way Roosevelt is doing his job as President?		
Approve	78%	80%
Disapprove	18	15
No Opinion	4	5
Vote in 1940		
Roosevelt	45	46.5
Willkie	31	33.5
Didn't vote	19	15
Others	3	5

Table 55 below gives the cross-section for a sample of 500 to be used in the field. This sample is a miniature of the usual stratified sample. The same instructions should go with this sample as with the earlier sample of 200, with some additional instructions about Negroes and farmers.

Conclusions. 1. The Latin Square technique of sampling gives very good results for small samples when stratification by economic status is used within cells.

2. On the questions tested, there were no reliable differences due to stratifying on any pairs of the four variables: economic status, sex, age, and education; consequently it seems reasonable to continue the use of economic status as an assigned control even in small samples.

3. Various types of small stratified samples have consistently produced smaller deviations than expected on the basis of random sampling.

SUMMARY OF ALL STUDIES REPORTED

1. What we know to date of the telegraphic poll and the use of small samples in general indicates that for a quick, inexpensive, and superficial sounding to get the drift of public opinion, the use of a small sample is surprisingly reliable.

2. Small samples were validated against three elections (a county, a state, and a national election) with an average error of less than five per cent.

3. Small samples were also validated against the regular national samples of polling organizations with an average error of less than five per cent.

4. Small samples were constructed in the laboratory from data already obtained on national surveys. Here again, deviations obtained were less than would be expected from random sampling. Economic status proved to be the most effective control.

TABLE 55. SAMPLE OF 500

	Relief	Poor	Average	Wealthy and Average Plus	Totals
New England					
Over 100,000	1	3	2	1	7
2,500-100,000	1	9	5	3	18
Rural nonfarm	0	4	2	1	7
Farmers					2
Middle Atlantic					
Over 100,000	4	34	14	9	61
2,500-100,000	3	16	7	4	30
Rural nonfarm	0	13	7	2	22
Farmers					9
Negroes					4
East Central					
Over 100,000	4	18	8	4	34
2,500-100,000	3	17	12	6	38
Rural nonfarm	0	5	2	1	8
Farmers					13
South and Southwest					
Over 100,000	2	4	3	1	10
2,500-100,000	4	19	6	4	33
Rural nonfarm	0	13	4	2	19
Farmers					34
Negroes					31
West Central					
Over 100,000	3	6	3	2	14
2,500-100,000	2	8	6	2	18
Rural nonfarm	0	6	4	3	13
Farmers					19
Rocky Mt. and Pacific Coast					
Over 100,000	4	10	4	2	20
2,500-100,000	0	8	5	2	15
Rural nonfarm	0	6	4	2	12
Farmers					9
					500

5. The results reported here should *not*, however, lead anyone to the conclusion that small samples are an adequate substitute for the regular national samples used by polling organizations. Some of their dangers and restrictions are:

    a. No cautious investigator—no matter how many accurate small samples he took—would feel safe or justified in reporting his results without rigid qualifications. Wherever he wanted a reliable gauge of opinion—whether to predict an election, discover information for a commercial client, form final policy, chart trends, or gather precise information for any theoretical reason—he would insist on the usual more adequate sampling.

b. Small samples are highly unlikely to represent opinion faithfully *unless* opinion is fairly uniform throughout an area and within different interest groups and *unless* such differences are already fairly well known and can be adjusted for in constructing the sample. They have little chance of predicting unexpected or unexplored differences and changes of opinion within a population group which, if not accommodated in the sample, may radically alter the over-all result.

c. Small samples allow no possibility of reliable breakdowns or other detailed analysis.

PART IV

GETTING AT OPINION DETERMINANTS

CHAPTER XIII

THE USE OF BREAKDOWNS[1]

AMONG the simplest and most powerful techniques available to the research workers in the field of public opinion is the breakdown of the sample on variables which may influence opinion. The breakdown is one of the few tools which provides an approach to the problem of causation. It gives us a method of attack on the questions of relative importance of two or more variables. It also furnishes a foothold for a study of the simultaneous relationship between variables when opinions are held constant.

The ease with which a breakdown can be performed on modern punched card equipment and the simple form of its tabulation give to this technique considerable practical advantage. But at the same time this simplicity—as well as other factors—appears to have lured many research workers into pitfalls. Conclusions drawn from breakdowns have frequently been vitiated because of poorly designed experiments, misinterpretation of the data, or because the problem has not been placed in its most general setting. The ancient slander, "You can prove anything with statistics," probably had as its source some dour old skeptic who had viewed conclusions inexpertly drawn from breakdowns.[2]

The use of breakdowns may be clarified at the beginning if we make a distinction between "descriptive" and "analytical" breakdowns. Although such a distinction is, of course, tenuous at best and depends entirely on the interests of the investigator, the distinction may be useful to students of public opinion. For, in general, they should find themselves dissatisfied with the simple descriptive breakdown which merely reports opinion among different groups. Such descriptive breakdowns are used by reporting agencies such as the American Institute of Public Opinion and *Fortune*. These reports often do little more than tantalize the person who wants to know what is behind opinion.

In Table 56 below there is an example of what we mean here by a "descriptive" breakdown. This was reported by AIPO on March 11, 1942.

---

[1] By Hadley Cantril.

[2] For a detailed discussion of the theory of stratified sampling and its relation to breakdowns, see Note 1 in Appendix 3 by Frederick Mosteller. A formula is indicated there for calculating the efficiency of a stratified sample.

TABLE 56

"After finding out what each person can do, should the government have the power to tell each citizen what to do as his part in the war effort, and require him or her to do it?" (March 1942—AIPO)

	For	Against	Undecided
National Total	61%	32%	7%
Section			
New England	57	36	7
Middle Atlantic	60	33	7
East Central	56	35	9
West Central	62	32	6
South	66	25	9
Rocky Mountain	69	24	7
Pacific Coast	63	33	4
Sex			
Men	66	29	5
Women	55	36	9
Economic Status			
Upper income group	62	34	4
Middle income group	61	33	6
Lower income group	60	30	10
Politics			
Democrats	67	26	7
Republicans	57	37	6
Age			
21-29	56	38	6
30-49	61	31	8
50 and over	62	30	8

An example of a single breakdown which gives more meaningful differences is another taken from AIPO, Table 57.

ANALYTICAL BREAKDOWNS

The background data concerning respondents obtained by most public opinion surveys concerns such variables as areas of the country, size of city, sex, age, political affiliation, income, education, religion and the like. This information allows us to place people in certain groups or subgroups. Such a procedure has its advantages for statistical purposes and is the only practicable way to proceed in a public opinion poll.

TABLE 57

"Are you in favor of labor unions?" (May 1942—AIPO)

	Yes	No
National Total	67%	33%
Occupation		
Farmers	52	48
Businessmen	66	34
White Collar	69	31
Professional	77	23
Skilled Workers	75	25
Unskilled	71	29

However, by the very nature of the method used, the background data we gather from all respondents are uniform and at best place people in broad population groups. They necessarily obscure much personal history or pertinent psychological information which may for many individuals be a great deal more important in "explaining" their opinions or behavior than any of the standard controls used. Furthermore, such rough background data give us no precise information concerning the role an individual may play within any group or how important any particular social affiliation is to him.

Briefly, the statistical method employed in public opinion polls can never in itself provide what most psychologists interested in motivation would call a real "explanation" of opinion. But analysis of public opinion data can point to many such explanations, can disprove many other explanations, and can get much closer to verifiable explanations of certain opinions of large numbers of people than psychologists have ever been before.

If the data obtained from the polls are to be used most effectively for purposes of analysis, it is necessary in this procedure, as it is in other scientific investigations, that the investigator have some definite theories to test out by means of breakdowns. The ease with which breakdowns can be made is all too likely to cause enormous waste of time, money, and effort if the investigator simply makes "a number of breakdowns" to see what he can find. Furthermore, such a procedure leads to facile rationalization when the investigator does discover some significant difference by means of breakdowns—rationalization that may not stand up long under more strenuous tests.

Probably the two most important and the two rarest qualifications for a good public opinion investigator are (1) his ability to slice public opinion issues in the most significant ways, and (2) his ability to plan systematic analysis ahead and to have his conceptual framework so well geared to the problems in hand that no significant breakdowns will escape him. When these qualifications are met, the investigator gets a relatively high percentage of significant information from the breakdowns he runs.

Several methods suggesting the use of breakdowns for analytical purposes are discussed below.

1. *Single variables held constant.* Frequently a division of the population into categories of a single variable (such as age or income) will completely hide some relationship between opinion and background which is really much more important as a determinant than the particular scale used. Therefore, this first variable must be held constant and other comparisons must be made within it if we are to discover more causal relationships.

The first two examples (Tables 58 and 59) show how straight breakdowns by age may obscure differences of opinion within single age-groups when these age-groups are divided into various economic classes. From comments obtained on earlier ballots, we noticed that both young people and old people in different income groups expressed different opinions about the war effort. In our subsequent survey, we set questions

TABLE 58

Proportions of Different Economic and Age Groups which Fall into the Isolationist, Sympathetic, and Interventionist Patterns. (June-July 1940)

| | Total | Economic Status | | |
		Upper	Middle	Lower
Isolationist				
Under 30	26%	30%	28%	22%
30-49	24	21	23	26
50 and over	26	17	23	34
Sympathetic				
Under 30	42	40	42	45
30-49	37	38	38	35
50 and over	40	39	40	40
Interventionist				
Under 30	32	30	30	33
30-49	39	41	39	39
50 and over	34	44	37	26

to bring out and systematize these variations in opinion. A breakdown by age and income was, therefore, planned in advance before the survey ever went into the field.

TABLE 59

"Do you think we are likely to have (greater) prosperity or another depression after the present war?" (July 1941—AIPO)

	Greater Prosperity	Depression	No Opinion
Age			
Under 30	13%	80%	7%
30-50	13	77	10
Over 50	13	75	12
Economic Status by Age			
Upper			
Under 30	3	90	7
30-50	13	80	7
Over 50	16	76	8
Middle			
Under 30	12	82	6
30-50	14	76	10
Over 50	13	78	9
Lower			
Under 30	17	76	7
30-50	11	77	12
Over 50	13	72	15

Table 58 illustrates particularly clearly the varying opinions of young people under 30 and older people over 50. We note, for example, that young people in the upper-income group are much more similar in their attitude to older people in the lower-income group than they are to young people in the lower-income group. In other words, the table illustrates how two distinctive groups—well-to-do young people and poor old people—may give essentially the same percentage response on a question. Such a situation immediately calls for further probing. People were asked, consequently, to give the main reason for their opinion as soon as that opinion had been expressed. In this instance, when the reasons given by the two groups were analyzed, we found that the two groups held similar opinions for entirely different reasons. The poor old people, feeling less than any other group that they would be personally affected by a German victory, saw no far-reaching implications in what was to them a very distant conflict. Also they had least to lose if Germany did win the war or if the social system in which they were at the bottom should be radically altered. On the other hand, the well-to-do young people— meaning essentially recent college graduates—were particularly cynical and realized that they would have a great deal to lose by any change in the status quo at the time (June 1940). Also noteworthy in Table 58 are the differences in the proportions of well-to-do old people and poor old people who fall in the interventionist pattern.

Table 59 shows again how young people in the upper-income group can differ from the young people in the lower-income group with respect to another issue, namely their optimism concerning the economic condition of the country when the war is over. A straight breakdown by age shows little difference between opinion with respect to the various age groups. But the further breakdown clearly shows the greater confidence in the future held by young people in the lower income bracket.

Table 60 indicates the importance of controlling religious affiliation. It shows first of all the opinion of persons in this country of Irish and Canadian ancestry on one of OPOR's standard pre-Pearl Harbor questions. When the Irish and Canadians are further separated by religion, we find a greater similarity within a single religious group than we do within a single nationality group.

In a country as large as the United States with various regions characterized by certain population groups or ways of life, it is often extremely important to hold section constant if comparisons are to be worth while, that is, to make the same comparisons within each section. For example, Southerners are on the whole less well educated than people in other sections of the United States: in most national surveys done by OPOR we find that about 45 per cent of our respondents say they have graduated from high school, whereas only about 30 per cent of the respondents in the South say they have graduated from high school. Hence any straight educational breakdown on a national population is apt to lose some of its significance, because the educational scale has a different distribution within different parts of the country. Table 61 illustrates this situation with respect to educational differences of opinion on the same question studied in Table 60.

We see from Table 61 that there was only a three-per cent difference between the opinions of grade-school and college graduates on the national sample, although except for two sections of the country (the East Central and the Rocky Mountain states) the difference between high-school and college graduates was at least eight.

TABLE 60. RELIGION BY NATIONALITY

"Which of these two things do you think is the more important for the United States to try to do—To keep out of war ourselves, or To help England win, even at the risk of getting into the war?" (October 1940—AIPO)

	Ireland	Canada
Total		
Keep out	50%	40%
Help England	45	54
No Choice	5	6
No. of cases	443	310
Catholic		
Keep out	55	48
Help England	39	42
No Choice	6	10
No. of cases	328	134
Protestant		
Keep out	30	33
Help England	67	62
No Choice	3	5
No. of cases	70	100

TABLE 61. DIFFERENCE BETWEEN GROUPS WITHIN EACH SECTION

% Help England, Even at Risk of War

Education	National Total	New England	Middle Atlantic	East Central	West Central	South	Rocky Mountain	Pacific Coast
Grade school	59%	49%	52%	53%	50%	69%	67%	66%
High school	61	60	60	52	62	79	69	65
College	62	61	63	52	60	77	70	55

2. Same breakdown on several questions. Whenever the opinion of a certain group seems particularly obscure or complex, the reasons for this obscurity or complexity may sometimes be brought out more sharply if the group can be compared with other groups or with the national population on several significant questions. For example, in January 1941, when OPOR asked one of its trend questions and separated the answers of Catholics from Protestants, results were as shown in Figure 15.

The conclusions from these figures might be that at the time Catholics were considerably more isolationist in general than were Protestants. That this interpretation is false because it is too broad is shown by the

FIGURE 15

Which of these two things do you think is the more important—That this country keep out of war, or That Germany be defeated (That the United States help England win), even at the risk of our getting into the war?

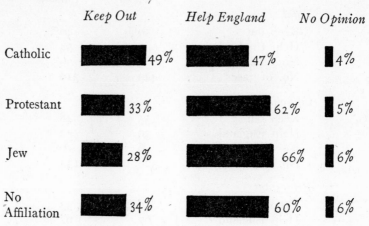

	Keep Out	*Help England*	*No Opinion*
Catholic	49%	47%	4%
Protestant	33%	62%	5%
Jew	28%	66%	6%
No Affiliation	34%	60%	6%

comparison of Catholic to Protestant answers to another question asked at the same time concerning the policy of the United States toward the Far East.

TABLE 62. AMERICAN OPINION ON FREEDOM OF SPEECH

Education	Age	Do you think that in America anybody should be allowed to speak on any subject any time he wants to, or do you think there are times when free speech should be prohibited? (July 1940—OPOR) Allow	If "Yes" on question at left, ask: Do you believe in free speech to the extent of allowing Fascists and Communists to hold meetings and express their views in this community? Allow
Grade school	Under 30	49%	26%
	30-49	50	26
	50 and over	41	28
High school	Under 30	43	34
	30-49	45	35
	50 and over	46	24
College	Under 30	41	72
	30-49	43	54
	50 and over	38	52

FIGURE 16

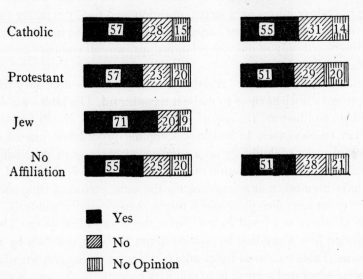

Do you think the United States should try to keep Japan from seizing the Dutch East Indies and Singapore?

(If "Yes" or "No Opinion") Do you think the United States should risk war with Japan, if necessary, in order to keep Japan from taking the Dutch East Indies and Singapore?

■ Yes

▨ No

▥ No Opinion

It appears, in other words, that when Catholics looked toward Europe, they tended to look on the European scene both as Americans and as Catholics; whereas when they looked toward the East, their religious frames of reference did not apply, and they held essentially the same nationalistic opinions as did Protestants.

Another illustration of the value of comparing the same group on several questions is shown in Table 62, where American opinion toward freedom of speech is recorded as of July 1940 (OPOR).

Here we see that, on the whole, well-educated people are somewhat more opposed than others to free speech. We also see, however, that when these people do favor free speech, they are willing to extend their tolerance to the logical conclusion of allowing Fascists and Communists to speak. Such a finding seems to indicate that these people are more burdened by the intellectual demand for consistency than are persons who have had less educational opportunity; who, though they are more in favor of free speech in general, are much less in favor when they are taken up on the general proposition.

3. *The use of higher-order breakdowns*. By a higher-order breakdown we mean that information is sorted in more than two ways. We may, for example, using two of the background variables such as education and age, segregate the people who have given a certain answer to a single opinion question; or we may first sort out the people who answer in certain ways to one opinion question, then divide these people further according to their opinions on a second question, and finally separate them a third time according to some background factor such as income. Or, if we are interested only in opinion relationships, we can compare answers to several opinion questions.

Whenever a higher-order breakdown is desired, it is necessary to be sure there are sufficient cases to make it meaningful. The tables we shall include here to illustrate the use of higher breakdowns are all based on more than 10,000 cases. In ordinary sampling procedures, one of the most useful ways of building up a number of cases is to pool ballots which have the same information on them.[3] Such a step is possible if the ballots have been taken at approximately the same period of time and if no major event has taken place which might change opinion suddenly.

Table 58 above is a good example of a three-way breakdown. There we separated first according to opinion about the war and then by age and income. Table 63 shows the results of a four-way breakdown where people were separated according to opinions concerning the war, according to preference for presidential candidate, according to income and to age. The resulting figures indicate rather clearly that in all income and age groups there was at this time a positive relationship between the vote for Roosevelt and a desire to risk war to help England.[4]

One of the important uses to which the polling mechanism can be put, and one which has hardly yet been exploited by social scientists or policy makers, is the gathering of straight information concerning the composition of our population, its habits, its needs, etc. Commercial market research has, of course, gathered vast amounts of information concerning people's radio and buying habits.

An example of the type of information that can be obtained from the polls and of the knowledge that higher-order breakdowns on these data provide the social scientist is illustrated in Table 64. The data on which

---

[3] For detailed discussion of this problem see Note 2 in Appendix 3.

[4] The ballots on which this table was based were taken during August and September of 1940, that is, before the elections but after the nomination of Roosevelt and Willkie.

TABLE 63. RELATIONSHIP BETWEEN OPINIONS ON AID TO ENGLAND AND
POLITICAL PREFERENCE IN 1940 ELECTION

(Economic Status and Age Held Constant)

Income	Age	Those Who Consider It More Important to Keep Out *% Voting for Roosevelt*	Those Who Consider It More Important to Help England *% Voting for Roosevelt*
Upper	Under 30	25	46
	30-49	24	34
	50 and over	22	29
Middle	Under 30	45	56
	30-49	38	53
	50 and over	33	50
Lower	Under 30	54	63
	30-49	62	70
	50 and over	55	63

this table is based could, of course, be percentaged in numerous different ways.

Table 64 shows that the ratio of Protestants in the population group tends to increase with the economic status of the group, and, conversely, that the ratio of Catholics in a population group tends to decrease with increasing economic status of the group. A higher concentration of Protestants within any educational group is found as economic status increases. With the exception of Catholics in the lowest educational group, the ratio of Catholics in a population group decreases as the economic status of the group increases. The exception is due to the heavy weighting of Southern Protestants in the lowest educational and income group as can be demonstrated by other tabulations.

4. *Patterns of opinion.* Since the social scientist, and frequently the policy-maker, are interested in conceptualizing information in such a way that the information will fit into a broad interpretation, and since in many instances questions which will fit into a broad conceptual scheme cannot be asked directly, it becomes necessary to try to get information on what are regarded as the most important components of the larger concept. Then the information on these components may be put together by cross-tabulations, so that in the end we have data that more nearly approximate the conceptual scheme than we could ever get by direct questioning.

TABLE 64. ECONOMIC STATUS DISTRIBUTION BY RELIGION WITH EDUCATION CONSTANT

(*Surveys Made in 1940*)

Education	Religion	Economic Status Lower	Middle	Upper	National %
College	Catholic	12%	10%	9%	10%
	Protestant	60	70	70	69
	Nonmember	28	20	21	21
		100	100	100	100
High School	Catholic	17	16	11	15
	Protestant	59	63	69	63
	Nonmember	24	21	20	22
		100	100	100	100
Grade School	Catholic	17	16	16	16
	Protestant	51	57	62	54
	Nonmember	32	27	22	30
		100	100	100	100
Less than Grade School	Catholic	13	12	20	13
	Protestant	55	57	58	55
	Nonmember	32	31	22	32
		100	100	100	100
National	Catholic	16	14	12	15
	Protestant	54	62	67	59
	Nonmember	30	24	21	26
		100	100	100	100

In Table 58 an age-by-economic-status breakdown was given for people in the United States who during the midsummer of 1940 were classified as isolationists, sympathetics, or interventionists. These three groupings of the population were obtained by comparing the answers of the people to two questions and grouping them accordingly. Table 65 shows how this grouping was obtained and relates other opinion concerning the war to the three more general patterns thus obtained.

Another example of clustering data so that they will more precisely fit a general concept is illustrated in OPOR's attempt to distinguish between "enlightened" and "unenlightened" people with respect to war issues. We defined enlightenment in terms of two components: (1) information as measured objectively by verifiable questions; and (2) felt-awareness of what the war is all about. Table 66 shows the way in

TABLE 65. CLUSTER OF OPINIONS OF THE ISOLATIONIST, SYMPATHETIC, AND INTERVENTIONIST GROUPS*

(June-July 1940)

Which of these two things do you think is more important for the U.S. to try to do?	At the present time, which of the following should the U.S. do about helping England?	Believe Germany would start war on U.S.	Believe they would be personally affected by a German victory	Think U.S. will get into the war	Think England will win	Favor conscription of 20-year-old men for one year
To keep out of war ourselves (61% of total)	Do less or no more than we are now doing (Isolationist: 23% of total)	26%	33%	22%	25%	51%
	Do more than we are now doing (Sympathetic: 33% of total)	40	66	25	49	60
To help England win, even at the risk of getting into war (35% of total)	Do more than we are now doing (Interventionist: 33% of total)	61	90	52	60	75

* About 6 per cent of the population cannot be classified in these patterns because they had no opinion.

which, in a survey made during the spring of 1942, enlightened and unenlightened groups were delineated from the total population. In constructing this table, we deliberately omitted those who were classified as "moderately informed" and who constituted 28 per cent of the total population, since we were interested in comparing only the two extreme groups.

TABLE 66. RELATIONSHIP BETWEEN AWARENESS AND AMOUNT OF INFORMATION

	Awareness Do you feel that you have a clear idea of what the war is all about?		
Information	Yes	No	Total
Well informed (38% of total)	60%	40%	100%
Uninformed (34% of total)	39	61	100

The "enlightened" people, then, we call those who are both well informed and who say they have a clear idea of what the war is all about. In the table this group amounts to 23 per cent of the total population. The "unenlightened" we call those who are both poorly informed and who do not have a clear idea of what the war is all about. This group amounts to 22 per cent of the total population.

It might be argued at once that the distinction between enlightened and unenlightened groups as thus derived is essentially the same distinction we would get if the population were broken down by income or education. This, however, is not the case. Figure 17, for example, shows that the expected relationship between enlightenment and income holds, with the upper-income group much more enlightened (according to our

FIGURE 17. ENLIGHTENED *vs.* UNENLIGHTENED BY INCOME

Cases	Income	Enlightened	Unenlightened	Mixture*
226	Upper	59%	10%	31%
524	Middle	46%	16%	38%
760	Lower	20%	22%	58%

* Mixture: either aware *or* informed but not both; either unaware *or* uninformed but not both.

FIGURE 18

Which of these two things do you think the United States should do?

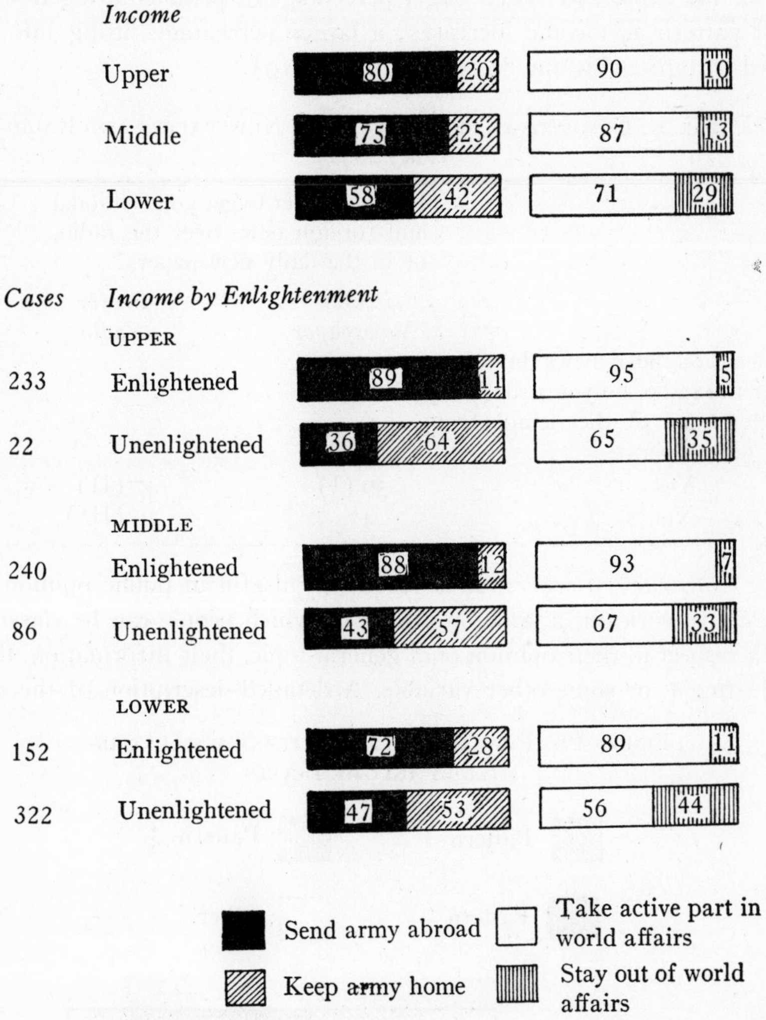

Income

Upper	[80] [20]	90 [10]
Middle	[75] [25]	87 [13]
Lower	[58] [42]	71 [29]

Cases   *Income by Enlightenment*

UPPER

| 233 | Enlightened | [89] [11] | 95 [5] |
| 22 | Unenlightened | [36] [64] | 65 [35] |

MIDDLE

| 240 | Enlightened | [88] [12] | 93 [7] |
| 86 | Unenlightened | [43] [57] | 67 [33] |

LOWER

| 152 | Enlightened | [72] [28] | 89 [11] |
| 322 | Unenlightened | [47] [53] | 56 [44] |

■ Send army abroad   □ Take active part in world affairs

▨ Keep army home   ▥ Stay out of world affairs

definition) than the lower-income group. When economic status is held constant (Figure 18), however, we find that the enlightened group is in every income bracket much more aggressive and interventionist in its position than is the unenlightened group.

A final example of the use of more than one question to divide the population into meaningful patterns is illustrated in our effort to compare the importance of radio and newspaper as media of communication for different population groups. Table 67 reports the two questions asked and shows the three patterns into which the population seems to fall. As we should expect, we find a larger percentage of persons fitting into the first pattern as income increases; a larger percentage fitting into the third pattern as income decreases (Figure 19).

TABLE 67. COMPARISON OF RELIANCE ON NEWSPAPERS AND RADIO
(*July 1942*)

	Do you prefer to get your national and foreign news over the radio, or in the daily newspapers?	
	Prefer Newspaper	*Prefer Radio*
When you hear news broadcast over the radio, do you usually try to get more of the details from the newspapers?		
Yes	30 (I)	47 (II)
No	4	19 (III)

5. *Constructing scores.* It is frequently useful in public opinion research to work out a scale by means of which people can be classified with respect to their opinion on a general topic, their information, their adjustment, or some other variable. A detailed description of the con-

FIGURE 19. HOW THE THREE PATTERNS ARE DISTRIBUTED BY INCOME LEVELS

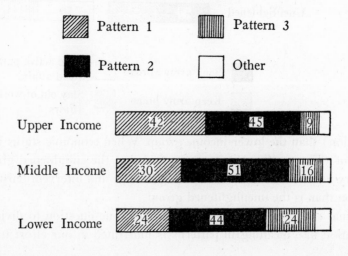

struction of an "information scale" is given in Chapter 15. In order to construct most scales, it is necessary to combine the answers to several questions in a single scale. For most members of the population, any refined attitude scale or rank-ordering is much too complicated to use in the usual interviewing situation, although the latter methods have been used with success when ballots were self-administrating. If several relatively simple questions can be devised to tap the same variable, then the answers of a single individual on these several questions can be pooled to place him on the scale with respect to the total population.

A single example will suffice to explain the procedure. Just before the Congressional election of November 3, 1942, OPOR designed a ballot to see if our understanding of why people voted or why they did not vote could be improved. Persons were very thoroughly interviewed before the election. After the election, interviewers called back on the same people to see whether or not they had voted and how they had voted. Among other problems studied was the individual's interest in the election as such. Previous experience had shown that a simple question asking "Are you interested in the coming election?" failed to differentiate in any significant degree between people who actually voted and those who failed to vote. So interest was broken down into several components and measured by the seven questions listed below.

1. Do you think it makes much difference one way or the other whether people vote in the coming elections for Congressmen?
       (*1*) Yes   (*o*) No   (*o*) No opinion

2. In general, how important does this coming election seem to you to be?
       (*2*) Seems extremely important
       (*1*) Only moderately important
       (*o*) Not at all important

3. a. Are you interested in the coming Congressional elections?
       (*1*) Yes   (*o*) No   (*o*) Not much
   b. Are you interested in the coming state elections?
       (*1*) Yes   (*o*) No   (*o*) Not much

4. Do you happen to know the names of any candidates running for office this November? If "Yes," do you know what their political party is and what office they are running for?
       (*2*) given for three or more correct
       (*1*) given for one or two correct
       (*o*) for all others—no answer and incorrect

5. How important is it to you that the (respondent's choice) candidate should be elected?
       (*2*) Extremely important
       (*1*) Only moderately important
       (*o*) Not at all important

6. Does it make a great deal of difference, or only a little difference which political party runs this state?

    (*1*) Great deal   (*o*) None at all

    (*o*) Only a little   (*o*) No opinion

7. Does it make a great deal of difference, or only a little difference which political party runs this country?

    (*1*) Great deal   (*o*) None at all

    (*o*) Only a little   (*o*) No opinion

The numbers beside the answer boxes show the weighting given the answers in making up the "intensity of interest" score. The total score possible was eleven. After the results were tabulated they were combined into the five groups as shown in Table 68.

TABLE 68. INTENSITY OF INTEREST SCORE

Score Group	Actual Score	Distribution in Population
4	10-11	22%
3	8- 9	34
2	6- 7	24
1	4- 5	12
0	0- 3	8
		100%

An average intensity of interest score was then computed for those who voted Republican, Democrat, and those who did not vote at all, as well as for persons with various background characteristics. Some of these results are shown in Figure 20. The intensity of interest score prepared in this study differentiated between voters and nonvoters, between Republicans and Democrats, and between persons in the various categories of age, income, sex, etc., much more sharply than did any single question or any score based on a combination of only two or three questions.

SUMMARY

1. The breakdown is one of the most useful techniques available for analysis of public opinion data. It gives some insight into causation by comparing the relative importance of variables. It points to more adequate and verifiable psychological explanation and helps to disprove other explanation.

2. But the breakdown of large sample populations cannot satisfy the psychologist with really adequate explanation because of the uniformity

FIGURE 20. INTEREST IN ELECTIONS COMPARED TO VOTE
AND BACKGROUND

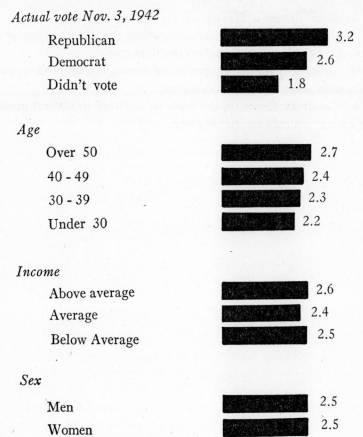

Average Interest Score

Actual vote Nov. 3, 1942

Republican	3.2
Democrat	2.6
Didn't vote	1.8

Age

Over 50	2.7
40 - 49	2.4
30 - 39	2.3
Under 30	2.2

Income

Above average	2.6
Average	2.4
Below Average	2.5

Sex

Men	2.5
Women	2.5

of background data which is bound to obscure significant personal information.

3. To obtain maximum results with breakdowns it is essential to plan breakdowns ahead of time and to design questions and surveys accordingly. This requires, of course, some systematic insight. This obvious point is repeated here because of the tendency of research workers to "fresh-fish" their data for significant differences without planning ahead of time. A certain amount of more or less random analysis is inevitable but, because of the usual expense and effort involved, it should be kept to a minimum and done only when there are genuine hunches to be followed through.

4. The use and value of five types of breakdowns are described and illustrated here. These are:

a. Hold a single variable constant and then compare other variables within it.

b. Make the same breakdown on related questions.

c. Use higher-order breakdowns where the relationships between several variables can be studied simultaneously.

d. Construct patterns of opinion by sorting out people who answer in certain ways to several questions.

e. Construct scores on the basis of answers to several questions so finer groupings can be obtained.

CHAPTER XIV

EDUCATION AND ECONOMIC STATUS AS DETERMINANTS OF OPINION[1]

THE science of public opinion measurement allows us to state statistically not only how many people hold specific viewpoints but also what groups within our population have decided tendencies to accept particular sides of a question. It has always been interesting to speculate whether membership in one group has more weight in the determination of opinion than membership in another group. For example, throughout the pre-war period it could be established that men (rather than women) were more interventionist-minded; and at the same time it was clear that Southern residents were also inclined to an interventionist position. Now, among Southern men which could be said to be more important in the determination of opinion: the variable, sex, or the variable, section of the country?

Two variables which are of particular interest to social scientists are education and economic status. Men with college training and men who are illiterate can be found at every income level. When social decisions are made by individuals who have disparate income and educational backgrounds, which of these factors plays a greater part in the molding of their judgments? What can be said about the relative influence of education or economic status upon the practical social thinking of the large majority of our population which is classified as average or poor in income and whose educational training involves only graduation from high school or less? Can we depend upon the indoctrination of our schools to give stability and historical maturity to their opinions? (Indeed, what is the general pervasive character of the indoctrination of our public schools?) Or, on the other hand, is the bald fact of economic distress or the satisfaction of an average income of more weight than the educational character of these people? Picture for a moment a needy man with a college degree talking to a wealthy alumnus of the same school; or think of an ignorant and penniless man in conversation with an uneducated captain of industry. How would the development of ideas in these two tête-à-têtes proceed? Where would disagreements arise? How could we attempt to account for them?

So many similar problems have arisen out of public opinion data that

[1] By Frederick Williams and Frederick Mosteller.

a method which will allow us to compare the importance of specific variables upon people's opinions is urgently needed. A careful statistical study was made of two variables whose interrelationship was obvious and whose relative importance, when established, would bear significant implications in itself. These two variables were "education" and "economic status." Our examination resolved itself into an attempt to find an answer to the question: *"Is it membership in an economic group or is it membership in a level-of-educational-attainment group which has more weight in the determination of the opinions of individuals?"*

METHOD

The educational levels of the members of the population were determined upon the basis of various questions designed to discover the respondent's last year of schooling. The economic levels were based upon the judgment of the interviewer. The following groups were used:

Education:[2]

    (1) Grade school nongraduate;
    (2) Grade school graduate and high school nongraduate;
    (3) High school graduate;
    (4) College nongraduate;
    (5) College graduate.

Economic Status:[2]

    (1) Wealthy and average plus;
    (2) Average;
    (3) Poor plus (some ballots did not request this category and it was consequently missing in those instances);
    (4) Poor;
    (5) All the relief groups.

Thus our data finally assumed the form of two-way tables of breakdowns of opinion in which there were four or five economic categories and five educational categories.

[2] While it is recognized that level of educational attainment is only a tenuous index to the training and abilities of an individual, these tests do attempt to assay the importance of these levels in the light of the educator's considerations of the problems involved. Similarly, the economic level within which one individual falls varies widely in relation to actual monetary income from section to section of the country or even from community to community. The assignment of a respondent to one economic level can in practice be based only upon a hurried, if keen, calculation by the interviewer.

We will use an index[3] W_{ed}/W_{eco} for our determination of relative importance of the variables. If W_{ed}/W_{eco} is greater than 1, we say education is more important; less than 1, economic status is more important; equal to 1, equally important. Before comparing the index we apply a test (chi-square) to the table of percentages to see if the whole table could have been drawn from the same population with proportion of "Yeses" equal to that of the national sample. If the table does not reject this hypothesis (at the .05 level of significance), we say both are unimportant. On Figures 22, 23, and 24 below, such points are indicated by an X on the line $W_{ed}/W_{eco} = 1$.

These two procedures were followed through on two tables where not only experience but also inspection of marginal percentages told us that education was more important, and on two questions where we could be sure that economic status was more important. One test for education was performed on the question: "Do you happen to know whether or not the Irish Free State (Eire) has gone to war against Germany?" The ratio returned was 4.17. The other educational test was made upon groups which had been scored on the basis of a barrage of information questions about the geography and history of the war. The well-informed and the moderately informed were balanced against the uninformed. The ratio returned was 3.31.

The first question inspected for possible return of a figure showing that economic status might be more important was, "Should the government forbid strikes in industries manufacturing materials for our national defense program, or should the workers in these industries continue to have the right to strike?" The ratio found was 0.50. The other question on this side of the test was "Are you better off, or worse off today than you were six months ago?" The ratio was 0.78.

Thus the procedure which we had outlined discriminated between the

---

[3] We have r rows (referring to different economic status levels) and c columns (referring to different levels of education) in our table. Let N_{ij} be the number of cases in the ith row and jth column, and let $\bar{n}_{ij}$ be the number of "yeses" in the same cell; then, holding column totals constant and letting $n._j$ equal the sum of the jth column, $\bar{n}._j$ the total number of "yeses" in that column, we compute for each column $\Sigma_i (\bar{n}_{ij} - \frac{\bar{n}._j}{n._j} n_{ij})^2$. We then add together such sums computed for all the columns. The result will be referred to as W_{eco}. We now compute the corresponding quantity for rows and call it W_{ed}. The ratio W_{ed}/W_{eco} is the index used. This quantity is plotted logarithmically on the figures. Naturally this index is completely arbitrary; many others could have been used.

importance of the two variables on questions where it was obvious in which way the direction of this importance lay.[4]

RESULTS

Certain areas were selected for investigation of our general problems and for carrying through our method of comparative analysis of the two variables.

The following topics were chosen:

(1) Information, estimates and awareness
(2) Social stereotypes
(3) Opinion on peace
(4) Intervention in the war
(5) Economic problems
(6) Political approval

We were interested in charting trends of opinion in relation to the war and in finding motivations behind such opinions. We were interested, too, in obtaining an estimate of the relative importance of education and economic status over a variety of topics to see whether or not changes in the relative importance of these two variables might cut across such categories. We were interested in deciding whether there were some questions dealing with economic problems in which the importance of education was greater than economic status, and vice versa. And, finally, we were interested in the social implications arising out of whatever interpretation could be made of these data.

Where education is more important. All of the questions subsumed under two of the categorized topics showed a greater importance allotted to education than to economic level. The first of these topics was called, *Information, estimates and awareness.* Answers to the questions in this group sharply distinguished between those people who showed an insight into the implications of recent history and those who did not, or those who had a store of factual information about the world in which we live and those who lacked this knowledge, or those people whose estimates and predictions of future events were seriously influenced by

[4] The data reported are based upon an examination of only 55 tables. Additional material should be gathered for more particular statements about the relative importance of the two variables. In addition, the intuitive method used to secure a figure representing the ratio of importance is not a mathematically rigorous test, nor can significance tests be applied to its results. Further material will be gathered in this office and the trends will be continued. The present chapter, it is hoped, will stimulate investigation of the problem. Such an investigation, if undertaken, could most profitably be directed toward the discovery of a more rigorous test for the relative importance of variables which influence the opinion of individuals.

their degrees of information and those people whose estimates and predictions were little if at all influenced by the scope of their information.

TABLE 69. INFORMATION, ESTIMATES AND AWARENESS

Question	Ratio
Do you happen to know whether or not the Irish Free State (Eire) has gone to war against Germany? (2-3-42) "No, it has not"	4.17
Do you think that, if the Nazis win the war, we would eventually have to do pretty much as they wanted us to, like the Poles? (3-12-41) "No"	3.90
Do you think the United States is doing all it possibly can to win the war?	
(3-10-42) "Yes"	3.69
(5-1-42) "Yes"	9.63
Well and somewhat informed on geopolitics. (11-19-41)	3.31
Do you think Japan will try to seize possession of Singapore and the Dutch East Indies? (12-11-40) "Yes"	3.29
If Germany defeats England in the present war, do you think you will be as free to do what you want as you are now? (3-12-41) "No"	3.12
Do you think the war against Japan will be a long war, or a short one?	
(12-10-41) "Long"	2.88
In England, public opinion has forced Churchill to change some members of his cabinet. Do you think Roosevelt should make any changes in his cabinet here?	
(3-18-42) "Yes"	2.39
Do you feel that you have a clear idea of what the war is all about?	
(11-19-41) "Yes"	1.91
Do you think that, if England falls, Germany will soon be in control of all our trade and foreign markets? (3-12-41) "Yes"	1.41

The second topic which returned ratios indicating the greater importance of education than of economic status was *Social stereotypes*. (Since only a few questions of this type were available, replication of these experiments are necessary to establish more reliably this conclusion.) Here were gathered questions whose answers indicated the individual's conception of an agreement with popular presuppositions involved in the socially founded attitudes of a majority of our people toward our society itself. These attitudes, cultivated in our educational system, form part of the indoctrination incorporated in the educational programs of our grade schools.

One other category of questions showed a tendency for education to be the more important determinant of opinion; this included questions concerning peace and the post-war world. While we cannot say that education will be a constant and consistently heavy weight operating upon this phase of opinion, the trend established by the first question in Table 71 offers room for speculation. We should expect, in the light of these

TABLE 70. SOCIAL STEREOTYPES

Question	Ratio
Do you think success is dependent mostly on luck, or ability, or on pull? (3-26-42) "Ability"	4.51
Do you think a poor man gets just as fair treatment in the law courts as a rich man? (3-26-42) "Yes"	1.52
Do you think most people can be trusted? (3-26-42) "Yes"	1.34
Some people say that teachers favor the children of parents who have the most money or the best position in the community. Do you agree? (7-10-40) "Yes"	1.23

returns, that the influence of education will become increasingly important as long as the balance of the war hangs in doubt. Since questions of this type presuppose a fairly high level of information and insight into the implications involved in international cooperation, it is further to be suspected that specific post-war problems will be similarly affected by education.

TABLE 71. OPINION ON PEACE

Question	Ratio
If England and France defeat Germany, should the peace treaty be more or less severe than the treaty at the end of the last war? (7-10-41) "More"	2.82
If Germany is defeated, do you think a peace that will last for at least 50 years can be worked out? (11-19-41) "Yes"	1.40
If Hitler offered peace now to all countries on the basis of not going farther, but of leaving matters as they are now, would you favor, or oppose, such a peace? (2-4-42) "Oppose"	1.85
(1-16-42)	0.32
(11-19-41)	0.91

TABLE 72. INTERVENTION IN THE WAR

Question	Ratio
Have you been following the discussion of the lease-lend bill regarding aid to England and other countries, which Congress is now considering? (1-22-41) "Yes"	0.54
Do you think it was a mistake for the United States to enter the last World War? (3-21-41) "Yes"	0.54
(12-10-41)	0.53
Do you think the United States will go into the war in Europe, or do you think we will stay out of the war? (7-10-41) "Go in"	0.72*
(9-17-41)	0.80
Should the United States take steps now to keep Japan from becoming more powerful, even if this means risking a war with Japan? (7-20-40) "Risk"	1.07*
(10-22-41)	0.62
(11-19-41)	1.84

Question   *Ratio*

Which of these two things do you think is the more important for the United
States to try to do—To keep out of war ourselves, or To help England win, even
at the risk of getting into the war?   (7-20-40) "Help"   1.81
                                               (9-17-40)   0.90
                                               (12-11-40)   0.41
                                               (1-22-41)   0.63
                                               (3-29-41)   0.76
                                               (7-10-41)   1.09
                                               (9-17-41)   0.73
                                               (11-19-41)   2.47

* Significance of total for these questions was between 0.01 and 0.05. Vide supra, p. 197.

Questions arrayed by the topic *Economic problems* deal with labor
problems, with the personal status of the respondent, and with other
general or specific problems whose implications or direct impact are
economic. The first two questions shown in Table 73 return ratios indicating the greater importance of income level. The question concerning
the freezing of wages and prices in Canada returned, however, a ratio
indicating greater importance allotted to education. Examination of the
problem posed by this question suggests that it is one in which acquaintance with the economic *implications* of its proposals is important. Consequently we could expect education to prove more important than economic status.

TABLE 73. ECONOMIC PROBLEMS

Question   *Ratio*

Should the government forbid strikes in industries manufacturing materials for
our national defense program, or should the workers in these industries continue
to have the right to strike? (7-20-40) "Forbid"   0.50

Are you better off, or worse off today than you were six months ago?
                                               (11-19-41) "Better"   0.78

A recent law in Canada keeps wage and salary rates from going higher than they
are now and also keeps all prices, including prices of farm products, from going
higher. Would you approve or disapprove of such a law in the United States?
                                               (3-18-42) "Approve"   2.52

Inspection of the marginal percentages on the various questions examined affords us an indication of some of the underlying factors which
allow the importance of education or economic status to be exerted. The
common denominator of the *educational* groups seems to be an *insight
into the implications* of the propositions upon which the respondents
were questioned. For example, a majority of the group of college graduates thought that Japan would take aggressive action in the Far East

and that, if we should become involved in war with her, the war would be long. But of the grade-school nongraduates only 38 per cent thought that Japan would take military steps to reach her goals.

The greatest differences found between the extremes of education and the intermediate levels of education exhibit definite shades of awareness in the expected direction.

This tendency is most obvious when we consider the proportions of the vote for aid to England even at the risk of war. The grade-school nongraduates most consistently were significantly less willing to tender help in the prewar period. At only one time (among all the cases examined in this study) were the grade-school graduates and the high-school nongraduates least in favor of this proposition. The high-school graduates, on the other hand, were twice in an extreme position. One of these extremes was in the direction of the smallest vote to aid England; the other was the largest proportion among all the educational groups in favor of such help. At all other times, the highest proportion of "Help England" votes was found among the college graduates.

Where economic status is more important. The remaining orders of questions ascribed, in general, superior importance to the other determinant, economic status. The topic *Intervention in the war* assembled questions relating to aid to England and China, as well as opinions even more relevant to the struggle between the isolationists and interventionists in this country. (See page 204 for discussion of the observed trends toward the greater importance of education.)

The greatest importance by economic status returned on any questions consistently resulted from the one inquiring into approval of President Roosevelt. The trend of this ratio, however, as will be seen below, shows some notable changes.

Inspection of the percentages by which *economic* groups accepted the various propositions, leads us to conclude that there is, among the lower-income levels, a desire for growth through change in the social structure, as opposed to the desire for growth without change in the social structure among the upper-income population.

Among the economic groups there is apparent homogeneity on each side if the groups are divided into two parts, with the poor and the relief groups opposed to the average and upper-income levels. This homogeneity, however, is biased as one would expect; while the high-income group favored in larger proportions participation in the war, they also gave a smaller vote of approval to the President. This complexion of opinion can be exemplified by noting that the highest proportions of

"Help England" votes fall in the upper half and the lowest proportions in the lower half of these income groups. The upper-income people, too, were most sure that the United States would go into the war. But these people believed at the same time that it was a mistake to enter the last war; and their approval of Roosevelt's work as President was always lowest.

It may be useful in considering the relationship between economic status and education to inspect the following schematic diagram.

FIGURE 21

FACTORS DETERMINING OPINION BY EDUCATIONAL AND
ECONOMIC LEVEL

EDUCATIONAL FACTOR		CORRELATION	ECONOMIC FRAME OF REFERENCE
implications not seen	*Low Education*	Narrow frame of reference	Growth through change (*Relief group*)
			Indecision as to change (*Poor*)
			Growth through preservation of position (*Average*)
implications seen	*High Education*	Broad frame of reference; some implications seen	Opposition to change; broad outlook (*Upper income*)

TRENDS

' The relationship between education and economic status is even more meaningful if an inspection is made of the ratios obtained from the same question over a period of time. Four such trends were followed through. All give an indication of a similar periodic influence upon the ratios. By and large, it seems clear that after the attack upon Pearl Harbor economic differences in the United States tended to level off, whereas the influence of education upon opinion not only did not decrease but may even have increased. At any rate, the *relative* importance of education became sharply apparent.

Figure 22 shows the ratio W_{ed}/W_{eco} for that curve for which the largest number of tests have been made. Popular sentiment was tested on the question of giving aid to England even at the risk of war. The first point, recorded just after the fall of France, indicates that at that time opinions were divided by educational level. It seems sensible that those who could assay the international situation and realize the position of the United States in the world at that time could more readily recognize the necessity for aid to England in her darkest hour. But by September 1940 the importance of economic status, as an expression of the quarrel over this particular question, asserted itself. This direction was to hold for the rest of the period before our declaration of war upon the

FIGURE 22

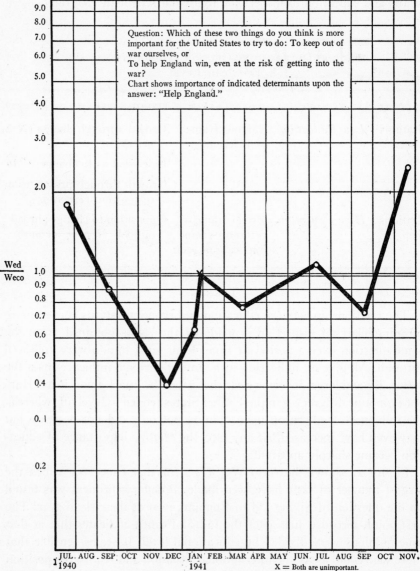

Question: Which of these two things do you think is more important for the United States to try to do: To keep out of war ourselves, or
To help England win, even at the risk of getting into the war?
Chart shows importance of indicated determinants upon the answer: "Help England."

$\dfrac{\text{Wed}}{\text{Weco}}$

JUL. AUG. SEP. OCT NOV. DEC JAN FEB. MAR APR MAY JUN. JUL AUG SEP OCT NOV.
1940   1941   X = Both are unimportant.

Axis. Throughout this time, however, there were changes—particularly after the speech of President Roosevelt at the end of the year, and after the introduction of the lease-lend bill into Congress in February 1941.

A later but similar directional influence can be seen in Figure 23, which shows the ratio of importance found among people who opposed arranging peace with our enemy at the limits of conquests of territory then held. This curve can be interpreted as a demonstration of growing awareness, on the part of our population, of the seriousness of the war and an increasing determination to see it through without compromise. Interestingly enough, more than a month after the outbreak of active hostilities more importance could be allotted to economic status on this question than could be before December 7, 1941.

One of the most interesting trends discovered was that, already reported, charting approval of the President (Figure 24). Though only two points are established between 1939 and 1941, both of these points are extremely similar. The growing awareness of the seriousness of the war probably induced (as will be elaborated below) the effect of the decreasing importance of economic status in relation to education.

FIGURE 23

Question: If Hitler offered peace now to all countries on the basis of not going farther, but of leaving matters as they are now, would you favor, or oppose, such a peace?
Chart shows importance of indicated determinants upon the answer "Oppose."

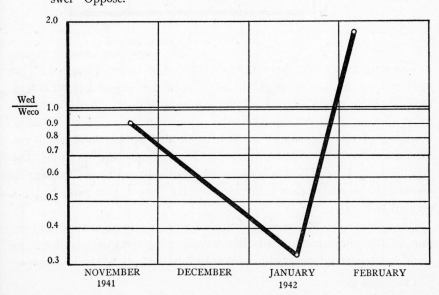

FIGURE 24

Question: In general, do you approve, or disapprove, of the way Roosevelt is handling his job as President today?

Chart shows importance of indicated determinants upon the answer "Approve."

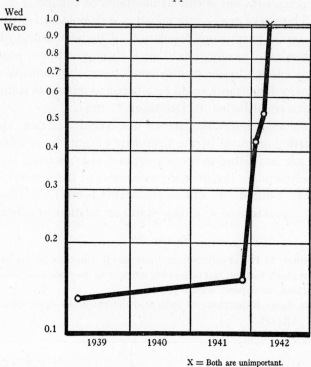

X = Both are unimportant.

The weight of events upon opinions cannot be overemphasized.[5] The figures just examined show graphically that this influence does cut across the topic lines which we had set up. Not only were the questions originally allotting greater importance to economic status affected, but a lessening of this importance could be seen also in questions which returned a ratio on the side of education. For example, the question, "Do you think the United States is doing all it possibly can to win the war?" showed in March 1942 a ratio of 3.69. By May 1 this ratio had increased to 9.63.

Even before the formal declaration of war, however, a trend on certain of the questions toward the increasing importance of education could be observed. Surveys of opinion in relation both to the importance

[5] Cf. Chapter 16.

of helping England at the risk of war and in relation to risking war with Japan demonstrated this effect in November 1941. It must be remembered that on October 17 the "Kearny incident" occurred and that the sinking of the "Reuben James" was announced on October 31. Just a few days before the loss of the "Reuben James" President Roosevelt publicly announced that "a shooting war has now begun." It was by then manifest to our people that selfish differences must necessarily be put aside; and it was clear to the more educated members of our population that the United States could not tolerate the assaults of the Nazis upon our shipping and convoys.

SUMMARY

1. A method is described by means of which the relative importance of two variables in determining opinion can be studied. The method is used in a comparative analysis of the two variables, education and economic status.

2. Education is found to be more important where factual knowledge gives an insight into implications, for example, in determining opinion toward a negotiated peace or toward post-war problems. Education is also apparently more important than economic status in creating, through more consistent indoctrination, greater allegiance to certain general social stereotypes as, for example, those toward law and the reward that comes from individual ability.

3. Economic status, on the other hand, determines opinion more than education on all issues where the chief impact or where the clear-cut implications deal with financial return. During the 1940-1941 period when these studies were made, the population tended to divide into two (rather than three) economic groups, in so far as economic status determined opinion toward the war. On one side were the poor people and those on relief, on the other side were the upper and average-income groups. The poor were least stable in their opinions, the upper income the most stable. The average-income group showed sympathy with the opinions of the poor but finally (around January 1941) accepted the position of the upper-income respondents. There is, then, at least some ground for inference that the population fundamentally tends to form two classes and that the demarcation between them can become marked under some circumstances.

The opinions of the poor group can be generally described as a desire for growth through change in the social structure; the opinions of the upper group as a desire for growth without change in the social structure.

4. The role of both of these important variables in determining opinion is, however, enormously affected by events. The major events of World War II shifted the relative standing of economic values and, therefore, changed the relative importance of education as a determinant. During the darkest period of the war (right after the fall of France), an interventionist position was more likely to be held by well-educated than by high-income people. The former group continued to see the implications of a German victory and wanted to help make it impossible while the latter group tended more to retreat into the temporary safety of the status quo. Immediately after the attack on Pearl Harbor, however, economic status seemed to disappear as a determinant of opinion and unity along economic class lines was clear. Even class differences in attitude toward President Roosevelt seemed, after Pearl Harbor, to have been rubbed out, at least temporarily, by a united confidence in him as a war leader.

CHAPTER XV

INFORMATION AS A DETERMINANT OF OPINION[1]

IN THIS chapter we attempt to discover something of the relationship between information and opinion. More specifically, the investigations reported here are concerned with: (1) the types of opinion where information apparently does and does not have some determining influence; (2) the influence of events upon the opinions of persons with varying degrees of information.[2]

When we say here that a person is "informed," we mean that he has the ability to verbalize specific answers which are publicly accepted as correct in reply to questions about verifiable matters. Thus, when we asked in January 1941, "Can you tell me what country controls Gibraltar?" we accepted "England" as the correct answer.

Although a high correlation (around .60) is found between information and education, we are not discussing here "education" as such. We are also, of course, not talking about "intelligence." In actual practice, however, these variables are so intimately related that they cannot be precisely distinguished from each other. It is also necessary to keep in mind the two-way relationship between information and interest. When we attribute differences of opinion to the factor "information" we are obviously talking about differences between an aware or interested group of people as opposed to those people who are unaware or uninterested. And in dealing with large groups of people it is even more difficult than with a single individual to know whether interest in a problem leads to acquisition of knowledge or whether interest springs from knowledge.[3]

Getting Data on Information

In order to discriminate between the well-informed and the uninformed populations, we must obviously ask questions the answers to which are readily verifiable. At different times, for example, OPOR

[1] By Frederick Williams.

[2] E. Roper, "So the Blind Shall Not Lead," *Fortune*, February, 1942. Cf. G. Gallup, "The People Are Ahead of Congress," *New York Times Magazine*, March 29, 1942. Also see Daniel Katz, "Three Criteria: Knowledge, Conviction, and Significance," *Public Opinion Quarterly*, 1940, 2, 277-284. OPOR has systematically gathered data on the information of respondents, scored information questions, and run breakdowns since July 1940. Isolated instances of information questions may be found in surveys taken by AIPO as early as February 1937.

[3] A. L. Edwards, "The Retention of Affective Experiences," *Psychological Review*, 1942, 49, 43-53.

asked for a statement of the names of the countries that Germany had conquered since the beginning of the war, or for the geographic location of many countries throughout the world. Table 74 shows some of the questions used.

In order to obtain information scores for comparison, weightings were assigned to answers. In the simplest case, for instance, each respondent was asked to find six countries on a map. A score of one was given to each correct answer and zero to each incorrect reply. The two tails of the distribution of the total population (after the assignment of these scores) were selected as the two groups in which we were interested. The "well-informed" (or those who answered all questions correctly) were found to be 25 per cent of the total cases, the "uninformed" (or those who answered none or only one question correctly) 27 per cent, and the remainder (48 per cent) the moderately informed. The

TABLE 74. SOME INFORMATION QUESTIONS

	Answer	Weight
Can you name any city in Central or South America which you think of as a big modern city like Chicago? (12-10-40)	Buenos Aires	2
	Rio de Janeiro	1
	Sao Paulo	1
	Santiago	1
	Mexico City	1
	Montevideo	1
London, England, is about 3,200 miles from New York. How far would you think it is from Buenos Aires, Argentina, to New York? (12-10-40)	5,000-6,999 miles	2
	4,000-4,999 "	1
	7,000-7,999 "	1
Can you tell me the name of the country where the armies of Greece and Italy are fighting? (1-28-41)	Albania	2
	Greece or Italy	1
Can you name four leaders of European countries and tell me what country each one heads? (1-28-41)		1 for each correct
Can you remember the names of five countries that Germany has conquered since the war began? (1-28-41)		1 each
Do you happen to know how many years Hitler has been in power in Germany? (1-28-41)	7, 8, 9 years	2
	6, 10 years	1
Here is a map of the world. Can you find Alaska, (Australia, China, Brazil, Iceland, India) on the map? (3-26-42)		1 for each correct

same principle of scoring was used in all other surveys. In some cases a weighting of more than one was given to an answer which was more exactly accurate than a second reply. Thus on one survey a score of two was given to all answers between 100 and 139 million in reply to the question, "About how many people do you think there are in Central and South America?" A score of one was allotted to estimates between 70 and 99 million or between 140 and 179 million.

Results

1. *Where information gives differences in opinion.* On a number of questions greater differences of opinion were obtained from breakdowns on information than on any other variable. As one would expect, the differences of opinion between the informed and the uninformed are due chiefly to *the ability of the informed to see the implications of events or proposals to their own self-interest.* Table 75 gives some typical results which point to this interpretation. The well-informed people of all income and age groups said they had a clearer idea of what the war is all about, they wanted to fight it more aggressively, they were more opposed to a negotiated peace.

There is some indication, too, that *the well-informed people accept less readily than the uninformed certain stereotyped, fatalistic, or emotional solutions to problems.* Table 76 indicates that the uninformed people were, for example, more in favor of a harsh peace treaty for Germany, more convinced that war is inevitable. Here, again, differences by information are more clear cut than differences by age or income.

2. *Where information does not give differences and why.* Answers to many of the questions asked showed no reliable differences by information groups. Differences were, however, given by other variables to each of the questions studied. For example, in December 1940, significantly more upper-income as contrasted to low-income people thought England would win the war; significantly more Democrats than Republicans thought the government was giving the public as much information about the war as it should. But, as Table 77 shows, no significant difference in opinion between the well-informed and the uninformed was found on these two questions.

An examination of the opinions where information did not seem to be a significant determinant indicates that there are at least three general conditions where we can expect a person's general level of information as such to be ruled out as an influence.

a. *Where standards of judgment are lacking*—that is, where the indi-

TABLE 75. RELATION OF DEGREE OF INFORMATION TO IMPLICATIONS FOR SELF-INTEREST

	Do you feel that you have a clear idea of what this war is all about?	Which of these two things do you think the U. S. should do when the war is over: Stay out of world affairs or take active part?	Which of these two things do you think the U. S. should do: Send army abroad, or keep our army at home?	If Hitler offered peace now to all countries on the basis of not going farther, but of leaving matters as they are now, would you favor or oppose such a peace?
	Yes	*Take active part*	*Send*	*Oppose*
Economic Status				
Well Informed				
Upper	75%	91%	75%	96%
Middle	69	91	72	96
Lower	73	89	66	93
Uninformed				
Upper	36	62	35	85
Middle	37	60	41	79
Lower	30	50	41	74
Age				
Well Informed				
Under 30	67	94	73	95
30-49	71	90	71	94
50 and over	74	89	71	96
Uninformed				
Under 30	33	57	35	69
30-49	31	53	45	77
50 and over	34	52	40	76

TABLE 76. RELATION OF DEGREE OF INFORMATION TO STEREOTYPED
SOLUTIONS

	If Germany is defeated, do you think a peace that will last for at least 50 years can be worked out?	If England defeats Germany and Italy should the peace treaty be more severe, or less severe, than the treaty at the end of the last war?
Economic Status	Yes	Less Severe
Well Informed		
Upper	62%	47%
Middle	57	40
Lower	56	31
Uninformed		
Upper	47	15
Middle	49	9
Lower	43	10
Age		
Well Informed		
Under 30	52	40
30-49	59	40
50 and over	58	38
Uninformed		
Under 30	43	15
30-49	44	8
50 and over	47	9

vidual has no knowledge he can rely on, no related experience, or no way
to check his opinion. In other words, under such circumstances, the individual himself feels that his "information" is tenuous. For example, on
the question, "Do you feel, in general, that the information you are getting about the war situation is true and accurate?" only a small handful
of highly placed officials would be in a position intelligently to compare
information given to the public with the true war situation.[4]

b. *Where the overwhelming majority of the population has common
standards of judgment* which they obtain almost exclusively from mass
media of communication reporting events and decisions soon known to
all. For example, in November 1941, almost everyone in the country had
the opportunity to size up for himself on the basis of common knowledge
the prospects of U. S. involvement in the war. It is, therefore, not sur-

[4] For other illustrations and a more complete discussion of this point, see Hadley
Cantril, *The Invasion from Mars*, Princeton University Press, 1940.

TABLE 77. EXAMPLES WHERE INFORMATION DID NOT AFFECT OPINION

Question	Answer	Well Informed	Uninformed
Which side do you think will win the war— Germany and Italy, or England? (12-11-40)	England	72%	64%
Do you think that in the long run Germany will win the war or lose it? (11-19-41)	Lose	91	91
Do you think the United States will go into the war in Europe sometime before it is over, or do you think we will stay out of the war? (1-28-41 and 12-11-40)	Go in	69 64	61 58
If Germany should defeat England and Russia in the present war, do you think Germany would start a war against the United States within the next ten years? (11-19-41)	Yes	69	72
Do you feel that, in general, the information you are getting about the war situation is true and accurate? (11-19-41)	Yes	30	27
Do you think the government is giving the public as much information as it should about the war? (11-19-41 and 3-26-42)	Yes	51 62	44 59
Some people say that the biggest job facing the country today is to help defeat the Nazi government. Do you agree or disagree? (11-19-41)	Agree	73	71
Do you think there are quite a few boys and girls now in high school who would be better off at work? (7-10-40)	Yes	55	53

prising that no significant differences were obtained between the well-informed and the uninformed on the question, "If Germany should defeat England and Russia in the present war do you think Germany would start a war against the United States in another ten years?"

c. *Where self-interest and wish fulfillment are involved* differences of opinion according to amount of information are likely to be obscured by the well-known distortion of perspective that comes when personal desire gets entangled with attempts at objective judgment. For example, when a month before our entrance into the war, we asked the question "Do you think that in the long run Germany will win the war or lose it?" the overwhelming majority of the American people identified themselves with the United Nations cause. In answer to the question, "Do you think the U. S. will go into the war in Europe sometime before it is over, or do you think we will stay out of the war?" there was undoubtedly the influence of a type of wish fulfillment consciously thought of by the individual in terms of what he *wanted* this country to do.

3. *Is information generalized?* The problem here is to discover whether or not information must be strictly in the same context as opinion if it is to have any influence on opinion. For example, if one individual is well-informed in areas A and B, and another individual is well-informed in areas C and D, are the opinions of the two individuals likely to be the same on questions which tap opinions relevant only to question B? Concerning this problem we can provide two bits of evidence.

In one study the opinions of persons who were well-informed about European affairs were compared to the opinions of people who were well-informed about Far Eastern affairs. Table 78 illustrates how two well-informed groups—whether their information was on the Far East or on Europe—held very similar opinions on questions concerning Europe and the Far East. Since a knowledge of Europe tends to presume a knowledge of Far Eastern affairs, or vice versa, respondents were sorted out into the four information groups indicated below.[5]

| | European Information | | |
Far Eastern Information	Good	None	Total
Good	438	79	517
None	317	705	1022
Total	755	784	1539

Each of these four groups was then compared on a number of opinion questions. These comparisons showed that there does not seem to be any great difference between an information question and an opinion question in the same context and an information question and an opinion question in a dissimilar context. By and large opinion changes with increasing information.

A second test on the problem was made by separating people who were able to give correct answers to all of the map questions; those who were able to find Peru, Brazil and Central America, but *not* Iceland, India and China; and those who found Iceland, India and China correctly but *not* Peru, Brazil and Central America. Table 79 shows that even the greater interest in South America, which can undoubtedly be attributed to those

---

[5] The small number of people who were well informed about the Far East but uninformed about the European question suggested that these people might have selected their correct answers by chance. However, if we assume that each answer has the same probability of being chosen, the odds that the two correct answers out of the five possible answers might have been picked by chance are one in ten, whereas the actual frequency of their selection was almost four times as great.

TABLE 78. INFORMATION AND CONTEXT

Question		Far Eastern Information		European Information	
		Well Informed	Un-informed	Well Informed	Un-informed
If peace could be obtained today on the basis of Britain keeping the British Empire as it now stands, and Germany holding the countries she has conquered so far, would you be in favor of such a peace?	Yes	15%	34%	13%	34%
	No	81	53	83	51
	No Opinion	4	13	4	15
Do you think that at the present time our navy is strong enough to defeat the Japanese navy?	Yes	90	66	91	66
	No	2	5	2	5
	Qual. Ans.	2	1	3	1
	Don't Know	6	28	4	28
Should the United States take steps now to keep Japan from becoming more powerful, even if this means we have to go to war against Japan?	Yes	75	55	73	57
	No	19	24	21	22
	No Opinion	6	21	6	21

TABLE 79. AREAS OF INFORMATION

Question	Generally Informed	Informed on S. A. only	Informed on World but not S. A.
Should our government help South American farmers sell their products?			
Approve	73%	68%	65%
Disapprove	18	24	27
Don't know	9	8	8
Danger South America will be invaded?			
Yes	59	60	65
No	34	29	26
Don't know	7	11	9
Thought about the effect of such an invasion?			
Yes	83	78	73
No	17	22	27

informed on South America alone, did not produce radically different opinions in this group from the opinions held by those who had a geographical blind spot for South America. The table also shows that those who are informed only on South America were, if anything, less aware of a German military threat to South America than were those people who were informed about non-South American areas.

These two studies seem to point to the conclusion that opinion is affected by the general amount of information rather than by specific type of information, providing, of course, that by "type of information" we mean a very specific body of knowledge within a general background of knowledge relevant to the problem in hand. Obviously we are not concluding that a person, for example, who knows a great deal about forestry or British poetry will, because of such knowledge, have different opinions about questions concerning U. S. foreign policy.

4. *Information and events.* At the same time OPOR repeated some trend questions, information questions were also included on the ballots so we might have some idea of the effect of events on the opinions of different information groups. Two conclusions emerge.

a. *The opinions of informed and uninformed persons concerning the war were influenced in the same direction by events.* This common shift in direction occurred on a wide variety of issues: approval of President Roosevelt's handling of his job, approval of the government's information policy, opinion toward Japan, Germany, and South America. Typical shifts of opinion among the informed and uninformed are charted in Figure 25.

b. *Differences of opinion between the well-informed and uninformed groups with respect to war issues were apparent as a difference of emphasis only.* Uninformed people lag behind the well-informed in their ability to see the implications of events. For example, on the question of aid to England during the 1940-1941 period, the uninformed seemed to feel that England was a sure winner and that continuance of nonbelligerent aid to England would be sufficient U. S. aid. The well-informed, on the other hand, were equally sure England would win but were quicker to realize that Germany's defeat would only be ensured by full U. S. intervention. As the war loomed closer to the United States and as its impact became more and more noticeable, there is little doubt that the general level of information of the total population about European affairs was raised. The radio, above all else, was cutting across educational and economic barriers and was bringing common news to everyone. This knowledge gained seemed to become functional as interest was aroused and opportunity was furnished to put it to use.

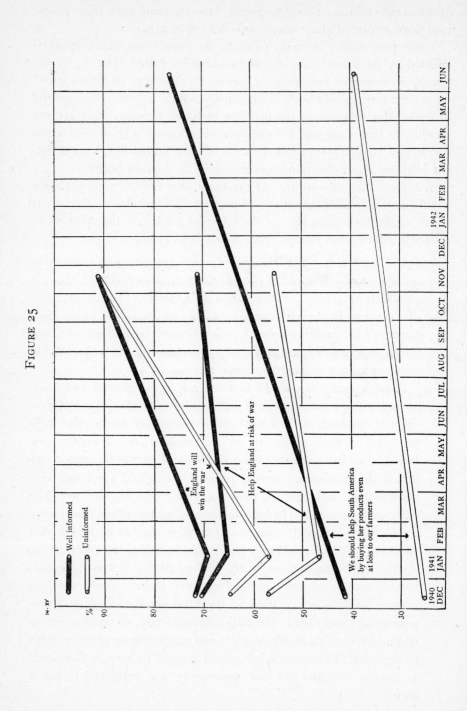

FIGURE 25

Summary

1. The population can be readily grouped into different information levels.

2. The chief effect of greater information is to make the well-informed more sensitive to the implications of events or points of view to their own self-interest.

3. No differences of opinion occur between persons generally well-informed and those generally uninformed when both groups are equally lacking in reliable standards of judgment, where both groups have in common essentially the same standards of judgment, or where wish fulfillment and personal desire cut across information lines.

4. Information tends to be generalized. Persons who are well-informed in one area tend to have the same opinions as persons well-informed in other areas.

5. The opinions of the well-informed and the uninformed were found to be affected in the same direction by the events which led up to the entrance of the United States into the war. The effect of these particular events on opinion can most accurately be described as an effect of emphasis. This does not imply, however, that any series of events would shift the opinions of the two groups in the same way. Obviously special circumstances appealing to special interests might produce the opposite effect.

CHAPTER XVI

THE USE OF TRENDS[1]

THE social scientist knows that any observation or interpretation is relative to the social context prevailing at the time his observation or interpretation is made; that he cannot control the variables affecting his results, cannot repeat his experiments precisely. He is, therefore, inevitably forced to rely heavily on a temporal analysis if he seeks interpretation that will be of more than limited validity. The wise man looks for trends.

Trends of opinion can show the experimentalist the effect of a single stimulus—such as a motion picture or a speech—upon the course of people's thoughts; they can give the psychologist concerned with motivation an insight into resistances, ego-involvements, suggestibility; they can give the historian or philosopher a sounder basis for his generalizations.

Modern sampling methods make it possible to chart trends of opinion with a high degree of accuracy. Questions which the investigator anticipates will be relevant during a given period can be repeated at regular intervals or as events seem to dictate. Social scientists of many interests might well peruse the thousands of questions asked by polling organizations since 1936 and find a considerable number which should be relevant and fascinating to repeat as the years go by. The cultural anthropologist might well use sampling methods to gather information and opinions in different cultures or different areas within a culture.

The trends shown in the accompanying charts are illustrations of a type of information afforded by repetition of the same question on comparable cross-sections of the population. The problem here was to study the effects of events on American opinion during the critical period between September 3, 1939, when World War II began and December 7, 1941, when the United States entered the conflict. The first two charts show some over-all national shifts of opinion; the last three charts break opinion on one question down by certain segments of the total population. OPOR kept many other trends during this period and each trend can, of course, be broken down in numerous ways to sift out the characteristic shifts and divergencies of opinion of specific groups.

Since the social context changes so rapidly with events, questions that make sense one week may be meaningless the next. It is therefore diffi-

[1] By Hadley Cantril.

FIGURE 26

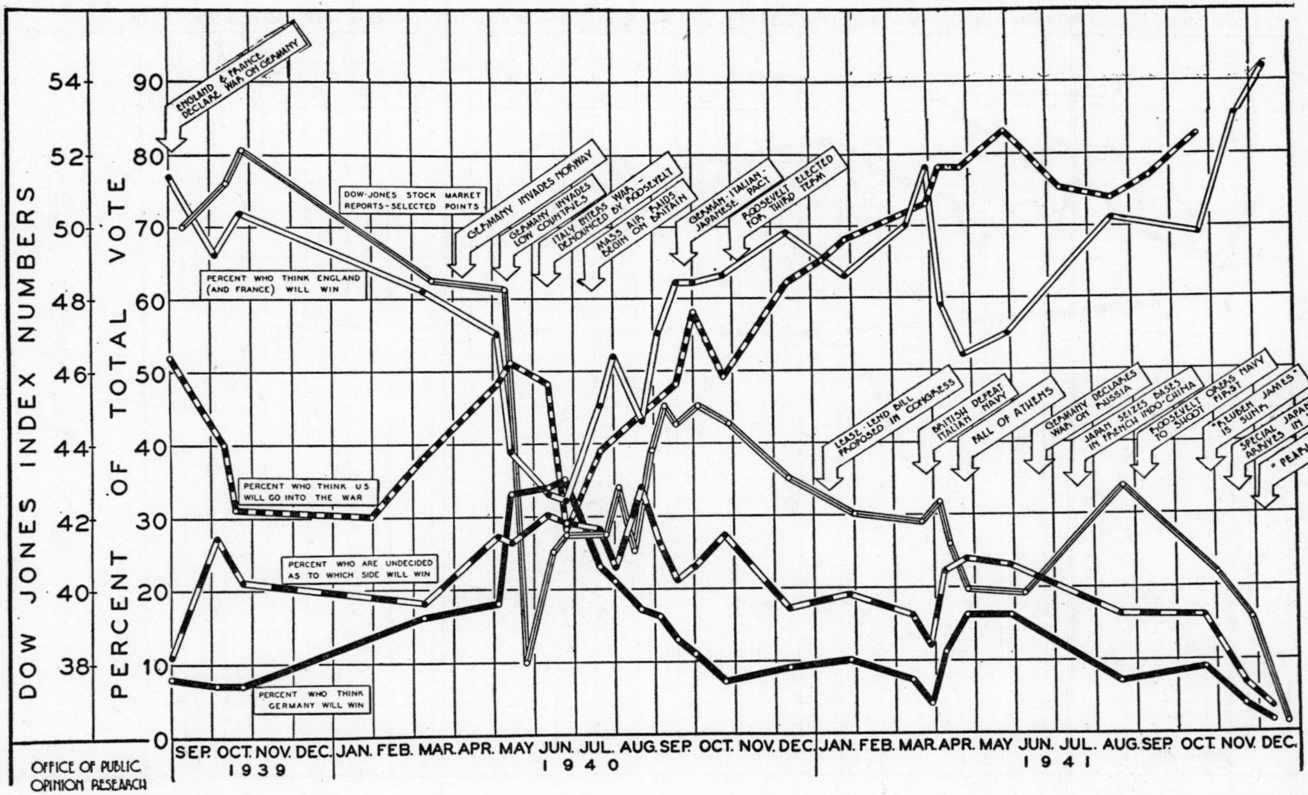

FIGURE 27

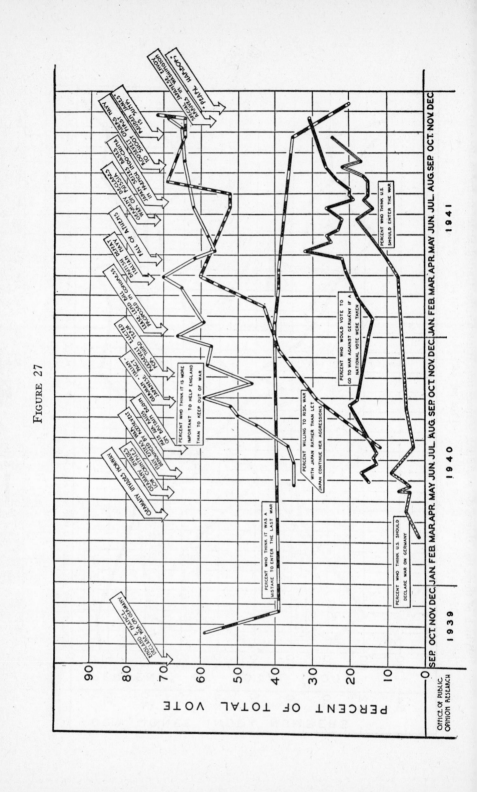

PERCENT OF TOTAL VOTE

OFFICE OF PUBLIC
OPINION RESEARCH

SEP. OCT NOV DEC JAN FEB MAR APR MAY JUN JUL AUG SEP OCT NOV DEC JAN FEB MAR APR MAY JUN JUL AUG SEP OCT NOV DEC
1939　　　　　　　　　　　1940　　　　　　　　　　　1941

PERCENT WHO THINK, U.S.
SHOULD ENTER THE WAR

PERCENT WHO WOULD VOTE TO
GO TO WAR AGAINST GERMANY IF A
NATIONAL VOTE WERE TAKEN

PERCENT WILLING TO RISK WAR
WITH JAPAN RATHER THAN LET
JAPAN CONTINUE HER AGGRESSIONS

PERCENT WHO THINK IT IS MORE
IMPORTANT TO HELP ENGLAND
THAN TO KEEP OUT OF WAR

PERCENT WHO THINK IT WAS A
MISTAKE TO ENTER THE LAST WAR

PERCENT WHO THINK, U.S. SHOULD
DECLARE WAR ON GERMANY

ENGLAND & FRANCE
DECLARE WAR ON GERMANY

GERMANY INVADES NORWAY

GERMANY INVADES
LOW COUNTRIES

ITALY ENTERS WAR
ANNOUNCED BY MUSSOLINI

DESTROYERS FOR
BRITISH BASES

GERMANY, ITALY,
JAPANESE TRIPARTITE

ROOSEVELT RE-ELECTED
FOR THIRD TERM

LEND-LEASE BILL
PROPOSED IN CONGRESS

BRITISH MEET
ITALIAN NAVY

FALL OF ATHENS

GERMANY DECLARES
WAR ON RUSSIA

JAPAN SEIZES INDO CHINA

ROOSEVELT ORDERS
TO SHOOT NAVY

RUDOLF HESS
FLIGHT TIMES

SPECIAL JAPANESE
ENVOYS IN WASHINGTON

PEARL HARBOR

help Britain, even at the risk of getting into the war, or to keep out of war ourselves?"

National
Men
Women

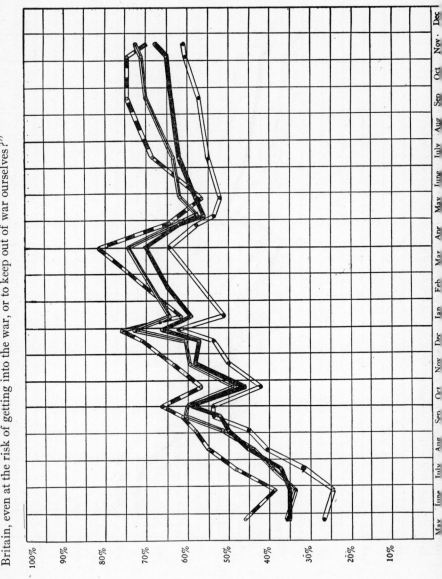

FIGURE 29. POLITICAL DIFFERENCES ON THE QUESTION:

"Which of these two things do you think is more important for the United States to try to do—To help Britain, even at the risk of getting into the war, or to keep out of war ourselves?"

"Which of these two things do you think is more important for the United States to try to do—To help Britain, even at the risk of getting into the war, or to keep out of war ourselves?"

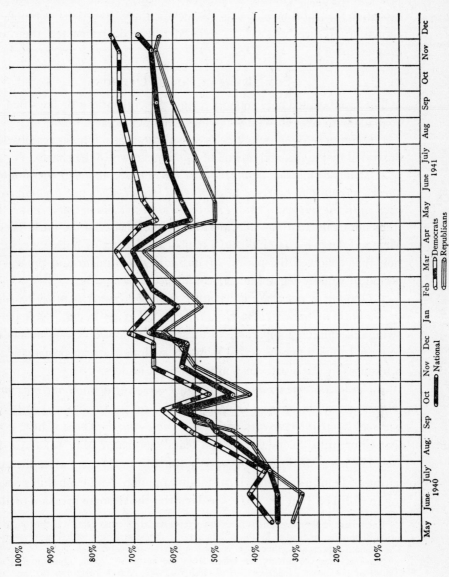

cult to frame many questions which can be repeated over a considerable period of time for trend purposes. But some questions have been appropriate since the beginning of the war in Europe, and others have been repeated for shorter intervals. Some of these trends of opinion are shown in Figures 26-30.[2] In general, these diagrams tell their own dramatic story.

Some Laws of Public Opinion

The trends noted here support certain generalizations or laws that can be made with respect to public opinion in a democracy.[3]

1. *Opinion is highly sensitive to important events.* This is readily demonstrated by the ups and downs of opinion shown in the charts.

2. *Events of unusual magnitude are likely to swing public opinion temporarily from one extreme to another. Opinion does not become stabilized until the implications of events are seen with some perspective.* The tremendous fluctuations in American opinion between the dark days of May and August 1940 indicate a temporary feeling of hopeless resignation that followed the period of unfounded optimism and preceded a period of rapidly regaining self-confidence.

3. *Opinion is generally determined more by events than by words— unless those words are themselves interpreted as an "event."* No extreme swings in opinion comparable to those that followed certain events can be traced to any purely verbal stimulus such as German propaganda or utterances by Axis or even United Nations leaders.

4. *Verbal statements and outlines of courses of action have maximum importance when opinion is unstructured, when people are suggestible and seek some interpretation from a reliable source.* There is little doubt that Churchill's "blood, sweat and tears" speech of May 14, 1940, followed by his realistic and courageous statement of June 5 after the evacuation of Dunkirk, did much to stabilize opinion. And Churchill's speech to the world on June 23, 1941, the day after the German invasion of Rus-

[2] Each point in the diagrams is based on a representative cross-section of the total population. The dates indicated by the points are the dates on which ballots were sent out. The opinion represented, therefore, is opinion for the subsequent ten days.

[3] Some of these comments are taken from the author's "Public Opinion in Flux," *Annals of the Amer. Academy of Pol. and Soc. Sci.*, March 1942, 136-152, and from "America Faces the War," *Public Opinion Quarterly*, 1940, 4, 387-407. Since these charts are included here mainly to illustrate the use of trends in public opinion research, their implication for the social psychologist concerned with motivation and propaganda is not spelled out in detail in a volume devoted to techniques of research. The "laws" suggested by a study of the trends as offered here will be amplified and discussed systematically in a later volume.

sia, clarified for millions of bewildered people the nature of the enemy, the war aims of Britain and the United States, and the role of the Soviet Union in the conflict.

5. *By and large, public opinion does not anticipate emergencies—it only reacts to them.* During the early period of the "phony" war, most Americans felt that we would not become involved. When hostilities began, more people thought we would be drawn in. For example, it was not until *after* Norway was successfully invaded and *after* the successful invasion of the Low Countries that the majority of people began to realize that a German victory would affect them personally.

6. *Psychologically, opinion is basically determined by self-interest. Events, words, or any other stimuli affect opinion only in so far as their relationship to self-interest is apparent.* For example, there is a close relationship between our desire to help Britain and our expectation of a British victory. We do not like to bet on a loser, even if he is a friend. The expectation that the United States would enter the war suddenly dropped in June 1940 when it seemed that our help would be too late. Throughout the period covered by the charts, the American people did not change their opinion concerning Britain's war aims. Approximately one-third of them believed at the beginning of the war that Britain was fighting to preserve democracy. This figure remained constant. We also find, for example, that women were less consistently interventionist than men and that older people with above average income were consistently more interventionist than older people with low incomes. It is clear from a close examination of the opinions of these groups that men and older people in higher income groups were more apt to identify their self-interest with an active interventionist policy than were women or older people not so well off.

7. *Opinion does not remain aroused for any long period of time unless people feel their self-interest is acutely involved or unless opinion— aroused by words—is sustained by events.* For example, President Roosevelt's fireside talk of December 29, 1940, increased by about eight per cent the number who thought it was more important to help England at the risk of war than to keep out of war. If this talk had been followed by some action, the rise in opinion might easily have been held. An example showing how public attention can be diverted is seen by the drop of over ten per cent in those who favored aid to Britain at the risk of war and those who thought we would become involved in the war during October 1940—the period when both major presidential candidates were minimizing the probability of actual intervention.

8. *Once self-interest is involved, opinion is not easily changed.* The signing of the German-Italian-Japanese pact of late September 1940, for example, did not scare Americans away from their policy of aid to Britain at the risk of war. And once the American people decided to resist what they clearly regarded as Japanese aggressions, there were no signs of appeasement. Furthermore, Hitler's talk of his Holy War against Communism made no impression on the American people. The effect of Russia's entrance into the war was only to lift American optimism concerning the war's outcome and to decrease slightly the number of people who thought we would enter the war.

9. *When self-interest is involved, public opinion in a democracy is likely to be ahead of official policy.* The polls showed this clearly during the period covered here with respect to the repeal of the arms embargo, conscripting man power, convoying, and the use of American ships and crews to carry supplies to England. In each case, a majority of the public was in favor of these measures on an average of four months before legislation was passed.

10. *When an opinion is held by a slight majority or when opinion is not solidly structured, an accomplished fact tends to shift opinion in the direction of acceptance.* Poll figures show that immediately after the repeal of the arms embargo, immediately after passage of the conscription laws, and immediately after favorable Congressional action on lend-lease and on the repeal of the neutrality laws, there was invariably a rise of around ten per cent in the number of people favorable to these actions.

11. *At critical times, people become more sensitive to the adequacy of their leadership—if they have confidence in it, they are willing to assign more than usual responsibility to it; if they lack confidence in it, they are less tolerant than usual.* Data from public opinion surveys in both England and the United States show that Prime Minister Churchill and President Roosevelt have increased their popularity whenever they have taken some bold action that the public has been waiting for, even though such action may in time of peace have been regarded technically as a usurpation of executive power. On the other hand, we know that the British were quick to resent Chamberlain's dilatory tactics and American opinion has been instrumental in the changes of subleaders of domestic affairs.

12. *People are less reluctant to have critical decisions made by their leaders if they feel that somehow they, the people, are taking some part in the decision.* For example, there was a higher percentage of people

who would "vote to go to war against Germany" than who thought we should "enter the war." Also we find greater differences of opinion by political affiliation during the spring of 1941 when the president and his close administration advisers were rapidly implementing the aid to Britain policy.

13. *People have more opinions and are able to form opinions more easily with respect to goals than with respect to methods necessary to reach those goals.* From the very beginning of the war, opinion was practically unanimous in agreeing that we wanted to see Germany and Japan defeated. However, on none of the methods proposed to realize this objective was there any such overwhelming agreement. A similar discrepancy existed with regard to the desire to aid Britain and opinion toward various measures effecting that aid.

14. *Public opinion, like individual opinion, is colored by desire. And when opinion is based chiefly on desire rather than on information, it is likely to show especially sharp shifts with events.* The curve most sensitive to the course of events is that indicating which side people think will win the war. Here wishes are most closely related to opinion. Also the average man has little solid and long-time strategic information on which to base his judgments. Furthermore, when separate trend curves of expectation are made by economic class, there is clear indication that persons of the upper income groups are more vacillating in their opinions than persons in the low income groups. Relationship between the curves representing those who think England will win and the unadjusted Dow-Jones Stock Index is close but not surprising. If upper income people are separated out, their expectations are found to approximate more closely the trends in the Dow-Jones Index.

15. *The important psychological dimensions of opinion are direction, intensity, breadth, and depth.*[4] Nearly all public opinion polls, including the charts above, report the dimension of direction only. The *intensity* of opinion, or the strength with which people hold their convictions, determines to a large extent the consistency and direction. With reference to the charts, there is little doubt that with the possible exception of the critical period in midsummer of 1940, "interventionist" opinion was by and large more "intense" than "noninterventionist" opinion. The *breadth* of opinion—its inclusiveness or generality—lends consistency to direction. That American opinion was general rather than specific during

[4] For an elaboration of these dimensions, see "Public Opinion in Flux," *op. cit.*, and Hadley Cantril, *Psychology of Social Movements* (New York: Wiley, 1941), Chaps. 1, 2, and 3.

the period covered is indicated by the consistency of reactions to various actions or statements issued by Germany on the one hand and Japan on the other. The American people were able to include within one basic frame of reference specific opinions pointing in the same direction. The dimension of *depth*, or the foundation of opinion, finally determines consistency, intensity, and breadth. American opinion during the period outlined became squarely rooted on standards of judgment difficult for any enemy propaganda to shake. The particular combination of these four dimensions characterizes the *stability* of an opinion.

16. *Although public opinion is by no means always consistent, many of the inconsistencies are more apparent than real when general frames of reference are discerned and when the basic standards of judgment are discovered from which specific opinions derive.* For example, the apparent inconsistency between the minority who said they would vote to go to war against Germany and the majority who said it was more important to help England even at the risk of war than it was to keep out of war, presented a dilemma to some observers of American opinion before December 7, 1941. "Interventionists" publicized one set of poll figures, while "isolationists" publicized another. However, when all data are taken into consideration, it becomes clear that the question of "voting to go to war against Germany" or any similar question is highly unrealistic, and fails to place opinion in terms of any contingency.

17. *By and large, if people in a democracy are provided educational opportunities and ready access to information, public opinion reveals a hard-headed common sense. The more enlightened people are to the implications of events and proposals for their own self-interest, the more likely they are to agree with the more objective opinions of realistic experts.* This conclusion has been argued at length since the days of the Founding Fathers. The trend data gathered here may some day be used by historians in debating the point. At the present time, however, it would seem likely that the "objective" appraisal by future experts of American opinion during this period would agree that the people acted in their own self-interest and that their actions could be roughly described as dictated by common sense. Given sufficient facts and motivated to pay attention to those facts, the common man will reach a decision based on his own self-interest as a member of a democratic community. His knowledge is functional.

PART V

THE POLLING TECHNIQUE APPLIED TO A SPECIFIC
PROBLEM

CHAPTER XVII

THE MEASUREMENT OF CIVILIAN MORALE[1]

MANY writers have been concerned about the morale of the American people since the fall of 1939. The public was said to be too jittery, too complacent, or too cynical, or too sentimental, or too tolerant, or not tolerant enough—the list can be made as long as you please. Yet presumably something was wrong with American morale somewhere, or so many people wouldn't be worried about it. An accurate diagnosis would be valuable.

We have also a practical interest in morale measurement. Governmental policies affect morale; and this effect must frequently be taken into account. Should we maximize or minimize our military losses? When a battleship is sunk, should the commentators emphasize how long one takes to build and how few we have, or should they argue that aircraft carriers are more important and that this battleship was an old one and not very good anyway?

It is no simple matter to estimate the effects on morale of these alter-

[1] By John Harding. Mr. Harding's chapter on the measurement of morale differs from the other chapters of this volume in that it combines a discussion of specific techniques with an application of these techniques to a broad area of inquiry. This research was planned with the hope of presenting the biography of a public opinion survey, from the original conception of the problem to the final conclusions derived from analysis of the data. The subject of morale was chosen as the theme of the story because of its intrinsic interest and because the attempt to measure it presented particularly thorny problems that illustrate better than simpler subjects some of the possibilities and limitations of the polling technique.

The length of this article and the complexity of its subject matter made it advisable to divide the account into two sections—a straightforward account of the investigation for the general reader, and a technical appendix (Appendix 1) for research workers and critically minded experts. This chapter states the main problems and presents all the important conclusions. Appendix 1 explains the assumptions underlying the research, presents all the data collected, and discusses the evidence for the conclusions advanced.

This experiment in morale measurement represents the work of several people. The idea of a morale index obtained by measuring morale components in a national survey resulted from a discussion of George Gallup and Hadley Cantril. The first list of morale components was prepared by Alfred Max, former director of the French Institute of Public Opinion. Gallup, Cantril and Gordon Allport and his morale seminar at Harvard University made further suggestions for the components of morale. The first survey—pre-Pearl Harbor—and the original analysis were made by Cantril. The cross-section was prepared by Donald Rugg. Frederick Mosteller worked out the tetrachoric correlations and made the investigation of morale scores.

Mr. Harding joined the Office of Public Opinion Research on a Rockefeller Fellowship in February 1942. Before this he had been working on morale measurement at Harvard. The second morale survey, including the construction of the ballot and its analysis, was his responsibility.—H.C.

native policies, but it will at least be helpful to know more about the nature of morale itself. If we know what are the components of morale, we can predict which of them are likely to be affected by a given policy and in what way. The way in which war news is reported, for example, will probably affect satisfaction with our progress toward our goal, awareness of the difficulties we are up against, confidence in our armed forces, and confidence in the news itself. A particular policy with respect to war information will usually have some advantageous effects and some disadvantageous ones. They must be weighed against each other. Thus it is desirable to know which components of morale are more important and which are less important. If it should turn out that awareness of the difficulties is more important than satisfaction with our progress, a less optimistic and more "realistic" news policy would be better from the standpoint of its effect on civilian morale.

As a means of diagnosing morale, public opinion polls have been repeatedly suggested. This chapter will present an analysis of the components of morale, show how they can be measured by polling methods, describe the interrelationship of the various components, and report on the state of civilian morale in the periods just before and just after American entry into the war.

THE DEFINITION OF MORALE

In defining morale we seek to distinguish a psychological factor which *makes a difference* to the success or failure of an enterprise when other factors—strength, ability, experience, technical equipment, etc.—are held constant. Morale is a condition which may vary both qualitatively and quantitatively from individual to individual, from group to group, from day to day. Behavior is the true test of morale. Avowals of interest and sentiment, protestations of belief are but a rough index of what an individual or group will *do* when called upon to act. For this reason wherever possible every measure of morale should be validated against some measure of actual performance.

The morale of a group must be estimated in relation to some designated goal of that group. For example, the morale of a group must be judged low if it is divided by factions working for independent goals or contending against each other, even though the morale of each faction (appraised in relation to its own goal) is good. High morale is a condition of mental soundness marked by a wholehearted, decisive resolution to achieve given goals, and by spirited, unyielding, coordinated efforts in the direction of these goals.

Components of Morale

To understand the components of morale which were measured by the first morale ballot of the Office of Public Opinion Research, we must go back to the atmosphere of the months immediately preceding American entry into the war. In the fall of 1941 the United States was legally at peace but had just been pledged by the Atlantic charter to "the destruction of Nazi tyranny." This was now the objective in terms of which morale could be measured. We asked of each proposed component of morale: Does this attitude tend to increase the contribution which an individual will make to the overthrow of Nazism? If not, we lost interest in that component.

Diplomatic relations were becoming weekly more tense. American troops had occupied Iceland, and the American navy was patrolling the North Atlantic in defiance of German threats. Though only 27 per cent of our people said they would vote for war with Germany if a referendum were taken, 64 per cent thought it was more important to continue helping England than to keep out of war. The Japanese had seized control of French Indo-China in July and were now threatening Thailand. By September, 66 per cent of the American people preferred risking war with Japan to allowing her to continue her aggressions.

In the autumn of 1941, 77 per cent of our people thought we would eventually get into the war. The question: Should we resist the Axis at any cost? was coming to be regarded as settled. The main issue was becoming: When will we fight?

For two months OPOR reviewed previous analyses of morale, and worked to find a set of questions which were simple and clear, which had the same meaning for people from all classes of society, but which were still adequate to the complex attitudes which make up morale. Finally we arrived at a set of morale components to be measured by the following list of questions:

I. *Awareness of the objective.*

Do you feel that you have a clear idea of what the war is all about?

What would you say the war *is* all about?

II. *Agreement with the objective.*

Which of these two things do you think is the more important:

That this country keep out of war, *or*

That Germany be defeated?

If Germany should defeat England and Russia in the present war, do you think Germany would start a war against the United States within the next ten years?

Some people say that the biggest job facing this country today is to help defeat the Nazi government. Do you agree, or disagree?

Should the United States take steps now to keep Japan from becoming more powerful, even if this means we have to go to war against Japan?

III. *Determination to achieve the objective.*

If peace could be obtained today on the basis of Britain keeping the British Empire as it now stands, and Germany holding the countries she has conquered so far, would you be in favor of such a peace?

If our present leaders and military advisers say that the only way to defeat Germany is for this country to go into the war, would you be in favor of this country's going into the war against Germany?

IV. *Belief that the objective can be attained.*

(a) That the war will be won.

Do you think that in the long run Germany will win the war or lose it?

If this country should get into a war against Japan, do you think we would win, or lose?

(b) That an enduring peace will be achieved.

If Germany is defeated, do you think a peace that will last for at least 50 years can be worked out?

Do you think that such a peace *will* be worked out?

V. *Awareness of the magnitude of the task.*

Do you think our own army, navy, and airforce will have to fight in the war against Germany before she is defeated?

If this country should get into a war against Japan, do you think it would be a difficult war, or do you think it would be a comparatively easy war for us to win?

Here are three ways to describe Germany's situation today. Which one of these statements comes closest to the way you feel?

(a) Germany is still very strong but will be defeated by Britain and Russia with the help of supplies from this country.

(b) Germany is the strongest military nation in the world. She can only be defeated if this country enters the war.

(c) Germany is so strong that she will never be defeated, whether we get into the war or not.

VI. *Confidence in the leader.*

In general, do you approve or disapprove of the way Roosevelt is handling his job as President today?

Some people say that President Roosevelt is taking advantage of the war situation to carry out some of his pet plans which have nothing to do with defense. Do you agree, or disagree with this?

(If "Agree") Do you approve, or disapprove of President Roosevelt's taking advantage of the war to carry out his plans not connected with defense?

VII. *Confidence in the armed forces.*

Do you think that at the present time our army is as strong as the German army?

Do you think that at the present time our airforce is as strong as the German airforce?

Do you think that at the present time our navy is strong enough to defeat the Japanese navy?

VIII. *Confidence in our allies.*

Do you believe the British are doing all they possibly can to win the war?

Do you think the Russians are doing all they possibly can to win the war?

IX. *Confidence in the news.*

Do you feel that, in general, the information you are getting about the war situation is true and accurate?

Do you think the government is giving the public as much information as it should about the war?

X. *Satisfaction with the progress of the group toward its goals.*

As far as you, personally, are concerned, do you think the United States has gone too far in opposing Germany, or not far enough?

Can you think of anything that a President of the United States should do that President Roosevelt has not done, or is not now doing?

XI. *Unity within the group.*

In general, do you feel that any of the following people are doing less than others for national defense?

(a) Farmers   (g) People on relief
(b) Negroes   (h) Factory workers
(c) Jews   (i) Labor leaders
(d) Foreign-born   (j) Businessmen
(e) Protestants   (k) Wealthy people
(f) Catholics   __None of these groups

This ballot was the first attempt in the history of public opinion research to measure morale systematically and on a nation-wide basis. Besides the questions listed above, the ballot included questions to measure the extent of respondent's information about the war, and all the usual background data.

CIVILIAN MORALE BEFORE PEARL HARBOR

On November 19, 1941, the morale ballot went out to a specially selected group of interviewers who were assigned a cross-section stratified according to census figures by section of the country, city size (including farmers), economic status, sex, and age. All the interviewing was completed before December 7. Two thousand five hundred forty-three ballots were returned.

On each of the questions on the ballot there were one or two answers which seemed clearly indicative of high morale (keeping in mind the components which the questions were designed to measure). The following table shows for each question the high-morale answers and the percentage of our sample which chose them out of the various possible alternatives:

TABLE 80. HIGH-MORALE ANSWERS

	Proportion of Answers Indicating High Morale
Awareness	
Clear idea about war.	50%
Agreement	
More important that Germany be defeated.	68
Germany would start war against U.S.	70
Biggest job is to help defeat Nazis.	72
Stop Japan, even if this means war.	64
Determination	
Against peace on present basis.	17
War against Germany if leaders say it is necessary.	70

Proportion of Answers
Indicating High Morale

War objective attainable

Germany will lose.   86%
We would win a war against Japan.   93

Peace objective attainable

A 50-year peace can and will be worked out.   32

Magnitude of the task

Our armed forces will have to fight Germany.   52
Germany can only be defeated if this country enters
the war.   30
A war with Japan would be difficult.   35

Confidence in the leader

Approve the way Roosevelt is handling his job.   72
Disagree that Roosevelt is taking advantage of the
war, *or* Agree, but approve.   58

Confidence in the armed forces

Our army is as strong as the German army.   23
Our airforce is as strong as the German airforce.   29
Our navy is strong enough to defeat the Japanese
navy.   79

Confidence in our allies

The British are doing all they possibly can.   60
The Russians are doing all they possibly can.   93

Confidence in the news

War news in general true and accurate.   39
Government is giving the public sufficient information.   48

Satisfaction with group progress

U. S. has *not* gone too far in opposing Germany.   76
President Roosevelt is doing everything a president
should do.   62

Sense of unity

None of these groups is doing less than others for
national defense.   18

It is reasonable to average the questions for a given component if the percentages of high morale are not too dissimilar. With this procedure we reach the accompanying picture of American morale just before Pearl Harbor (Figure 31).

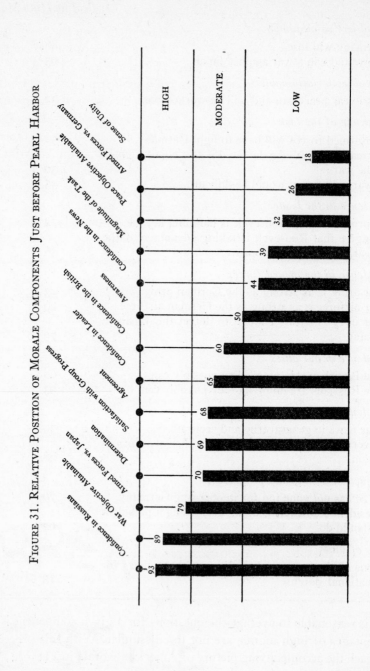

FIGURE 31. RELATIVE POSITION OF MORALE COMPONENTS JUST BEFORE PEARL HARBOR

PATTERNS OF MORALE

How are these morale components related to one another? Do they vary independently, or are they highly correlated? Are the correlations the result of a single common factor, degree of morale? Or are there different types of high morale found in different kinds of people?

To answer such questions we correlated each item with every other item and did a simple factor analysis of the table of intercorrelations. It was evident that the attitudes represented by these questions did not vary independently, since the average correlation was .21. But this average does not give us a good idea of the degree of relationship between any two specific components, since many of the correlations were as high as .5 or .6, while others were close to zero or even negative. The high and low correlations form a peculiar and interesting pattern.

The questions most highly correlated with the others are those measuring *Agreement with the objective* and *Determination*. These two components are undoubtedly essential to high morale; from their correlations it is clear that they best represent that single factor which is common to all the questions, and consequently that a man's answers to these questions will be a good index of the degree of his morale. Examination of the content of these questions shows that all of them are concerned in some way with American intervention in the war. In the fall of 1941 the stand which he took on this question was the main contribution which the average citizen could make to the goal of "the destruction of Nazi tyranny." So it is natural that on our ballot interventionism should turn up as equivalent to high morale.

But there is another factor, common to many of the questions, which cuts across this first factor at right angles. The questions measuring *Awareness of the objective* and *Amount of information* are highly correlated with each other and moderately correlated with the Agreement and Determination questions. On the other hand, *Confidence in the leader, Confidence in the armed forces, Confidence in the news*, and *Satisfaction with group progress* are also highly correlated with each other and moderately correlated with Agreement and Determination. *But their correlations with Awareness and Information are low or negative.*

This pattern of correlations results from the fact that these questions are measuring not only degree of morale but another factor which we will call "degree of sophistication." Sophisticated people tend to be high on Awareness and Information but to lack confidence in the President and the armed forces. They also tend to lack confidence in the government's information policy, and to be dissatisfied with the rate of our progress toward our goal. These people are usually above average in education and economic status. They tend to vote Republican.

Unsophisticated people are less informed and less aware of what the war is all about. They are not so well educated, nor so well off financially; the majority of them are Democrats. These people characteristically have confidence in the President. They tend to be satisfied with the way things are going, with the armed forces, and with the news.

There were thus two main types of high morale in the fall of 1941. The morale of sophisticated people was usually the result of their realization of the consequences of a Nazi victory to their own positions and freedoms, while the morale of unsophisticated people sprang essentially from their confidence in President Roosevelt and all he stood for.

Group Differences in Morale

If knowledge of the state of morale is to bear fruit in a practical morale-building program, it is important to know which sections of the population have high morale and which do not, as well as something about the causes of these differences. We obtained from the answers to the most discriminating questions on the ballot a score representing degree of morale, and made all of the usual breakdowns on it.

As we should expect, nationality background is an important factor in morale. People whose parents were from any of the other United Nations had higher morale than the national average—represented by those whose parents were born in this country—and people of German and Italian origin had much lower morale. In *Two Way Passage* Louis Adamic has given a vivid picture of the way in which old-world loyalties affect the attitudes of Americans toward the present war.

Even more important than nationality background is political affiliation. People who voted Democratic in 1940 were substantially above the average in morale, whereas people who voted Republican and people who did not vote at all were both well below the national average. The low morale of Republicans and nonvoters reflects their lack of confidence in the President and his policies.

Geographical region also enters the picture as a determinant of morale. The traditionally isolationist Middle West was definitely below average in morale, and the South higher than any other section of the country. The causes of these sectional differences are very complex, but the differences themselves are fairly stable; the South has been the most interventionist section of the country since the beginning of the present war.

There were no consistent differences in morale by education, economic status, or age. Women in the upper economic brackets had somewhat lower morale than men, and women in the lower brackets considerably lower morale.

Protestants, the dominant religious group in this country, were exactly average in morale. Catholics were slightly below, while Jews were strikingly above average. On this ballot the Jews—representing only three or four per cent of our population—were higher in morale than any other group studied.

There were some differences in morale among the various occupations, but these were rather slight. Businessmen and skilled workers tended to be above average in morale, with domestic servants, unskilled workers, and unemployed people below average.

Even before Pearl Harbor two-thirds of our people were agreed on the issue of American participation in the war. The most important lines of cleavage were ethnic, political, and geographical. Yet these were not so great as to imperil the unity of the country, as we shall see from our analysis of American morale during the first four months of war.

A New Morale Ballot

Although our twelve morale components were presumably as valid after Pearl Harbor as before, it was necessary to find new questions to measure many of them, and we took this opportunity to revise the whole ballot. It was now possible to include a measure of participation in war activities open to civilians as a criterion of morale against which questions and components could be validated. Because this objective test of validity was planned, we felt we could experiment with new questions and new components, relying on the process of validation to sort the wheat from the chaff. The new ballot included sixteen components of morale, with the following questions to measure them:

I. *Awareness of the objective.*

Do you feel that you have a clear idea of what the war is all about?

What would you say the war *is* all about?

Which do you think is our No. 1 enemy in the war—Japan or Germany?

II. *Awareness of the threat.*

Do you think that if Germany and Japan should win this war, they would keep their armies over here to police the United States?

III. *Agreement with the objective.*

If Hitler offered peace now to all countries on the basis of not going farther, but of leaving matters as they are now, would you favor or oppose such a peace?

Which of these two things do you think the United States should try to do when the war is over: Stay out of world affairs as much as we can, *or* Take an active part in world affairs?

IV. *Determination to achieve the objective.*

Which of these two things do you think the United States should do: Send most of our army abroad to fight the enemy wherever they are, or Keep most of our army at home to protect the United States?

After finding out what each person can do, should the government have the power to tell each citizen what to do as his or her part in the war effort, and require him or her to do it?

V. *War objective attainable.*

What will bring the war to an end?

VI. *Peace objective attainable.*

After the war is over, do you think there will be jobs for everyone or lots of unemployment?

Do you think your children twenty years from now will be better off or worse off than you are now?

VII. *Awareness of the magnitude of the task.*

About how much longer do you think the war will last?

VIII. *Confidence in leaders.*

In general, do you approve or disapprove of the way Roosevelt is handling his job as President today?

As you know, a lot of new government offices have been set up in Washington especially to deal with national defense and war problems. From what you have heard, do you think most of these offices are doing a good job, or a poor one?

IX. *Confidence in the armed forces.*

Which do you think has the smartest military leaders at present—Germany or Russia or the United States?

Which do you think has the strongest navy at present—Japan or England or the United States?

X. *Confidence in our allies.*

Do you think the British are doing all they possibly can to win the war?

Do you think Russia can be trusted to cooperate with us after the war is over?

XI. *Confidence in the news.*

Do you think the government is giving the public as much information as it should about the war?

XII. *Satisfaction with group progress.*

Do you think we are now doing all we can to defeat Japan and Germany, or could we be doing more?

XIII. *Unity within the group.*

Do you think any of these groups is taking unfair advantage of the war to get money or power for themselves?

(a) Farmers   (g) People on relief
(b) Negroes   (h) Factory workers
(c) Jews   (i) Labor leaders
(d) Foreign-born   (j) Congressmen
(e) Protestants   (k) Businessmen
(f) Catholics   (l) Wealthy people
                    ___None of these groups

XIV. *Hatred of the enemy.*

If we win the war, how do you think we should treat the people in Germany?

How should we treat the Nazi leaders?

XV. *Feeling of participation.*

Do you feel that you personally are doing something that is important in helping to win the war?

XVI. *Basic values.*

Do you think a poor man gets just as fair treatment in the law courts as a rich man?

Do you think most people can be trusted?

Do you think success is dependent mostly on luck, on ability, or on pull?

On March 26, 1942, the new morale ballot went out to a cross-section stratified in the same way as in our previous survey. Two thousand five hundred thirty-nine complete interviews were returned.

In addition to the questions already listed, the ballot included questions to measure information, participation in the war effort, and the usual background data. There were four participation questions. If respondent answered "Yes" to the question: "Do you feel that you personally are doing something that is important in helping to win the war?" he was asked further: "What sort of thing are you doing?" and given one point if his answer included serving in the armed forces, working in war industry, working for the government, raising farm products, reducing purchases, psychological or ideological work, social-service work for the army, military training, or training for war work. Everyone was then asked: "Are you doing any work in the civilian defense program such as air-raid warning, first aid, and the like?" "Have you or your family bought any defense bonds or defense stamps?" and "Are you or your family saving materials such as metal, rubber, or waste paper?" One point was given for participation in each of these activities. This gives us a total participation score ranging from 0 to 4 points.

VALIDATION OF MORALE COMPONENTS

If a given attitude is really important for morale, the people having that attitude should on the average be doing more to help win the war than the people without that attitude. And we can determine not only whether or not an attitude is important for morale, but how important it is by examining the extent to which the performance of the people with the attitude differs from the performance of those without the attitude.

To validate our questions we calculated for each possible answer to each question the average participation score of the people choosing that answer. We called a question "good" if there was some answer to it (other than "No Opinion") so that people giving that answer made participation scores significantly higher or lower than the scores of people choosing the other answers to the question. The rank of a question was determined by the size of the differences in participation associated with the various answers to the question.

Because some of our components were measured by several different questions, each component was given the rank of the best question measuring it. The following list shows the components which turned out to be important *for actual performance in the war effort*, in order of their importance:

1. Agreement with the objective.
2. War objective attainable.

3. Awareness of the objective.
4. Basic values.
5. Determination to achieve the objective.
6. Confidence in the news.
7. Sense of unity.
8. Awareness of the magnitude of the task.
9. Confidence in leaders.
10. Hatred of the enemy.
11. Peace objective attainable.

It is significant that for American civilians the enemy includes only the Nazi leaders. Only 12 per cent thought the German people should be treated harshly after the war, and their participation scores were definitely below average rather than above.

One of our components, Feeling of participation, could not be validated by its relation to the participation score because the two are linked directly; their degree of relationship is not, as with the other questions, a measure of their mutual dependence on morale.

Satisfaction with group progress seems, if anything, to be negatively related to morale. The people who say we are *not* doing all we can to defeat Japan and Germany tend to be participating in war activities a little more than the people who say we are doing all we can.

The other three components, Awareness of the threat, Confidence in armed forces, and Confidence in our allies, are not related either positively or negatively to performance in the war effort, and so presumably were not important for civilian morale as of March 1942. This is a revealing discovery. It tells us, in the first place, that the problem of what would happen to us *if* we lost the war is unreal to the vast majority of the American people. Their support of the war is not dependent upon their notion of what defeat would mean.

An important problem for some of them, however, is: Can we win a real victory? That this belief in victory is very important for morale is shown by the high rank of War objective attainable on the list of components. The 6 per cent of our people who believe that we cannot achieve a victory are giving the most half-hearted kind of support to the war effort; they do not expect the war to end in our defeat, but only in a stalemate.

The crucial importance of this belief in ultimate victory gives us the explanation of the fact that opinion concerning the strength of our armed forces *at present* is of no significance for morale. Since it is belief in ultimate victory that counts, and since the great majority of the people believe that our army and navy will eventually be adequate to their task, their opinion of the present strength of the armed forces makes no difference to their enthusiasm for the war.

The unimportance of Confidence in our allies is more difficult to explain. There seems to be a widespread feeling that this is our private war against the dictators and that it will end when *we* clean up on them. Of the large majority who believe we should take an active part in world affairs after the war, very few seem to have any real faith in international cooperation. They see our role as that of a corporation which dominates a whole industry and by sheer size and power establishes a code of trade practices which everyone must follow. The characteristics of its competitors and customers are interesting, perhaps, but not fundamentally important.

TRENDS IN MORALE

What effect did our entry into the war have upon civilian morale in the United States? The following graphs show the trend of opinion on all morale questions which were asked more than once in the period beginning with our first morale ballot on November 19, 1941, and ending with our second morale ballot on March 26, 1942. The date given for each question is the date on which the ballot containing that question was sent out to the interviewers. From these graphs we see that the general trend of morale was upward during these four months.

FIGURE 32. AWARENESS OF THE OBJECTIVE

Do you feel that you have a clear idea of what the war is all about?

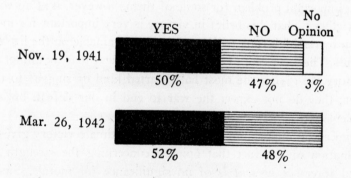

FIGURE 33. AGREEMENT WITH THE OBJECTIVE

If peace could be obtained today on the basis of Britain keeping the British empire as it now stands, and Germany holding the countries she has conquered so far, would you be in favor of such a peace?

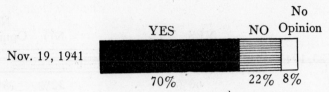

                                    No
                    YES   NO Opinion

Nov. 19, 1941

                 70%   22% 8%

If Hitler offered peace now to all countries on the basis of not going farther, but of leaving matters as they are now, would you favor, or oppose such a peace?

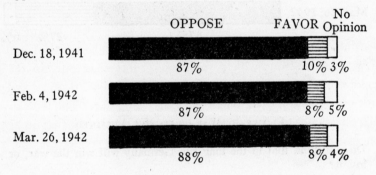

                                          No
                OPPOSE   FAVOR Opinion

Dec. 18, 1941

                 87%   10% 3%

Feb. 4, 1942

                 87%   8% 5%

Mar. 26, 1942

                 88%   8% 4%

FIGURE 34

Which of these two things do you think the United States should try to do when the war is over: Stay out of world affairs as much as we can, or take an active part in world affairs?

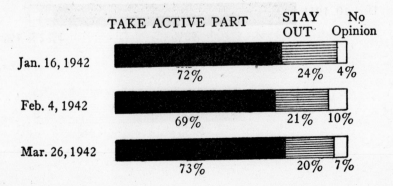

                                      STAY   No
          TAKE ACTIVE PART   OUT   Opinion

Jan. 16, 1942
                 72%   24%   4%

Feb. 4, 1942
                 69%   21%   10%

Mar. 26, 1942
                 73%   20% 7%

FIGURE 35. DETERMINATION TO ACHIEVE THE OBJECTIVE

After finding out what each person can do, should the government have the power to tell each citizen what to do as his part in the war effort and require him or her to do it?

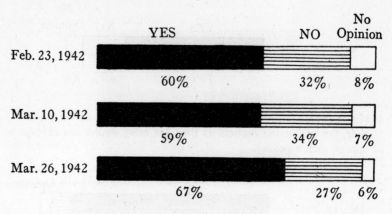

FIGURE 36. WAR OBJECTIVE ATTAINED

Do you think that in the long run Germany will win the war, or lose it?

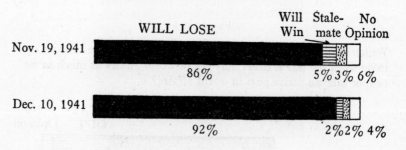

FIGURE 37. AWARENESS OF THE MAGNITUDE OF THE TASK

About how much longer do you think the war will last?

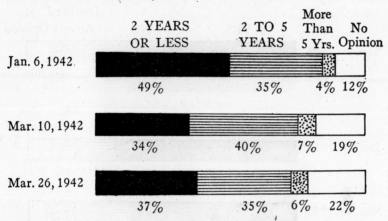

FIGURE 38. CONFIDENCE IN THE LEADER

In general, do you approve or disapprove of the way Roosevelt is handling his job as President today?

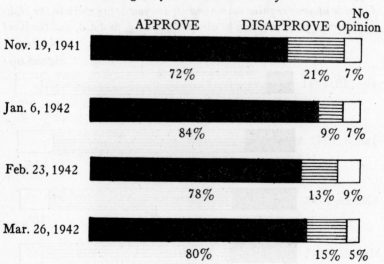

FIGURE 39. CONFIDENCE IN THE NEWS

Do you think the government is giving the public as much information as it should about the war?

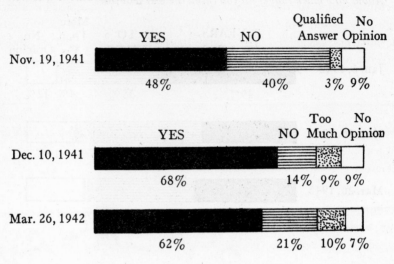

FIGURE 40. PARTICIPATION IN THE WAR EFFORT

Outside of your regular employment, are you doing work in the civilian defense program such as air raid warning, first aid, and the like?

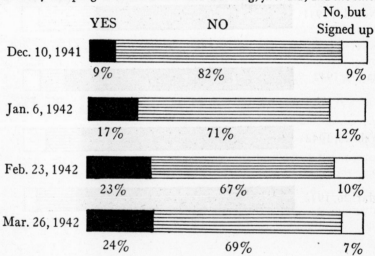

AMERICAN MORALE AFTER FOUR MONTHS OF WAR

The performance criterion not only tells us which of our questions are actually diagnostic of morale, but gives us an objective method of deciding which of the various possible answers to a question indicate high morale and which low. The following table gives for each question the answers associated with better-than-average participation and the percentage of our sample which chose them:

TABLE 81. HIGH MORALE ANSWERS

Awareness	Proportion of Answers Indicating High Morale
Clear idea about war.	52%
Germany is No. 1 enemy.	47
Agreement	
Oppose peace on present basis.	88
U. S. should take an active part in world affairs.	73
Determination	
Send most of our army abroad; send some abroad and keep some home.	65
Government should have power to tell everyone what to do in the war.	67
War objective attainable	
War will end in Allied victory.	79
Peace objective attainable	
Children will be better off twenty years from now.	43
Magnitude of the task	
War will last from two to five years more.	35
Confidence in leaders	
Approve the way Roosevelt is handling his job.	80
Government war offices are doing a good job, or doing the best they can.	51
Confidence in the news	
Government is giving the public enough (or too much) information about the war.	72
Sense of unity	
None of these groups is taking unfair advantage of the war.	16

	Proportion of Answers Indicating High Morale
Hatred of the enemy	
Nazi leaders should be killed after the war.	43%
Feeling of participation	
Respondent feels he is doing something that is important in helping to win the war.	56
Basic values	
A poor man gets just as fair treatment in the courts as a rich man.	36
Most people can be trusted.	66
Success is dependent mostly on ability.	70

Averaging the questions for a given morale component, we arrive at the picture comprising Figure 41—civilian morale after four months of war.

That the six components which our analysis showed to be most important for morale were all at a moderate or high level in March 1942 is encouraging. The greatest weakness in American morale in March as well as in November seems to be a feeling of disunity, a belief that certain groups are not doing as much as they should for national defense, or are taking unfair advantage of the war to get money or power for themselves. Labor leaders, foreign-born, and people on relief are most commonly accused of the former; labor leaders, businessmen, wealthy people, Congressmen, factory workers, and Jews of the latter. The tendency to pick scapegoats within the United States is especially characteristic of well-educated, upper-income people.

THE DIMENSIONS OF MORALE

On the new ballot we also correlated every question with every other question and performed a factor analysis, this time by a somewhat different method. Instead of pulling out a single general factor representing degree of morale, we analyzed morale into three different aspects, independent of one another, but all related to participation in war activities. These are not "components" of morale in any concrete sense, but abstract "dimensions" along which the morale of individuals can vary. We called them *Reasoned determination to achieve the objective, Confidence in leaders,* and *Satisfaction with traditional values.*

This tridimensional scheme gives a method of classifying morale components. Though each component represents to some extent all three dimensions, we can group together those whose variance is primarily

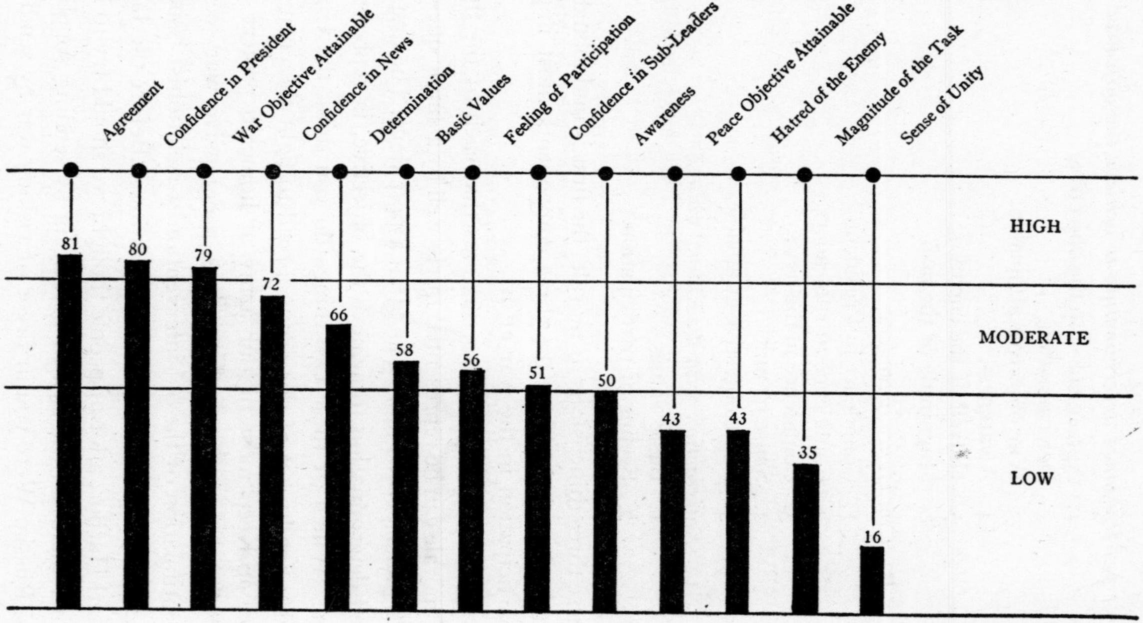

FIGURE 41. RELATIVE POSITION OF MORALE COMPONENTS AFTER FOUR MONTHS OF WAR

concentrated in the first dimension, and similarly those which represent primarily the second, and the third. In the following table the morale components are arranged according to this scheme:

A. *Reasoned determination to achieve the objective*
  1. Agreement with the objective.
  2. Determination.
  3. War objective attainable.
  4. Awareness.
  5. Hatred of the enemy.
  6. Magnitude of the task.

B. *Confidence in leaders*
  1. Confidence in President.
  2. Confidence in subleaders.
  3. Confidence in the news.
  4. Sense of unity.
  5. Peace objective attainable.

C. *Satisfaction with traditional values*
  1. Basic values.
  2. Feeling of participation.

Of these three dimensions of morale, the first is undoubtedly the most significant, since it includes the three components most important for actual participation in the war effort.

It turns out from the intercorrelations that each of the three dimensions of morale can be represented fairly well by a single question, which measures that aspect of morale and that aspect alone. The first dimension, Reasoned determination to achieve the objective, is represented by the question: "Which of these two things do you think the United States should do: Send most of our army abroad to fight the enemy wherever they are, *or* Keep most of our army at home to protect the United States?" The issue of an offensive *vs.* a defensive war seems to be a direct continuation of the old interventionist-isolationist issue, since our new question correlates .49 with the question: "Before the Japs attacked us at Pearl Harbor, a lot of people thought we should try to keep out of war rather than run the risk of getting in by sending supplies to England and Russia. Were you in favor of risking war by sending supplies to England, or were you in favor of trying to keep out of war?"

The second dimension of morale, Confidence in leaders, is represented by the question: "In general, do you approve or disapprove of the way Roosevelt is handling his job as President today?" and the third dimension, Satisfaction with traditional values, by the question: "Do you think most people can be trusted?"

This third dimension is an aspect of morale not tapped at all by our November ballot. The questions measuring it on the second ballot were mostly taken from a study by Rundquist and Sletto of *Personality in the Depression*, and it corresponds essentially to the factor of "general adjustment" which they found running through all their scales. It is worth noting that the best measure of this rather intangible factor—"Do you think most people can be trusted?"—is a question which is so vague that it seems to justify the worst invective of the critics of public opinion polls (cf. Chapter 1 of this volume). Yet it is precisely for this reason that it is a good question for the present purpose. Answers to it tell us, not what respondents think, but *how they feel*; and this turns out to be very important for their morale.

GROUP DIFFERENCES IN MORALE

Although we made all the customary breakdowns on the questions representing the three dimensions of morale, there were few significant group differences except those by education and economic status. We can take educated, upper-income people as typical of the "sophisticated" group on our November ballot, and uneducated, lower-income people as typical of the "unsophisticated." Analysis shows that sophisticated people are considerably above unsophisticated people on the first and third dimensions of morale—Reasoned determination and Satisfaction with traditional values—but unsophisticated people are higher on the dimension of Confidence in leaders. On the November ballot the number of questions representing the first dimension was about equal to the number representing the second, with the result that the total morale scores of sophisticated and unsophisticated were the same.

The strong point of the unsophisticated is a simple faith that their leaders are trustworthy, from the President on down; and that however bad things look now, they will eventually turn out all right. Sophisticated people tend to be critical of the way the war is being run, perhaps because they realize so much more clearly the things we must do if we are to win. Thus 74 per cent of these people come out for an offensive war, as compared with 55 per cent of the unsophisticated. Eighty-five per cent of the sophisticated believe the United States should take an active part in world affairs after the war, but only 59 per cent of the unsophisticated. *In these new contexts unsophisticated people still tend to be isolationist.*

In March, political, religious, and nationality differences were not as prominent as they had been in November. People of German background were still low on the first morale dimension (measured by the question of an offensive *vs.* a defensive war). Italians and people from occupied countries were unusually high in Confidence in leaders (measured by the question on approval of Roosevelt). This may represent a tendency to overconform, bred of a feeling of insecurity, rather than genuinely high morale.

Jews continue to be far above the other religious groups in all three dimensions of morale. Catholics and Democrats tend to be high in Confidence in leaders, while Republicans are high in Satisfaction with traditional values. But on the most important dimension—Reasoned determination to achieve the objective—Catholics and Protestants, Republicans and Democrats are alike.

Sectional differences have become insignificant. Occupational differences follow the pattern of sophistication-unsophistication we have already discussed. There is, however, a difference between men and women with respect to Reasoned determination which is almost as great as the difference between sophisticated and unsophisticated. For many women low morale seems to be the result of plain indifference to international affairs; others, however, have a sincere emotional dislike of war in any form.

It seems fairly certain that these group differences in morale do not constitute any threat to national unity in the war effort. Sophisticated and unsophisticated do not have different programs for political action any more than do men and women. Isolationism persists not as an organized political movement, but as a point of view, an emotional attitude which in 1942 seemed to be gradually breaking down under the impact of the contemporary world.

CONCLUSIONS

In this chapter we have shown how the principles of public opinion measurement can be applied to the problem of gauging the nation's morale. We have presented a set of questions which provide an objective measure of morale in any section of the adult civilian population. These questions have been validated by their relation to actual performance in the war effort. Though there are other, and perhaps better, methods of measuring morale in wartime, we have shown that ours is sufficiently accurate to describe in detail changes in the level of morale, and to reveal something of its complex pattern.

PART VI

APPENDICES

APPENDIX I

The Measurement of Civilian Morale: Technical Notes[1]

The aim of this appendix will be to describe in detail certain methods used in treating the data provided by the two morale ballots, and to include enough of these data so that it will be possible for the reader to see on precisely what evidence the conclusions in the text are based. Each of the sections in this appendix refers to a specific section of the text, which is indicated in the margin. Copies of the two morale ballots used will be found at the end of this appendix.

The definition of morale is taken from G. W. Allport and H. A. Murray. See "Notes on the Definition of Morale" in the *Worksheets on Morale* of the Department of Psychology, Harvard University. January 1942.

> p. 234.
> The definition of morale.

The reader is referred to Hadley Cantril, "Public Opinion in Flux" in the *Annals of the American Academy of Political and Social Science*, March 1942, for a full account of American attitudes toward the war from its outbreak until our own entry.

> p. 235.
> American public opinion in the fall of 1941.

In wartime, respondents with unpopular views may refuse to express their true opinions; this may seriously bias any survey of morale. The bias may take two forms: (1) low-morale people may refuse to be interviewed, making the cross-section actually obtained unrepresentative; or (2) they may answer the questions, but in a way that reflects majority opinion rather than their own attitudes.

> pp. 238 f.
> Cross-sections for the morale ballots.

We investigated the first possibility by instructing our interviewers on the March ballot to keep a record of *every person approached for an interview*, including the characteristics and the reasons for refusal of the people who could not be interviewed. Four hundred twenty-nine refusals were recorded, as compared with 2,539 complete interviews. The reasons for failing to complete the interview were given by the interviewers as follows:

Reason	Per cent of Cases
Respondent refuses to talk about anything—too busy, not interested, or suspicious.	76%
Respondent refuses to talk about the war.	6
Interview discontinued—respondent can't understand questions, or talks at random.	12
Interruptions.	2

[1] By John Harding. More complete description of all the methods used together with a bibliography will be found in the writer's doctoral thesis "The Measurement of Civilian Morale" on file in Widener Library, Cambridge, Mass.

Respondent is sick.	3		
Respondent cannot be included in interviewer's assignment—interviewer has approached the wrong person.	1		
Number of Cases	429		

About the only thing this table tells us is that only a tiny fraction of respondents explicitly refuse to talk about the war. Examination of the objective characteristics of the people who are approached but not interviewed shows that they deviate from the regular cross-section in directions which might be expected—more women, more poor people, more old people—but by amounts which do not exceed 10 per cent. (See Chapter 9 of this volume for a more complete discussion of this problem.)

pp. 238 f.
Cross-sec-
tions for the
morale bal-
lots.

Since the reported vote in 1940 was a fairly good index of morale on both ballots we can use this to check the extent of the combined bias in our estimates of national morale resulting from interviewing too many high-morale people, and getting too many high-morale answers from low-morale people.

The following table shows the actual distribution of the presidential vote in 1940 among those old enough to vote; the distribution for the AIPO cross-section (the average of two polls taken in December 1940); and the distribution on each of our morale ballots:

TABLE 82. REPORTED VOTE IN 1940

	Roosevelt	Willkie	Other*	Didn't Vote
Election Figures	32.5%	26.6%	.3%	40.6%
AIPO cross-section Dec. 1940	44	40	2	14
Ballot 810 Nov. 1941	47	37	1	15
Ballot 813 Mar. 1942	48	35	1	16

* On the polls this category includes people for whom nothing was recorded except the fact that they voted.

Two things stand out in this table. The first is that the people interviewed on each of the polls voted to a much greater extent than did the rest of the population. This is true because the AIPO cross-section, which is essentially the cross-section we used on the two morale ballots, was designed to represent the voting population and systematically underrepresents the South, the uneducated, and the lower-income groups. In the text we refer to the opinions of "the American people" for purposes of convenience when we really mean the opinions of the voting public; our figures must be corrected for the differences in morale between voters and nonvoters to become unbiased estimates of the morale of the adult population as a whole.

The second fact which stands out from Table 82 is that while the AIPO cross-section began by overrepresenting the Willkie voters, our morale ballots give Roosevelt an even larger majority than he actually obtained. If we assume that the proportion of people who actually did vote for Roosevelt was the same on all of the cross-sections, the figures show that a year after the elections more people *said* they voted for Roosevelt. If we assume that the reported vote for Roosevelt on the December ballots, taken immediately after the election, represents the proportion of the AIPO cross-section who actually *did* vote for Roosevelt, then our figures show that a year later more people *said* they voted for Roosevelt than really had. This difference has been verified on many AIPO ballots taken in 1942; it represents a tendency toward conformity with majority opinion.

On a ballot sent out June 17, 1942 we asked: "Before the Japs attacked us at Pearl Harbor, a lot of people thought we should try to keep out of war rather than run the risk of getting in by sending supplies to England and Russia. Were you in favor of risking war by sending supplies to England, or were you in favor of trying to keep out of war?" Thirty-five per cent said they had favored trying to keep out of war. One year earlier—June 10, 1941—we had asked: "Which of these two things do you think is more important for the United States to try to do: To help Britain, even at the risk of getting into the war, *or* To keep out of war ourselves?" and 34 per cent had answered: "To keep out of war ourselves." At the same time 32 per cent thought it was more important that we keep out of war than that Germany be defeated. By November 1941 only 28 per cent of our cross-section thought it was more important that we keep out than that Germany be defeated. In other words, after six months of war the number of people admitting to isolationist views before Pearl Harbor *is greater than the number that actually held such views.* Here is the band-wagon effect in reverse.

Our conclusions from the available evidence are: (1) biases in our morale surveys resulting from the unwillingness of low-morale people to express their true opinions are small in size and are confined to particular questions. There is no evidence for any general distortion of answers resulting from people's desire to appear more "war-minded" than they actually are. (2) However, our cross-section represents the voting population of the country rather than the total adult popu-

pp. 238 f. Cross-sections for the morale ballots.

lation, and both our surveys show higher morale among voters than among nonvoters. This fact must be taken into account in generalizing from our findings. For a discussion of the AIPO political cross-section, the reader is referred to Chapter 11.

pp. 238 f.,
253 f. Figs.
31, 41. The
method of
measuring
level of mo-
rale.

If we wish to answer questions such as: What was the general level of civilian morale at a certain date? and What were the strong and weak points in morale? we need some scheme of evaluating responses to the various questions on a ballot. Any such scheme must be rather arbitrary. Our conclusions about the general level of morale will depend on the standards we set for high morale, and our conclusions concerning the level of the various components will depend on the extent to which the questions measuring them are comparable.

If we have some external criterion of morale we can determine the high-morale answers to a question objectively by noting which answers agree most closely with the criterion. If we do not have such a criterion we must simply use our own judgment as to which answers indicate high morale and which do not. On our first ballot we used the latter procedure; on our second ballot the former.

Having determined which answer to a question indicates high morale, we describe the morale of the people of the United States as *high* with respect to that question if 75 per cent or more of them choose the high-morale answer; *moderate* if between 50 per cent and 75 per cent of them choose the high-morale answer; and *low* if less than 50 per cent of them choose the high-morale answer.

Averaging the results of the questions measuring a given component enables us to compress our data somewhat and also to generalize our findings. Though the questions measuring them have changed, there is a strong tendency for the components of morale to occupy the same positions in March as in November. This may be verified by examining Figures 31 and 41; a tabular summary is given in Table 83.

pp. 241 f.
Interrelation-
ship of ques-
tions and
components
on first sur-
vey.

For a preliminary study of this problem we considered all the possible combinations of answers to the questions measuring a given morale component, and classified these *combinations* into those indicating high morale, those indicating moderate morale, and those indicating low morale. By this means it was possible to assign each individual a score for each morale component; the scores were given the arbitrary values of 0 for low, 2 for moderate, and 4 for high morale on a particular component. These scores were then punched on the cards and each component was run against every other component. A statistic similar to the fourfold point correlation coefficient was computed to measure the intensity of association between each pair of components. The conclusions in the

TABLE 83. POSITION OF MORALE COMPONENT IN NOVEMBER

	High	Moderate	Low	Absent
High in March	War objective attainable.	Confidence in the leader. Agreement.		
Moderate in March		Determination. Awareness.	Confidence in news.	Basic values. Feeling of participation. Confidence in subleaders.
Low in March			Peace objective attainable. Magnitude of the task. Sense of unity.	Hatred of the enemy.
Not Validated in March	Confidence in Russians. Armed forces vs. Japan.	Confidence in British. Satisfaction with group progress.	Armed forces vs. Germany.	

pp. 241 f.
Interrelation-
ship of ques-
tions and
components
on first
survey.

text concerning patterns of morale were reached from an examination of these coefficients of association. (Cf. *A Survey
of Morale*, Office of Public Opinion Research, February 6,
1942.)

To verify these conclusions and to study the value of the
individual questions as measures of morale, we computed tetrachoric correlations between each question and every other
question. The answers to a question were dichotomized by
giving the value 1 to the answer which we thought indicated
high morale (see pp. 238 f. in the text) and the value 0 to
all other answers. With the use of Thurstone's *Computing
Diagrams* (obtainable from the University of Chicago Book-
store), it is possible to compute tetrachoric correlation coefficients in an average time of only ten or fifteen minutes, including all operations. The intercorrelations of the questions on
the first morale ballot are presented in Table 84.

An examination of these correlation coefficients will verify
the statements made in the text. The average correlation among
the Awareness and Information questions is .43; among the
questions measuring Confidence in the leader, Satisfaction
with group progress, Confidence in the news, and Confidence
in the armed forces the average correlation is .32 if we exclude
question 8, which has a substantial positive correlation with
information and hence does not belong with this group. The
average correlation of this group (excluding question 8) with
the questions measuring Awareness and Information is —.04.

We extracted two centroid factors from the correlation
matrix, following Thurstone's rules of procedure. They account for 24 per cent and 11 per cent of the question variance,
respectively. Table 85 shows the saturations of the questions
with these two factors.

Six out of the eight questions most highly saturated with
Factor I are included in the two morale components Agreement and Determination; no question measuring these two
components ranks lower than eighth. Loadings on the first
centroid factor represent essentially correlations with the sum
or average of all the questions in the battery.

Examination of question 1a, 25, and 28 shows that Factor I
is essentially interventionism. It is interesting that the question
with the fourth highest loading on this factor is No. 19 on
approval of Roosevelt. At this time, approval of Roosevelt may
have been largely determined by approval of his foreign policy.

We can interpret the loadings on Factor I as validations of
the various questions by the criterion of internal consistency.
All of the questions satisfy this criterion to a moderate degree
except 12a and b. The "high" group on this question were

TABLE 84. TETRACHORIC CORRELATIONS—FIRST BALLOT

	Ia	2	3a	4b	6	7	8	10	11	12 a,b	13	14a	15a	17a	18	19	20	22a	24 a,b	25	26	27 a,c	28
Ia		59	30	36	-04	03	30	27	51	-01	21	18	23	57	63	44	12	35	39	63	21	23	72
2			36	22	-18	-04	35	13	36	-04	33	11	30	39	35	27	05	20	20	46	41	19	42
3a				18	-08	00	24	20	23	-04	30	06	27	14	08	04	-21	10	07	16	40	19	18
4b					13	12	19	04	16	01	05	23	20	26	25	50	25	38	10	44	10	19	38
6						66	09	-03	07	-10	-24	12	-09	07	08	22	27	12	09	12	-32	09	10
7							23	-03	10	-07	-18	06	-05	07	13	22	19	11	03	23	-24	10	12
8								17	31	-17	35	-01	30	18	06	18	-13	16	10	27	39	14	19
10									27	-24	10	00	19	20	11	10	-03	07	45	16	08	06	27
11										-03	23	12	23	43	39	32	01	25	32	44	17	24	52
12a&b											00	03	04	00	07	00	00	07	11	-01	-03	-05	03
13												-07	36	04	-01	02	-24	06	05	14	59	-10	09
14a													15	25	29	32	21	16	08	31	-07	07	28
15a														30	07	08	-18	20	07	21	36	25	13
17a															52	38	21	28	28	52	05	21	57
18																41	23	29	37	53	-05	16	57
19																	56	64	15	60	-03	15	54
20																		34	05	25	-35	04	22
22a																			09	46	05	23	35
24a&b																				27	-02	14	40
25																					14	30	63
26																						04	07
27a&c																							26
28																							

Mean of the absolute values of the coefficients = .21.

TABLE 85. FACTOR SATURATIONS ON FIRST BALLOT

	Question	Factor I	Factor II	Morale Component
pp. 241 f.	1a	.78	.09	Agreement.
Interrelation-	25	.77	—.18	Satisfaction with group progress.
ship of ques-	28	.75	—.12	Determination.
tions and	19	.66	—.45	Confidence in leader.
components	17a	.63	—.07	Agreement.
on first sur-	11	.61	.14	Agreement.
vey.	2	.60	.32	Determination.
	18	.59	—.20	Agreement.
	22a	.54	—.27	Confidence in leader.
	4b	.51	—.20	Confidence in news.
	8	.46	.35	Confidence in armed forces.
	24a & b	.39	.07	Magnitude of task.
	15a	.38	.30	Confidence in allies.
	3a	.36	.38	Awareness.
	27a & c	.34	—.04	Peace objective attainable.
	10	.32	.28	Magnitude of task.
	14a	.31	—.25	Confidence in allies.
	13	.26	.60	(Information.)
	7	.25	—.38	Confidence in armed forces.
	26	.25	.64	(Information.)
	20	.24	—.60	Satisfaction with group progress.
	6	.20	—.46	Confidence in armed forces.
	12a & b	—.05	—.08	Magnitude of task.

those who thought that we would win a war against Japan but that it would be difficult. Since nearly everybody thought we would win, the discriminating part of the question is that concerning the difficulty of the war. We counted as "high" the 35 per cent of our sample who thought the war would be difficult, but this opinion seems if anything to have indicated a tendency toward low morale.

Factor II we have named *sophistication*. The average saturation of the Awareness and Information questions with this factor is .57; the average saturation of the questions measuring Confidence in the leader, Satisfaction with group progress, Confidence in the news and Confidence in the armed forces (excluding question 8) with Factor II is —.36. Factors I and II are, of course, uncorrelated.

Nineteen of the questions seemed from their saturations with Factor I to be most diagnostic of general morale. These were 1a, 25, 28, 19, 17a, 11, 2, 18, 22a, 4b, 8, 24a & b, 15a, 3a, 27a, 27c, 10, 14a, and 20. An individual was given one point for each high-morale answer on these questions and the points were added to give a total morale score. Its distribution is given in Table 86.

Tables 87 and 88 show the morale scores of various groups as of November 1941.

TABLE 86

Score	Number of Cases	Score	Number of Cases
19	20	9	167
18	74	8	134
17	135	7	100
16	216	6	105
15	238	5	79
14	254	4	57
13	269	3	40
12	251	2	17
11	199	1	9
10	176	0	3

p. 242. Total morale scores.

N = 2543.
Mean = 11.69.
Standard deviation = 3.89.

TABLE 87. MORALE BY NATIONALITY BACKGROUND

	Score	Number of Cases
Both parents U. S.	11.8	1707
United Nations	12.9	276
Ireland	11.9	98
Germany and Italy	9.8	194
Other foreign	12.1	237

pp. 242 f. Group differences in morale.

TABLE 88. MORALE BY ECONOMIC STATUS AND VOTE IN 1940

	Democrats		Republicans		Other	
	Score	No. Cases	Score	No. Cases	Score	No. Cases
Upper	13.6	132	10.8	185	10.8	30
Middle	13.2	390	10.9	373	11.5	111
Poor	12.7	472	10.5	287	10.7	290
Relief	12.3	127	9.5	34	9.8	62

Table 88 shows that when political affiliation is held constant there is a tendency for morale to increase with economic status, especially among Democrats.

There is in the total sample, however, an insignificant cor-

TABLE 89. MORALE BY SECTIONS

	Score	Number of Cases
South	12.9	327
Rocky Mountain	12.5	86
New England	12.4	187
Pacific Coast	12.0	241
Middle Atlantic	11.7	743
West Central	11.4	386
East Central	10.9	573

TABLE 90. MORALE BY EDUCATION AND ECONOMIC STATUS

| | Grade School | | High School | | College | |
	Score	No. Cases	Score	No. Cases	Score	No. Cases
Upper	11.0	54	11.9	122	12.1	152
Middle	12.2	167	11.9	396	12.0	260
Poor	11.5	404	11.8	468	11.7	105
On Relief	11.0	130	11.5	61	14.2	6

pp. 242 f.
Group differences in morale.

TABLE 91. MORALE BY ECONOMIC STATUS AND AGE

| | Under 30 | | 30-49 | | 50 and Over | |
	Score	No. Cases	Score	No. Cases	Score	No. Cases
Upper	11.4	34	12.0	157	12.0	141
Middle	12.0	173	11.8	445	12.2	226
Poor	11.5	262	11.9	473	11.3	287
On Relief	12.0	21	11.4	73	10.9	126

TABLE 92. MORALE BY ECONOMIC STATUS AND SEX

| | Men | | Women | |
	Score	No. Cases	Score	No. Cases
Upper	12.1	220	11.5	125
Middle	12.2	468	11.7	402
Poor	12.0	466	11.3	572
On Relief	11.8	99	10.7	123

TABLE 93. MORALE BY RELIGION

	Score	No. of Cases
Protestants	11.7	1502
Catholics	11.3	439
Jews	14.0	69
Non-Church Members	11.8	504

TABLE 94. MORALE BY OCCUPATION

	Score	No. of Cases
Businessmen	12.3	290
Skilled workers	12.1	322
Clerical	12.0	449
Professional	11.9	330
Farmers	11.5	429
Semiskilled	11.5	257
Housewives	11.3	136
Unskilled	11.2	178
Servants	11.0	27
Unemployed	10.5	40
Retired and No Occupation	10.3	37

relation between morale and economic status, probably because so many upper-income people are Republicans.

A special study was made of the 67 people with morale scores of 0 to 3 to find out whether their low scores were the result of actual negative attitudes on all the questions or merely of indifference to the issues involved. The following distribution of "No opinions" and "No answers" was obtained:

TABLE 95

Number of Questions Answered "No Opinion" or Not Answered	Number of Cases
0	15
1 to 5	29
6 to 10	12
11 to 15	11
More than 15	0

Mean = 4.4. This is 23% of the 19 questions studied.

While this percentage is high, compared with that of the rest of our sample, it is nevertheless true that more than three-fourths of the low morale tallies made against these individuals were for negative attitudes rather than for failure to take a stand.

These low-morale individuals came from all sections of the population, with no one group being much overrepresented. This bespeaks the importance of personal, subjective factors as determinants of morale. Most of the variance in morale score remains unaccounted for by the determinants which we were able to study; it is literally true that the *causes* of high and low morale remain a mystery.

This low-morale group can best be described as intensely isolationist. Though 90 per cent thought it was more important that we keep out of war than that Germany be defeated, only two people seemed from their comments to be actually pro-German. Twelve per cent approved of the way Roosevelt was handling his job as President, and only 3 per cent thought the government was giving them as much information as it should about the war. Only 4 per cent thought we should take further steps against Japanese aggression. Only one person thought that a lasting peace *could* be worked out after the war, and he did not believe it would be.

pp. 242 f. Group differences in morale.

The distribution of participation scores on the second ballot is presented in Table 96.

According to our definition, morale is a psychological factor which makes a difference to the success or failure of an enterprise. In the present investigation we are concerned with social

TABLE 96

pp. 245 f.
Critical dis-
cussion of the
validation
procedure.

Score	Number of Cases	Per cent of Sample
4	127	5%
3	730	29
2	1045	41
1	490	19
0	147	6

Mean = 2.08   N = 2539

attitudes as indicators of morale, and we have assumed that a given attitude indicates high morale if it is associated with a high degree of participation in those war activities open to civilians.

p. 241. The
morale com-
ponent the-
ory.

The notion of "morale components" can be viewed as a working hypothesis to explain the relationships which we find to exist between certain attitudes and performance in the war effort. It assumes (1) that there are a number of generalized attitudes which work together as motivating factors, as *causes of performance*; (2) that the explanation of the relationship between participation score and the answers to various specific questions is that these questions measure, to a greater or less degree, these generalized attitudes; and (3) that the integrated total of these generalized attitudes is what we mean by morale.

We cannot claim to have demonstrated this hypothesis, though all our data are in accord with it. A strong point in favor of the morale component theory is that out of twenty-five questions which were expected to be diagnostic of differences in performance because they represented various "components of morale," eighteen actually turned out to differentiate significantly between high-participation people and low-participation people when education and economic status were held constant. Also for all except one of these eighteen questions (15a) the differences in performance were in the direction which the morale component theory had predicted.

p. 254. Inter-
correlations
on second
survey.

On the second morale ballot we calculated tetrachoric correlations by the same method as before, using a dichotomous classification of "high-morale" and "low-morale" answers. The "high-morale" answers for the 18 questions measuring morale components are given on pp. 238 and 239. We also included in the correlational analysis question 13, measuring information; question 15a, measuring *lack* of hatred of the German people; and the seven questions which were not related to participation score (apart from their mutual dependence on education and economic status). On these "non-morale component" questions we classified the answers according to the scheme in Table 97.

TABLE 97

Question	"High-morale" answers	"Low-morale" answers
13	4 or more countries correctly identified.	All others.
15a	Treat them kindly; treat them kindly *but* firmly.	All others.
2a	Could be doing more.	All others.
5	United States.	All others.
6	United States.	All others.
8	Yes.	All others.
12a	Yes; They won't win.	All others.
16	Yes.	All others.
21	Jobs for everyone; some unemployment but not a great deal; unemployment for a while, but then recovery.	All others.

This classification is of course arbitrary in most cases. However, we need it to interpret the sign of the correlation coefficients in Table 98.

The questions on the second ballot were more heterogeneous than those on the first, and as a result the average of the absolute values of the correlations is .14 as compared with .21 on the November ballot. On the earlier ballot we needed a single factor to represent degree of morale, because this was the only criterion we could use to validate our questions. On the later ballot we have validated the questions by an external criterion, participation score, and so can represent degree of morale by several independent factors if we wish.

pp. 254-257. The method of factor analysis used on second ballot.

One of the objections to multiple factor analysis is the difficulty of interpreting the factors once they have been obtained. We can avoid this difficulty, and save ourselves a great deal of work at the same time, if we can define each factor by a single question on our ballot. If we look at the questions in our first cluster of high correlation coefficients (3, 7, 13, 14), No. 3 seems to be the one which has the best combination of high correlations with the other questions in that cluster and near-zero correlations with the questions in the other two clusters (17, 18b, 24 and 16, 19, 20, 21, 22, 23, respectively). This question, offering a choice between an offensive and a defensive war, is the one which most nearly corresponds to the intervention-isolation questions which formed the core of the first ballot. For these reasons it seems well fitted to define a factor.

If we take question 24 as the central question in our second cluster we can define a second factor, independent of the first.

It is noteworthy that in March approval of Roosevelt, measured by question 24, correlates only .06 and .04 with questions 3 and 7, measuring support of the war. On the November ballot, approval of Roosevelt correlated .44 with

Table 98. Tetrachoric Correlations—Second Ballot

	2a	3	4	5	6	7	8	9a	10	11	12	13	14	15a	15b	16	17	18b	19	20	21	22	23	24	25a	29
1	17	19	12	-09	04	28	07	14	03	19	11	27	24	10	00	15	08	-03	09	17	07	13	10	09	08	23
2a		23	-05	-21	12	34	-20	18	09	07	04	36	27	08	09	09	-18	-30	04	16	00	01	-04	-24	04	12
3			17	-08	01	52	10	32	09	33	17	34	41	08	12	21	-01	-06	10	28	09	18	11	06	06	30
4				11	06	24	20	11	01	15	18	04	16	10	04	10	24	13	10	17	13	15	11	36	-10	18
5					27	-03	06	00	-13	12	20	-31	-07	-03	-01	-02	25	18	01	-02	09	05	06	14	13	-01
6						05	09	10	02	15	03	-07	05	-05	09	11	15	16	11	-03	14	10	10	13	02	05
7							-02	26	18	44	29	41	46	09	24	19	-05	-16	15	34	10	15	15	04	14	23
8								07	01	18	05	-09	03	-06	16	16	25	20	11	04	13	14	14	24	02	09
9a									11	23	03	32	30	05	06	18	08	02	03	23	09	13	18	07	14	06
10										09	12	13	14	06	05	-01	02	-10	04	12	-04	02	02	21	06	20
11											25	19	33	03	19	14	07	-02	09	-04	10	19	09	14	13	17
12												06	21	02	17	09	05	-09	01	24	01	08	05	-17	07	22
13													49	20	01	12	-14	-22	26	18	11	14	14	15	11	28
14														23	-16	24	05	-14	24	40	19	30	17	05	12	13
15a															08	-05	-07	-03	24	43	26	11	05	-01	-02	19
15b																05	-05	-14	-08	24	01	-03	15	14	03	07
16																	20	03	14	-02	22	24	22	47	10	14
17																		38	12	15	15	17	20	36	06	07
18b																			05	02	05	07	25	05	12	02
19																				-04	18	20	25	03	11	17
20																					15	35	17	19	11	21
21																							17	28	08	13
22																								08	04	19
23																									04	08
24																										27
25a																										00

question 1a (Keep out of war *vs.* Defeat Germany) and .27
with question 2 (Peace at present basis).

We have already observed that in November approval of
Roosevelt seemed to be determined to a considerable extent
by approval of his foreign policy—in other words, at this time
the question measured not only Confidence in the leader but
also Agreement with the objective. But in March, with the
United States actually in the war, Roosevelt's foreign policy
was no longer an issue, and it was possible for approval of
Roosevelt and support of the war to vary independently. Con-
firmation of this change is found in the fact that while Democrats were considerably higher than Republicans on the interventionist questions in November, the March morale ballot
finds Republicans and Democrats equally in favor of an offensive war (and equally against a negotiated peace).

Question 19 is the one in the third cluster which correlates
least with the two questions we have already chosen; we can
use it to define a third factor uncorrelated with the other two
which will represent the new questions on the second ballot
which have no counterpart on the first.

In precise terms, we are assuming three orthogonal common
factors in terms of which we propose to describe all the questions on the ballot and explain all the intercorrelations in our
table. We assume that question 3 is highly correlated with the
first of these hypothetical factors but uncorrelated with the
other two; that question 24 is highly correlated with the second
but uncorrelated with the first and the third; and that question
19 is highly correlated with the third but uncorrelated with the
first two. These latter assumptions require us to regard the
observed correlations between our three criterial questions
(.06, .10, and .05) as the result of sampling error. This is very
unlikely since the standard errors of these coefficients are
somewhere around .03 or .04, but, since we are interested only
in a rough and approximate analysis, our assumptions are
sufficiently accurate for working purposes.

The goal of our analysis is to find the saturations of the
various questions with our three factors. To do this we must
make some assumption about the saturation of each of our
criterial questions with the factor it represents. Looking again
at our table of intercorrelations, we find that question 3 is
most highly correlated with question 7 and that their correlations with the other questions form a similar pattern. It is
reasonable then to assume that their factorial compositions are
similar, and specifically that their saturations with Factor I are
about the same. Since Factor I is the only factor which they
can have in common (because we are assuming that the saturation of question 3 with the other two factors is 0), their satura-

pp. 254-257.
The method
of factor
analysis used
on second
ballot.
(Cont.)

tion with this factor should be equal to the square root of their correlation with each other (.52). In other words, the saturation of question 3 with the first factor is approximately .7.

If we apply a similar process of reasoning to explain the correlation of question 24 with question 17 (which is the question most like it in the table), we arrive at an estimate of .7 for the saturation of question 24 with Factor II. Because there is no question which is really similar to question 19, we have no grounds for any empirical estimate of its saturation with Factor III. But as a first approximation we can assume that it also is .7.

pp. 254-257.
The method
of factor
analysis used
on second
ballot.
(Cont.)

Since the correlation between any two questions is equal to the sum of the products of their saturations with the factors they have in common, we estimate the saturations of all the questions with each of the three factors from their correlations with our three criterial questions. The next step is to use these estimated factor saturations to attempt to reproduce the observed correlations between the various questions themselves. If we subtract from the observed correlations the theoretical correlations deduced from the factor saturations, the residuals should be equal to zero (within the limits of sampling error) if all our assumptions have been correct, *and if there are no common factors other than the three we have postulated.*

Actually we find that the mean of the absolute values of the residuals is .065, if we ignore the residuals involving our three criterial questions, which are of course all 0. This is a great deal less than .14, the mean of the absolute values of the correlations from which we started, but still is a considerable distance from 0.

It is possible, theoretically, to estimate the factor saturations of a question from its correlations with *any* group of questions whose factor saturations are known. Since we are now assuming that we know approximately the factor saturations of all our questions, it is legitimate to change our estimate of the factor saturations of a single question if this will give us an improved estimate of its correlations with all the other questions, even though it worsens our estimate of its correlations with the criterial questions. On this principle we changed twelve of our eighty-one estimated factor saturations, and recalculated our theoretical correlation matrix. The mean of the absolute values of the residuals (including those involving the three criterial questions) is now .04. This is about as good a fit as can usually be obtained with three common factors in a matrix of this size. We have probably not exhausted all the common factors present in the questions—e.g. there is still a residual correlation of .23 between questions 5 and 6, and we can attribute this to a factor of "confidence in the armed forces" which is common to these two questions but not to any others on the ballot. However, if we were to continue any further, our original aim of simplifying our description of the questions would be largely nullified.

It is clear from the rough-and-ready methods we have adopted that we take a nominalist rather than a realist position concerning factor analysis. We regard it as essentially a method of classification, not as a means of bringing to light hidden causes.

Table 99 gives the factor saturations of all our questions. The sum of the squares of the factor saturations of a given question represents the proportion of its total variance which is attributable to the three common factors; this sum is called the *communality* of the question. The remainder of the variance of a question is called its *uniqueness*. Its size represents the extent to which a question is uncorrelated with the others

pp. 254-257.
The method
of factor
analysis used
on second
ballot.
(Cont.)

TABLE 99. FACTOR SATURATIONS ON SECOND BALLOT

Question	Factor I	Factor II	Factor III	Communality	Uniqueness
7*	.74	.10	.10	.57	.43
3*	.70	.00	.00	.49	.51
14*	.59	.01	.34	.46	.54
13*	.49	—.24	.37	.43	.57
11*	.47	.20	.10	.27	.73
9a*	.46	.10	.19	.26	.74
2a	.33	—.34	.06	.23	.77
29*	.30	.20	.24	.19	.81
16	.30	.20	.20	.17	.83
1*	.27	.13	.13	.11	.89
12	.24	.20	.01	.10	.90
15b*	.17	.01	—.11	.04	.96
10*	.13	.10	.06	.03	.97
24*	.00	.70	.00	.49	.51
17*	—.10	.67	.17	.49	.51
4*	.24	.51	.14	.34	.66
22*	.26	.40	.29	.31	.69
18b*	—.30	.40	.10	.26	.74
8	—.10	.34	.16	.15	.85
21	.13	.27	.26	.16	.84
5	—.11	.20	.01	.05	.95
6	.01	.19	.16	.06	.94
19*	.00	.00	.70	.49	.51
20*	.40	.04	.51	.42	.58
23*	.16	.11	.36	.17	.83
15a*	.11	—.03	.26	.08	.92
25a	.09	.06	.17	.04	.96
Total Variance	2.99	2.18	1.68	6.86	20.14

APPENDICES

and sufficient unto itself. In the table the questions are grouped according to the factor with which they are most highly saturated. The starred questions are those diagnostic of actual performance in the war effort.

What psychological meaning can we give to these factors? We cannot identify them completely with our three criterial questions because only half the variance of each question is attributable to the common factor; the rest being specific to that question, or attributable to errors of measurement. We must also take into account the other questions which are saturated with the common factors.

pp. 254-257. The method of factor analysis used on second ballot. (Cont.)

We want a name for that part of a belief in an offensive war which represents not only Determination but Agreement with the objective, Awareness, and Belief that the objective can be attained. This factor might be called *Reasoned determination to achieve the objective*. It accounts for 11 per cent of the question variance and is the dominant factor in the four questions most diagnostic of performance. It is the legitimate successor of the "Interventionist" or "General morale factor" on the first ballot.

Factor II represents *Confidence in leaders*, not only in President Roosevelt but also in government officials, military leaders, and our foreign allies. It is natural that this factor should be dominant in questions 22 and 21, which represent in a general way confidence in the post-war world. This factor accounts for 8 per cent of the question variance. It is not the same as our factor of sophistication-naive faith on the first ballot because that factor was defined as uncorrelated with general morale. However, Factor II on this ballot represents one aspect of morale, although not such an important aspect as Factor I, since the questions with high saturations in it do not rank so high in diagnostic value for performance.

Factor II is more difficult to interpret. Question 19: "Do you think most people can be trusted?" is correlated only .05 with question 18b: "Are there any people or groups here in the United States that you think are taking unfair advantage of the war to get money or power for themselves?"; which seems to indicate that question 19 represents more lip-service to a principle than actual "confidence in other members of the group." The three questions which are highest in Factor III are the ones which were designed to measure "Basic values." They are highly correlated with education and economic status. The factor which is common to them, and independent of our other two factors, seems to be a *Satisfaction with traditional values*, which corresponds approximately to the general factor in the Rundquist-Sletto scales from which questions 19 and 23 were taken. This factor accounts for only 6 per cent of the question variance, but the questions saturated with it are all highly diagnostic of performance, and it is the only factor that is appreciably correlated (.17) with question 25a, which measures the feeling of participation.

PRINCETON UNIVERSITY
OFFICE OF PUBLIC OPINION RESEARCH

1. a. Which of these two things do you think is the more important—
   ☐ That this country keep out of war, or
   ☐ That Germany be defeated?   ☐ No choice
   b. What is your chief reason for thinking it is more important that (this country keep out of war); (Germany be defeated)?
   ....
   ....
   ....

   If "Germany be defeated" or "No choice" on a, ask:
   c. If you were asked to vote today on the question of the United States entering the war now against Germany and Italy, how would you vote—to go into the war now, or to stay out of the war?
   ☐ Go in   ☐ Stay out   ☐ No Opinion
              (Only voters who want to go in NOW should be marked "Go in")

2. If peace could be obtained today on the basis of Britain keeping the British Empire as it now stands, and Germany holding the countries she has conquered so far, would you be in favor of such a peace?
   ☐ Yes   ☐ No   ☐ No Opinion
   COMMENT ....

3. a. Do you feel that you have a clear idea of what the war is all about?
   ☐ Yes   ☐ No   ☐ No Opinion
   b. If "Yes", ask: What would you say the war is all about? ....
   ....
   ....

4. a. Do you feel that, in general, the information you are getting about the war situation is true and accurate?
   ☐ Yes   ☐ Qualified answer ....
                                ☐ No   ☐ Don't know
   COMMENT ....
   b. Do you think the government is giving the public as much information as it should about the war?
   ☐ Yes   ☐ Qualified answer ....
                                ☐ No   ☐ Don't know
   COMMENT ....

5. What problems do you think this country will be likely to face when the war is over?......................
   ....
   ....☐ Don't know any

6. Do you think that at the present time our army is as strong as the German army?
   ☐ YES!   ☐ NO!   ☐ Our army is stronger   ☐ Don't Know
   ☐ Yes   ☐ No   ☐ Qualified answer ....
                        (YES! and NO! are for emphatic answers)
   COMMENT ....
   ....

7. Do you think that at the present time our airforce is as strong as the German airforce?
   ☐ YES!   ☐ NO!   ☐ Our airforce is stronger   ☐ Don't know
   ☐ Yes   ☐ No   ☐ Qualified answer ....
   COMMENT ....
   ....

8. Do you think that at the present time our navy is strong enough to defeat the Japanese navy?

☐ YES! ☐ Yes ☐ NO! ☐ No ☐ Don't know

☐ Qualified answer ....

COMMENT ....

....

9. Do you have any relatives or close friends who are in the army or navy now?

☐ Yes ☐ No

10. Here are three ways to describe Germany's situation today. Which one of these statements comes closest to the way you feel? (HAND CARD TO RESPONDENT)

☐ a ☐ b ☐ c ☐ No choice ☐ Can't read

☐ Other ....

11. Should the United States take steps now to keep Japan from becoming more powerful, even if this means we have to go to war against Japan? .

☐ Yes ☐ No ☐ No Opinion

COMMENT ....

....

12. a. If this country should get into a war against Japan, do you think we would win, or lose?

☐ Win ☐ Lose ☐ Stalemate ☐ No Opinion

b. If "Win", ask: Do you think it would be a difficult war, or do you think it would be a comparatively easy war for us to win?

☐ Difficult ☐ Easy ☐ Don't Know

COMMENT ....

....

13. Which of the following territories have been occupied by Japan since the beginning of the present war with China? (HAND CARD TO RESPONDENT)

☐ Korea ☐ Australia

☐ Nanking ☐ Unable to answer

☐ French Indo-China ☐ Can't read

☐ Dutch East Indies

14. a. Do you believe the British are doing all they possibly can to win the war?

☐ Yes ☐ No ☐ No Opinion

b. If "No", ask: What more do you think they could do? ....

....

....

15. a. Do you think the Russians are doing all they possibly can to win the war?

☐ Yes ☐ No ☐ No Opinion

b. If "No", ask: What more do you think they could do? ....

....

....

16. Are you better off, or worse off today than you were six months ago?

☐ Better off ☐ Worse off ☐ About same ☐ No Opinion

COMMENT ....

17. a. Some people say that the biggest job facing this country today is to help defeat the Nazi government. Do you agree, or disagree?

☐ Agree ☐ Disagree ☐ No Opinion

COMMENT ....

b. If "Disagree", ask: What do you think is the biggest job facing this country today? ....

....

18. If Germany should defeat England and Russia in the present war, do you think Germany would start a war against the United States within the next ten years?

☐ Yes ☐ No ☐ No Opinion

19. In general, do you approve, or disapprove, of the way Roosevelt is handling his job as President today?
☐ Approve   ☐ Disapprove   ☐ No Opinion

20. Can you think of anything that a President of the United States should do that President Roosevelt has not done, or is not now doing?
☐ Yes   ☐ No

If "Yes", ask: What? ....

21. What plans do you think Roosevelt is most anxious to have carried out while he is President?...............
....
....☐ Don't know

22. a. Some people say that President Roosevelt is taking advantage of the war situation to carry out some of his pet plans which have nothing to do with defense. Do you agree, or disagree with this?
(Important not to explain this, or any other question to the respondent)
☐ Agree   ☐ Disagree   ☐ No Opinion   ☐ Don't understand question
b. If "Yes", ask: Do you approve, or disapprove, of President Roosevelt's taking advantage of the war to carry out his plans not connected with defense?
☐ Approve   ☐ Disapprove   ☐ No Opinion

23. In general, do you feel that any of the following people are doing less than others for national defense? (HAND CARD TO RESPONDENT AND ASK HIM TO GIVE THE LETTER OR NAME TO YOU.)

☐ (a) Farmers   ☐ (e) Protestants   ☐ (i) Labor leaders
☐ (b) Negroes   ☐ (f) Catholics   ☐ (j) Business men
☐ (c) Jews   ☐ (g) People on relief   ☐ (k) Wealthy people
☐ (d) Foreign-born   ☐ (h) Factory workers

☐ Any others ....
☐ None of these groups ☐ Can't read   ☐ Don't know
COMMENT ....
....

24. a. Do you think that in the long run Germany will win the war, or lose it?
☐ Will Win   ☐ Will Lose   ☐ Stalemate   ☐ No Opinion
b. If "Will lose", ask: Do you think our own army, navy, and airforce will have to fight in the war against Germany before she is defeated?
☐ Yes   ☐ Qualified answer ....
☐ No   ☐ No Opinion
COMMENT ....
....

25. As far as you, personally, are concerned, do you think the United States has gone too far in opposing Germany, or not far enough?
☐ Too far   ☐ About right   ☐ Not far enough   ☐ Don't know

26. Would you name as many countries as you can that have been conquered or occupied by Germany since the beginning of the war? ....
....
....
....☐ Can't name any

27. a. If Germany is defeated, do you think a peace that will last for at least 50 years can be worked out?
☐ Yes   ☐ No   ☐ No Opinion

b. If "No", ask: Why not? ....
....

c. If "Yes", on a, ask: Do you think that such a peace will be worked out?
☐ Yes   ☐ No   ☐ No Opinion
ASK EVERYBODY:
d. Do you happen to have any ideas that you would like to see put into a peace plan?.........................
....☐ No ideas

28. If our present leaders and military advisors say that the only way to defeat Germany is for this country to go into the war, would you be in favor of this country's going into the war against Germany?
☐ Yes   ☐ No   ☐ No Opinion

29. a. Do you remember FOR CERTAIN whether or not you voted in the 1940 Presidential election?
     ☐ Yes, voted   ☐ No, didn't vote   ☐ No, too young to vote
     b. If "Yes", ask: Did you vote for Willkie, Roosevelt or Thomas?
     ☐ Willkie   ☐ Roosevelt   ☐ Thomas   ☐ Other...................

30. Are you a member of a church?
☐ Yes   Which denomination?...   ☐ No

31. In what country were your parents born?   Father........................   Mother ....

32. Can you remember the name of a teacher you had in your last year of schooling—who was it?
     Name   Subject   Grade or Year   Name and Location of School

     INTERVIEWER: If respondent cannot recall names of any teachers in last year of schooling, record remaining information.

☐ Wealthy   ☐ AV   ☐ P   ☐ OR—WPA ☐ Car   ☐ Tel   ☐ Man   ☐ Wh.
☐ AV+   ☐ OAA   ☐ OR—Home Relief ☐ No Car   ☐ No Tel   ☐ Woman   ☐ Cl.
SPECIFIC OCCUPATION _____ ESTIMATE AGE_____
STREET _____ CITY _____

Is there a telephone in your home (place where you live)?   ☐ Yes   ☐ No
If "yes", ask: Is the telephone listed either under your name or the name of a member of your immediate family?   ☐ Yes   ☐ No

Interviewer _____

Date this interview was made...

N.º   2734

HAVE YOU CHECKED ANSWERS ON EACH QUESTION?

PRINCETON UNIVERSITY
OFFICE OF PUBLIC OPINION RESEARCH

1. Which do you think is our No. 1 enemy in the war—Japan or Germany?
   ¹· ☐ **Japan**   ²· ☐ **Germany**   ³· ☐ **Both**   ⁴· ☐ **No Opinion**

2a. Do you think we are now doing all we can to defeat Japan and Germany, or could we be doing more?
   ⁵· ☐ **Doing all we can**   ⁶· ☐ **Could be doing more**   ⁷· ☐ **No Opinion**
   If "Could be doing more" ask:
b. What more could we be doing? ....
   ....
   ....

3. Which of these two things do you think the United States should do:
   ¹· ☐ **Send most of our army abroad to fight the enemy wherever they are, or**
   ²· ☐ **Keep most of our army at home to protect the United States?**

   ³· ☐ **Qualified answer** ....
   ....⁴· ☐ **No Opinion**

4. Do you think the government is giving the public as much information as it should about the war?
   ☐ **Yes**   ☐ **No**   ☐ **Too much**   ☐ **No Opinion**
   Comment ....
   ....

5. Which do you think has the smartest military leaders at present—Germany or Russia or the United States?
   ¹· ☐ **Germany**   ²· ☐ **Russia**   ³· ☐ **United States**   ⁴· ☐ **No Opinion**

6. Which do you think has the strongest navy at present—Japan or England or the United States?
   ⁵· ☐ **Japan**   ⁶· ☐ **England**   ⁷· ☐ **United States**   ⁸· ☐ **No Opinion**

7. If Hitler offered peace now to all countries on the basis of not going farther, but of leaving matters as they are now, would you favor or oppose such a peace?
   ¹· ☐ **Favor**   ²· ☐ **Oppose**   ³· ☐ **No Opinion**

8. Do you think the British are doing all they possibly can to win the war?
   ⁴· ☐ **Yes**   ⁵· ☐ **No**   ⁶· ☐ **No Opinion**

9a. Do you feel that you have a clear idea of what the war is all about?
   ☐ **Yes**   ☐ **No**   ☐ **Qualified answer**.............................
   ....
   If "Yes" or a qualified answer, ask:
b. Briefly, what would you say the war IS all about? ....
   ....
   ....

10. About how much longer do you think the war will last? .... ☐ **No Opinion**
    (Please record in terms of years and months)

11. What will bring the war to an end?...
    ....
    ....

12a. Do you think that if Germany and Japan should win this war they would keep their armies over here to police the United States?
    ¹· ☐ **Yes**   ²· ☐ **No**   ³· ☐ **They won't win**   ⁴· ☐ **No Opinion**
    If "No" ask:
b. Why not? ....
   ....

HAVE YOU CHECKED ANSWERS ON EACH QUESTION?

13. (HAND MAP TO RESPONDENT) Here is a map of the world. (MAKE SURE THAT RESPONDENT UNDERSTANDS WHERE THE UNITED STATES, EUROPE, AND ASIA ARE ON THE MAP)

a. Can you find Alaska on the map
and tell me the number there?　　　　　　　　d. Brazil?

.... **Number**　　　☐ **Don't know**　　　　.............. **Number**　　　☐ **Don't know**

b. Can you find Australia?　　　　　　　　　　e. Iceland?

.... **Number**　　　☐ **Don't know**　　　　.............. **Number**　　　☐ **Don't know**

c. China?　　　　　　　　　　　　　　　　　f. India?

.... **Number**　　　☐ **Don't know**　　　　.............. **Number**　　　☐ **Don't know**

☐ **Can't understand map**

14. Which of these two things do you think the United States should try to do when the war is over:

☐ **Stay out of world affairs as much as we can, or**

☐ **Take an active part in world affairs?**　　　　　　　　　☐ **No Opinion**

MAIN REASON ....

....

15a. If we win the war, how do you think we should treat the people in Germany? ....

....

b. How should we treat the Nazi leaders? ....

....

16. Do you think Russia can be trusted to cooperate with us after the war is over?

☐ **Yes**　　　　　　　　　　☐ **No**　　　　　　　　　☐ **No Opinion**

MAIN REASON ....

....

17. As you know, a lot of new government offices have been set up in Washington especially to deal with national defense and war problems. From what you have heard, do you think most of these offices are doing a good job, or a poor one?

1.☐ **Good job**　　　　　　2.☐ **Poor job**　　　　　　3.☐ **Fair job**

4.☐ **Doing the best they can**　　　　　　　　　　　　5.☐ **No Opinion**

18a. Are there any people or groups here in the United States that you think are taking unfair advantage of the war to get money or power for themselves?

.... ☐ **None**

b. (HAND CARD TO RESPONDENT) Do you think any of these groups are taking unfair advantage of the war to get money or power for themselves?

1.☐ **Farmers**	5.☐ **Protestants**	9.☐ **Labor leaders**
2.☐ **Negroes**	6.☐ **Catholics**	0.☐ **Congressmen**
3.☐ **Jews**	7.☐ **People on relief**	v.☐ **Business men**
4.☐ **Foreign-born**	8.☐ **Factory workers**	x.☐ **Wealthy people**
1.☐ **None of these groups**	2.☐ **Can't read**	3.☐ **No Opinion**

19. Do you think most people can be trusted?

1.☐ **Yes**　　2.☐ **No**　　3.☐ **Qualified answer**......................................

.... 4.☐ **No Opinion**

20. Do you think success is dependent mostly on luck, on ability, or on pull?

5.☐ **Luck**　　　　6.☐ **Ability**　　　　7.☐ **Pull**　　　　8.☐ **No Opinion**

21. After the war is over, do you think there will be jobs for everyone or lots of unemployment?

1.☐ **Jobs for everyone**　　　　2.☐ **Lots of unemployment**

3.☐ **Qualified answer**...

.... 4.☐ **No Opinion**

22a. Do you have any children?　　　　　　☐ **Yes**　　　　　　　　☐ **No**

If "Yes" on a, ask:

b. Do you think your children twenty years from now will be better off or worse off than you are now?

1.☐ **Better**　　　　2.☐ **Worse**　　　　3.☐ **Same**　　　　4.☐ **No Opinion**

If "No" on a, say:

c. Well, suppose you had some children. Do you think that if you had some children they would be better off or worse off twenty years from now than you are now?

5.☐ **Better**　　　　6.☐ **Worse**　　　　7.☐ **Same**　　　　8.☐ **No Opinion**

HAVE YOU CHECKED ANSWERS ON EACH QUESTION?

23. Do you think a poor man gets just as fair treatment in the law courts as a rich man?
¹· ☐ **Yes**   ²· ☐ **No**   ³· ☐ **No Opinion**

24. In general, do you approve or disapprove of the way Roosevelt is handling his job as President today?
⁴· ☐ **Approve**   ⁵· ☐ **Disapprove**   ⁶· ☐ **No Opinion**

25a. Do you feel that you personally are doing something that is important in helping to win the war?
¹· ☐ **Yes**   ²· ☐ **No**   ³· ☐ **Qualified answer**...

....
If "Yes" or a qualified answer, ask:
b. What sort of thing are you doing?...,...............
....

26. Are you doing any work in the civilian defense program such as air raid warning, first aid, and the like?
¹· ☐ **Yes**   ²· ☐ **No**   ³· ☐ **No, but signed up**

27. Have you or your family bought any defense bonds or defense stamps?
⁴· ☐ **Yes**   ⁵· ☐ **No**

28a. Are you or your family saving materials such as metal, rubber, or waste paper?
☐ Yes   ☐ No
If "Yes," ask:
b. What materials are you saving?...

29. After finding out what each person can do, should the government have the power to tell each citizen what to do as his part in the war effort, and require him or her to do it?
☐ Yes   ☐ No   ☐ No Opinion
COMMENT ....
....

30a. Do you remember FOR CERTAIN whether or not you voted in the 1940 Presidential election?
¹· ☐ **Yes, voted**   ²· ☐ **No, didn't vote**   ³· ☐ **No, too young to vote**
If "Yes," ask:
b. Did you vote for Willkie, Roosevelt, or Thomas?
⁴· ☐ **Willkie**   ⁵· ☐ **Roosevelt**   ⁶· ☐ **Thomas**   ⁷· ☐ **Other**..............

31. Are you a member of a church?
☐ Yes   Which denomination?..   ☐ No

32. In what country were your parents born? Father....................... Mother ....

33a. Do you remember the name of the last school you attended? ....
b. How far did you go in that school?
                                                                          ☐ No schooling
¹· ☐ **Grammar school, incomplete**   ⁴· ☐ **High school, graduated**
²· ☐ **Grammar school, graduated**   ⁵· ☐ **College, incomplete**
³· ☐ **High school, incomplete**   ⁶· ☐ **College, graduated**
   ☐ **Other** ....

| ☐ Wealthy | ☐ AV | ☐ P | ☐ OR—WPA | ☐ Car | ☐ Man | ☐ Wh |
| ☐ AV+ | | ☐ OAA | ☐ OR—Home Relief | ☐ No Car | ☐ Woman | ☐ Cl. |

SPECIFIC OCCUPATION _____ ESTIMATE AGE_____

STREET _____ CITY _____

Is there a telephone in your home (place where you live)?   ☐ Yes   ☐ No
If "Yes", ask: Is the telephone listed either under your name or the name of a member of your immediate
family?   ☐ Yes   ☐ No

Place of interview: ☐ Home   ☐ Office   ☐ Street   ☐ Other _____

Interviewer ....

Date this interview was made ....
HAVE YOU CHECKED ANSWERS ON EACH QUESTION
AND ALL VITAL INFORMATION?

APPENDIX II

Correcting for Interviewer Bias[1]

The following formulae show why an even distribution of interviewers is the best one can do in a practical situation. They also indicate how an investigator may set limits on errors due to interviewer bias under various assumptions.

Formulae to adjust for interviewer bias. Let us suppose that on the average all interviewers interview the same number of respondents, or at least that:

$$\frac{\text{number of respondents interviewed by favorable interviewer}}{\text{number of respondents interviewed by not favorable interviewer}} = \frac{\text{number of favorable interviewers}}{\text{number of not favorable interviewers}}$$

Let us assume the following data:

(1)
p = true population proportion in favor of issue
n_1 = number of favorable interviewers
n_2 = number of unfavorable interviewers
$n = n_1 + n_2$ = total number of interviewers
$100\delta_1$ = percentage increase of favorable responses due to favorable interviewers
$100\delta_2$ = percentage decrease of favorable responses due to unfavorable interviewers.

Now in order to get the true population proportion as our sample estimate (assuming no sampling error) we must have

(2)
$$\frac{(p + \delta_1)n_1 + (p - \delta_2)n_2}{n_1 + n_2} = p,$$

which on rearranging gives the condition

$$\frac{\delta_1}{\delta_2} = \frac{n_2}{n_1}.$$

This means in order to get the proper proportion if we have

$$\delta_1 = .05, \ \delta_2 = .10$$

and a total of 150 interviewers, we must have 100 favorable interviewers and 50 not favorable interviewers. However, this situation is not likely to occur in practice.

The interviewers' opinions are more likely to be distributed in approximately the true population proportion, i.e.

$n p$ = number favorable interviewers
$n(1 - p)$ = number not favorable interviewers.

[1] By Frederick Mosteller.

Then evaluating the left side of (2) we find since $n_1 + n_2 = n$ that the expected sample proportion, $\bar{p}$, when the interviewers bias their respondents according to condition (1) is

(3) $\qquad \bar{p} = p - \delta_2 + (\delta_1 + \delta_2)p.$

Let us suppose that $\delta_1 = .05$, $\delta_2 = .10$ and $p = .70$ then the expected $\bar{p}$ would be $.70 - .10 + .15 \times 70 = .705$.

For a given value of p we may set up the condition for $\bar{p} = p$, i.e. that $-\delta_2 + (\delta_1 + \delta_2)p = 0$. This equation determines in the δ_1, δ_2—plane a straight line through the origin with slope $p/(1-p)$. If the point (δ_1, δ_2) is above the line, $\bar{p} < p$, on the line, $\bar{p} = p$, below the line, $\bar{p} > p$.

Since p is unknown and there is usually no information about the relative values of δ_1 and δ_2 the above formulae usually have practical interest only in so far as they place an upper bound on the amount of error which may be introduced by interviewer bias.

A battery of questions on the main issue may be given to the interviewers. On the basis of the several questions it is then possible to classify interviewers as pro or con the issue or middle-of-the-roaders. If we then assume that middle-of-the-road interviewers induce no bias in the responses, it is possible to get estimates of δ_1 and δ_2.

Generally we can estimate $\delta_1 + \delta_2$. Frequently a reasonable assumption is that $\delta_1 = \delta_2 = \frac{1}{2}(\delta_1 + \delta_2) = \delta$. If this hypothesis is true and previous assumptions hold, the estimate of $\bar{p}$ from (3) becomes

(4) $\qquad \bar{p} = p + \delta(2p - 1).$

From (4) we see that $\bar{p} \overset{>}{\underset{<}{=}} p$ according as $p \overset{>}{\underset{<}{=}} .50$.

We are now ready to consider the effect of arbitrarily using equal numbers of interviewers favoring and not favoring an issue. In this situation if $\delta_1 \neq \delta_2$ then the expected value of $\bar{p}$ is just $p + \frac{1}{2}(\delta_1 - \delta_2)$. This means that the estimate of the population proportion will be increased or decreased by the difference in interviewer bias. In the example previously considered where $\delta_1 = .05$, $\delta_2 = .10$, $p = .70$, the expected $\bar{p} = .675$, a result considerably further from the true one than when interviewers were used who fell into approximately the true population proportions.

This result, of course, is not an invariant property of the two methods. If we again take $p = .70$, but $\delta_1 = .10$, $\delta_2 = .05$, we find that the result of the above example is reversed. In this case, using equal numbers of favorable and unfavorable interviewers, we get $\bar{p} = .725$, while with interviewers proportional to the true population we get $\bar{p} = .755$. In this case the equal numbers method gives a result closer to the true value.

A more general result concerning the range of error by each method is as follows: (1) In the case where equal numbers of interviewers are assigned to each side of the issue if the sum of the biases $\delta_1 + \delta_2 = k$, and no other information is known and we do not consider sampling errors, the expected

$\bar{p}$ must be between $p + \dfrac{k}{2}$ and $p - \dfrac{k}{2}$; (2) In the case where interviewers are distributed according to the actual population proportions the $\bar{p}$ will be between $p + kp$ and $p - k(1 - p)$. In case (1) the range is symmetrical about p, whereas in case (2) it is asymmetric unless $p = .50$. However, the total range of error in (1) is k, and the total range for interviewer bias in case (2) is the same. Thus there seems to be considerable justification for the preference of case (1) due to symmetry. Of course, if p approximates .50, there will be little difference in the methods.

APPENDIX III

Sampling and Breakdowns: Technical Notes[1]

Note 1. The efficiency of stratified sampling.[2] The ordinary idea of stratified sampling is that we know something about the population we are working with, for example that half the people are over 40 years of age. In this case we are trying to get additional information about age, such as what the average age is or what the spread (standard deviation) of ages is. Our information would indicate that we should take half our sample at random from the people over 40 years, and similarly for the other half. It is well known that this procedure gives better estimates for the average and the standard deviation than merely taking random samples from the whole population.

Actually this concept of stratification is not useful in public opinion polling.

The principal reason for stratification in public opinion sampling is to make it possible to take a sample which will be representative of the population. It is clear that the ordinary polling agency does not have access to a list of the complete population it is sampling, nor is it economically feasible for such an agency to enumerate its population. Thus random sampling of the universe cannot be seriously considered in nationwide polls (except perhaps in the case of polling done by government agencies where census data and considerable funds are available).

In practice stratification has usually been performed in the following manner. The population has been stratified jointly by region, city size, and economic status, and marginally by age and sex. This means that within a particular region, a particular city size, and a particular economic status category a subsample is drawn of size approximately proportional to the population of that group as compared with the universe we are sampling. Furthermore, the whole sample is drawn in such a way that men and women appear in the sample in the same proportions that they appear in the population, with a similar result holding for age groups. This procedure roughly gives the basis for our sample, although occasional technological difficulties may produce some changes.

Thus far we have taken the attitude that our stratification is made on an

[1] By Frederick Mosteller.
[2] Note 1 refers to pages 139-141 in Chapter 10 on sampling.

ideal population about which we have sufficient information concerning the probability density function so that we can draw subsamples exclusively from each stratum. Practically, such is not always the case.

Of course we can draw subsamples from regions and be sure the person sampled was in the region at the time. City size and sex present no problem, but economic status and age are not the same type of variables. Elsewhere the latter type of control has been distinguished from the others by the term *variable control*. By this term we mean that different observers may evaluate the same respondent differently according to these controls. For example, two interviewers in Oklahoma may be expected to class the same respondent as being in that state, but we do not necessarily expect these interviewers to give the same estimate of the respondent's age or economic status.

This gives rise to a situation in breakdowns which is frequently overlooked. Theoretically we have stratified on economic status, but actually we have done a quite different thing. We have obtained groups of respondents classed Wealthy, Average Plus, Average, Poor, and On Relief. Supposedly in order to stratify the population, we have knowledge of the proportions in which each group makes up the population. However, due to the inability of interviewers to rate respondents according to the absolute scale necessary for stratified sampling (on account of the difficulty and relativity of the definition of the variable), we find that a group called Average is not made up of Average people, but of a few Wealthy, some Average Pluses, more Averages, and some Poor. In fact if we take the comparison of a first interviewer's estimate with a second interviewer's estimate of economic status as an approximation of what happens when we compare an interviewer's estimate with an absolute scale we find the makeup of a group called Average to be about:

Wealthy	Average +	Average	Poor
2%	23%	70%	5%

The same type of dispersion occurs throughout each economic category. Thus technically we have failed to stratify the sample, although we have managed to draw a sample and, considering the manner in which these dispersed groups add when measured on an absolute scale, it seems likely that the national totals (when each respondent is rated on an absolute scale) will give approximately the correct proportions in each economic group.

Empirically it is fairly clear that no very great national bias has been present, otherwise presidential predictions by such organizations as the American Institute of Public Opinion and *Fortune* poll would have missed their estimates by wider margins.

The foregoing brings us to the first type of error made in statements about breakdowns. Any breakdown of a question by economic status must be considered as merely a first approximation to the true sample breakdown. If there are differences due to economic status, it must be recognized that these differences have been blunted by the heterogeneity within economic categories. For example, if the group classed by interviewers as Wealthy is composed on an absolute scale of 50 per cent Wealthy, 35 per cent Average

Plus, and 15 per cent Average (and there is evidence that the composition is at least this bad), we may be interested to see approximately how the true Wealthy sample votes on a question as compared with the votes of the group classified Wealthy by interviewers.

Let us suppose that the true Wealthy group votes 70 per cent for, 30 per cent against; the true Average Plus 60 per cent, 40 per cent; and the true Average 50 per cent, 50 per cent on a question. Then the interviewers' Wealthy group, if distributed over the true Wealthy, Average Plus, Average in proportions of 50 per cent, 35 per cent, 15 per cent, would have an expected vote of 63.5 per cent, 36.5 per cent on the question.

It might be worth while to construct a hypothetical table supplying such an example for the entire table and demonstrating how differences really due to economic status may be obfuscated by this sampling difficulty.

CLASSIFICATION ON ABSOLUTE SCALE

		Wealthy	Average+	Average	Poor
Interviewers'	Wealthy	50%	35%	15%	
Classification	Average +	5	60	35	
	Average	1	15	70	14%
	Poor			20	80

		Proportions in true population			Proportions expected in observed population		
		Yes %	No %			Yes %	No %
Absolute	Wealthy	70	30	Wealthy		63.5	36.5
Classification	Average+	60	40	Average +		57.0	43.0
	Average	50	50	Average		50.3	49.7
	Poor	40	60	Poor		42	58

Of course these results are obtained under the hypothesis that we know the distribution of the interviewers' classifications on an absolute scale, and further that we know in what proportions the absolute groups vote on the question. In practice, of course, we know neither of these things, and no real solution is available. It can be remarked, however, that relationships between variable controls and an issue may be expected to be decreased because of this lack of reliability in classification of respondents.

In order to improve this situation we are trying to increase the validity and reliability of the interviewers' estimates by experiments in which category limitations are sharpened by experimenting with definitions which operate locally while fitting into a national economic-status scale.

It is clear that the discussion above may be generalized to include breakdowns by any variable control where the responses to the question are not independent of that control.

The reader has already realized that the advantages of stratification when we are attempting to estimate unknown quantities connected with distribution functions do not directly apply to the problem of estimating population proportions on given questions. However, if the variables on which the stratification has been made are correlated with the responses, the estimates of the population proportions from the sample will tend to be more stable than estimates from random samples; that is, the variances of estimates of population proportions are smaller when related variables are stratified than when the sample is drawn at random.

Since this fact has generally been taken for granted in public opinion literature, we indicate a general formula and supply an easy example to show how the variance of the estimate of a population proportion decreases when the population is stratified on a variable correlated with the opinion on a question (cf. note 2 *infra*).

Note 2. Effect of stratification in practical polling.[3] In the simplest situation we have a variable such as economic status and a dichotomized opinion question. Then the true proportions will form a table like the following:

QUESTION

Economic Status	Yes	Other	Total
High	p_{11}	p_{12}	$p_{1.}$
Low	p_{21}	p_{22}	$p_{2.}$
Total	$p_{.1}$	$p_{.2}$	1

If we have stratified by economic status, that is, taken a sample of $n_{1.}$ high-economic-status people and $n_{2.}$ low-economic-status people, where we know that the proportions in high and low are $p_{1.} = n_{1.}/n$, $p_{2.} = n_{2.}/n$ respectively, then we are interested in the standard deviation, or variance of the estimate of the proportion of "Yeses" as estimated by $n_{.1}/n$ (where n is the size of the sample). We will call the true proportion of "Yeses" $p_{.1}$, and its variance in the case of random sampling is $p_{.1} p_{.2}/n$.

In the case of stratified sampling the variance of the estimate of $p_{.1}$ is

$$(\text{I}) \quad \sigma^2_{p_{.1}} = \frac{\text{I}}{n} \left(\frac{p_{11} p_{12}}{p_{1.}} + \frac{p_{21} p_{22}}{p_{2.}} \right).$$

Here, of course, the p_{ij}'s are the true values.

If economic status is not correlated with the response to the question, it turns out that the variances in random sampling and in stratified sampling are the same. When these variables are correlated, the variance for stratified sampling is smaller.

To take an example of the latter case, we consider the following table:

Economic Status	Yes	Other	Total
High	.35	.15	.50
Low	.15	.35	.50
Total	.50	.50	1

In the case of random sampling, the variance of the estimate of the proportion of "Yeses" in a sample of size n is $.25/n$. In the case of stratified

sampling, it would be $\dfrac{\text{I}}{n} \left(2 \dfrac{.35 \times .15}{.50} \right) = .21/n$. Essentially this means that

[3] Note 2 refers to pages 139-141 in Chapter 10.

if we stratify in this case we only need a sample of size $.21n/.25 = .84n$ to get the same accuracy as a sample of n taken at random. However, actual situations from the field seldom give this much improvement.

To extend equation (1) to more categories or more variables we only add terms of the same sort, namely the product of the proportion of "Yeses" by the proportion of "Others" in a category divided by their sum until there is a term of this type for each category in the stratification. A generalization of formula (1) is:

$$\frac{1}{n} \sum_{i, j, k, \ldots, m} \frac{p_{ijk\ldots m}\, p'_{ijk\ldots m}}{p_{ijk\ldots m} + p'_{ijk\ldots m}}$$

where $i, j, k, \ldots, m$ are the category numbers of the first, second, third, etc., variables, p the proportion of "Yeses," p' the proportion of "Others," n the size of the sample. Of course

$$\sum (p_{ijk\ldots m} + p'_{ijk\ldots m}) = 1.$$

As an example of the type of setup used in practice we have the following table:

Question: Which of these two things do you think the United States should do: Send most of our army abroad to fight the enemy wherever they might be, or keep most of our army home to protect the United States?

Economic Status	Send Army Abroad		Other		Total
Upper					
Men	167	69%	75	31%	242
Women	121	67	59	33	180
Middle					
Men	393	69	175	31	568
Women	284	56	223	44	507
Lower					
Men	403	59	281	41	684
Women	359	49	372	51	731
Total	1727	59.3%	1185	40.7%	$n = 2912$

Assuming that the numbers in the table are representative of the true population proportions, we compute the variance of the estimate of the proportion wishing to "send army abroad" for random sampling as $.24/n$, for stratification on sex only, $.24/n$, on economic status only, $.24/n$, while for economic status and sex simultaneously it is $.235/n$. This means that with respect to this question, we need only have taken a sample of size $.975n$ to get the same accuracy as that obtained from a random sample of n. In other words, for practical polling purposes, even when the other variables city size, section of country and age are taken into account, we may expect no great gain from the stratification over random sampling.

Note 3. Pooling ballots.[4] Sometimes it is useful to pool ballots which have been taken on the same question in order to obtain sufficient cases to study the reactions of small interest groups or to get cases enough for meaningful higher order breakdowns. It is clear that rigid restrictions must be met before such a pooling arrangement is valid.

When we are studying the relationships between variables and opinions, it is not sufficient that the national population has not changed its proportions. We must be able to treat this pooled ballot as if it were a single sample from our population. From the point of view of the polls, we must be able to consider this pooled sample as having been taken instantaneously. Actually interviewing on a single OPOR or AIPO ballot is usually taken over a period of about a week. Usually no event whose impact upsets the population proportions takes place in the interval; consequently the sampling may be considered to have been taken instantaneously if no trend is occurring during the period. When several successive ballots are added together, however, we are working over a longer period; thus trends and fluctuations are much more likely to be taking place. If important changes *are* taking place, these will be blunted or nullified when we treat several ballots as a single sample.

A further consideration in cumulating ballot results, in some types of investigation, is that the context of the ballots be similar. For example in a ballot whose main issue is problems of the present war, the question: "What do you think is the most important problem facing this city?" may elicit distinctly different results from the same question asked on a ballot concerned with problems of urban planning.

Even if the national percentages do happen to be the same, the fundamental reasons and interpretations by respondents may be entirely different. Consequently, before the pooling of the results of questionnaires, considerable investigation needs to be made to verify that such a procedure is valid. Otherwise investigations of causes will have little meaning.

A common situation is that in which we are attempting to study three variables simultaneously. We may desire to attempt the ordering of the relative importance of three variables with respect to opinion on a question.

Let us consider the example given in Table 100, where we have broken down economic status by education by section on the question:

"Which of these two things do you think is the more important for the United States to try to do: To keep out of war ourselves, or to help England win, even at the risk of getting into the war?"

Three ballots have been cumulated in order to obtain sufficient data for investigation. The hypothesis that the three ballots were drawn from a single population (with respect to the particular question and the related variables) was not refuted; therefore, there is no evidence that we should not pool the ballots. Naturally, the cross-sections remained the same.

As our criterion for ordering the importance of the three variables, we shall take the probability associated with goodness of fit within the table

[4] Note 3 refers to pages 184 f. in Chapter 13 on breakdowns.

TABLE 100. "HELP ENGLAND" PERCENTAGES FOR CUMULATION OF THREE BALLOTS

UPPER-ECONOMIC STATUS

Section	Grade School	Cases	High School	Cases	College	Cases	Total Per cent	Total Cases
1	60%	10	60%	51	53%	30	58%	91
2	66	56	66	108	68	144	67	308
3	75	28	50	104	47	127	51	259
4	53	47	57	58	60	92	57	197
5 & 8	75	20	94	33	76	70	81	123
6	75	8	75	24	52	21	66	53
7	83	18	67	39	57	67	64	124
Totals	67	187	63	417	60	551	62	1155

MIDDLE-ECONOMIC STATUS

Section	Grade School	Cases	High School	Cases	College	Cases	Total Per cent	Total Cases
1	56%	55	57%	209	62%	71	58%	335
2	56	367	61	595	61	260	59	1222
3	56	307	53	466	53	212	54	985
4	55	262	63	346	59	181	59	789
5 & 8	75	168	82	248	78	153	79	569
6	70	63	70	122	74	106	71	291
7	68	90	68	154	56	126	64	370
Totals	60	1312	63	2140	62	1109	62	4561

LOWER-ECONOMIC STATUS

Section	Grade School	Cases	High School	Cases	College	Cases	Total Per cent	Total Cases
1	43%	75	64%	92	86%	7	56%	174
2	47	448	54	285	62	55	51	788
3	49	386	50	204	41	39	49	629
4	51	188	59	161	66	44	56	393
5 & 8	62	177	69	124	72	29	66	330
6	62	55	65	74	67	18	64	147
7	59	86	60	83	46	26	58	195
Totals	51	1415	58	1023	60	218	55	2656

ECONOMIC-STATUS TOTALS

Section	Grade School	Cases	High School	Cases	College	Cases	Total Per cent	Total Cases
1	49%	140	60%	352	61%	108	58%	600
2	52	871	60	988	63	459	58	2318
3	53	721	52	774	52	378	52	1873
4	53	497	62	565	60	317	57	1379
5 & 8	67	365	78	405	77	252	75	1022
6	67	126	69	220	70	145	69	491
7	66	194	65	276	55	219	62	689
Totals	56	2914	61	3580	62	1878	59	8372

when we hold each variable constant separately. Thus we take the grand marginal percentages of a given variable and compute the chi-square value within each layer, cumulate for the layers, and find the probability associated with this number for the appropriate degrees of freedom (usually it is unnecessary actually to obtain the probability levels, as the order will be apparent from the chi-square values).

In the case of Table 100, we find on holding education constant:[5]

$$\chi^2 = 263, \qquad \text{d.f.} = 60 \qquad \text{c.r.} = 12.$$

Holding economic status constant:

$$\chi^2 = 247, \qquad \text{d.f.} = 60 \qquad \text{c.r.} = 11.3.$$

Holding section constant:

$$\chi^2 = 126, \qquad \text{d.f.} = 56 \qquad \text{c.r.} = 5.3.$$

In the above data we have supplied the critical ratio (c.r.) which would be associated with the chi-square value for a normal distribution rather than the probability.

We shall interpret this to mean that section of the country is the most important variable of the three considered. When section appears in combination with economic status or education, the chi-square value is large; but when section is held constant, the chi-square value due to variations in the other two variables is relatively small. Between the chi-square values for education and economic status, there appears to be no difference not readily accounted for by sampling variations, so we shall not distinguish between the importance of these two variates.

Thus far we have considered loose conditions under which ballots may be pooled in order to obtain sufficient data to investigate the relative effect of several variables on opinion. We have further suggested a criterion for this relative importance, or ranking of variables which lends itself to rapid computation.

There are many other occasions when one may wish to pool ballots, and among them are occasions when we may relax the conditions on pooling still further. For example, in attempting to predict national elections it is frequently necessary to attempt the prediction of single states rather than merely national proportions. In that case it may be necessary to cumulate results of ballot after ballot in states with small representation in the cross-section in order to obtain reliable figures. Even if trends are apparent, it may be necessary to make adjustments and attempt to pool the results.

In order partially to iron out sampling discrepancies and get a better picture of the true trend, a method of linked averages is sometimes used, where

[5] We apply the formula $\chi^2 = \Sigma \dfrac{n_{ijk}(p_{ijk} - p_{i..})^2}{p_{i..}(1 - p_{i..})}$ and the two corresponding formulae utilizing $p_{.j.}$, $p_{..k}$. In this case $i = 1,2,3$ refers to education layers, while $j = 1,2,3$ refers to economic-status layers, while $k = 1,2,...7$ refers to section layers, when we consider the cells as forming a rectangular parallelepiped. As usual the occurrence of two dots in the subscript is indicative of a marginal proportion.

the results of each ballot are averaged in with the material from the immediately preceding ballot. Of course if sampling errors are small in comparison with the trends, such a method results in a lag, unless the average nature of such figures is taken into consideration.

An alternative to pooling ballots. Sometimes, as indicated above, certain interest groups, sections of the country, city sizes, etc., are of particular importance to the study, and it may become necessary to have sufficient cases at hand to compare these groups.

Instead of pooling ballots, we may design the experiment in such a manner that these groups will have sufficient cases to make reliable estimates of their opinion proportions.

For example, in a recent survey on urban planning[6] it was desired that certain city sizes in each section of the country be adequately represented for comparison; and at the same time, on account of cost, it was possible to take only a sample of about 2,500. Furthermore, there was no possibility of pooling ballots.

The following cross-section was arranged:

SECTION

City Size by Thousands	New England and Middle Atlantic	South	East Central	West Central	South-west	Pacific	Total
5-25	417	16	245			72	750
25-100	100	100	100	100	100	100	600
100-500	100	100	100	100	100	100	600
Over 500	100	100	100	100	100	100	600
Totals	717	316	545	300	300	372	2500

It will be noticed that large cities are sampled in proportion to their population, whereas each of the smaller cities in each section was assigned equal quotas of 100 (it was felt that this was the smallest sample for which differences could reliably be compared).

One might feel that a special sample such as this makes it necessary to weight the results according to the true population cross-section in order to get unbiased national totals and breakdowns. In this particular case, however, national totals as indicated by the weighted and unweighted totals were in no case as much as one half of one per cent apart, while on first order breakdowns deviations of at most three per cent appeared in the cells.

This circumstance made it possible to use unweighted results with very little error. Naturally the context of a ballot and variation in response over the groups which are not sampled proportional to the population have much to do with the amount of error incurred by such a system.

[6] Melville C. Branch, Jr., *Urban Planning and Public Opinion: National Survey Research Investigation*, Bureau of Urban Research, Princeton University, 1942.

APPENDIX IV

Charts Indicating Confidence Limits and Critical Differences Between Percentages[1]

Charts for finding the confidence limits on a percentage, and also for testing the significance of differences between percentages, are often useful to the research worker in public opinion polls, both in the design of his experiment and analysis of the results.

It is well known that for large samples of size n drawn at random from a binomial or "yes-no" distribution in which p is the proportion of "yeses," $\bar{p}$, the observed proportion of "yeses," is approximately normally distributed about the mean p, with standard deviation $\sqrt{pq/n}$. This means that if we take samples of size n and set limits a certain number of standard deviations above and below p, we can estimate the proportion of times $\bar{p}$ will fall in this interval. Suppose we take 2.58 standard deviations, the probability that

$$p + 2.58\sqrt{pq/n} > \bar{p} > p - 2.58\sqrt{pq/n},$$

is about .99. In other words $\bar{p}$ will fall between these limits at least 99 times out of 100 in the long run. However, this formula can practically never be used in a real life experiment, since we seldom know p, the proportion of "yeses," say.

The problem we are interested in is not the one above, but, If we have observed $\bar{p}$, between what limits does p lie a certain proportion of the time? The confidence limit approach can answer this problem without the fallacious assumption, $p = \bar{p}$, necessary in solving this problem by the approach given above. A confidence solution to this standard problem in public opinion polling is given for specified values of n for a .99 probability level by the "football" shaped chart on page 298.

The other charts (Figures 43-45) also use the confidence limit approach to ascertain whether or not statistically significant differences occur between or within samples. Confidence limits are employed as before to avoid fallacious assumptions in the computations of standard errors necessary to obtain significance levels of differences between percentages by the ordinary critical ratio method.

Of the following charts, Figures 42-44 are reproduced from an article by S. S. Wilks.[2] A more complete explanation of their meaning, use, and computation appears in that article. Figure 45 is similar to Figure 44 with the exception that a .90 significance level is used instead of .99.

It should be understood that the limits supplied are conservative, and that the charts are applicable only when the sampling has been done correctly.

Examples of the use of these charts follow from the text of Wilks' article.

[1] By Frederick Mosteller.
[2] S. S. Wilks, "Confidence Limits and Critical Differences between Percentages," *Public Opinion Quarterly*, 1940, 4, 332-338. These charts are reproduced with the permission of the *Public Opinion Quarterly*.

   As an example of the use of Figure 42, suppose a representative sample
of 1,000 is drawn from a large population, and suppose 20 per cent of the
people in the sample answer "yes" to a certain question. Using $\bar{p} = 20$ per
cent in the chart and finding where the vertical line through 20 cuts the two
curves for $n = 1,000$, the two confidence limits are seen to be about 17 per

FIGURE 42

Curves giving 99 per cent confidence limits of a population percentage p corresponding to each value of the sample percentage p for sample sizes 50, 100, 200,
500, 1,000, 3,000 and 10,000.

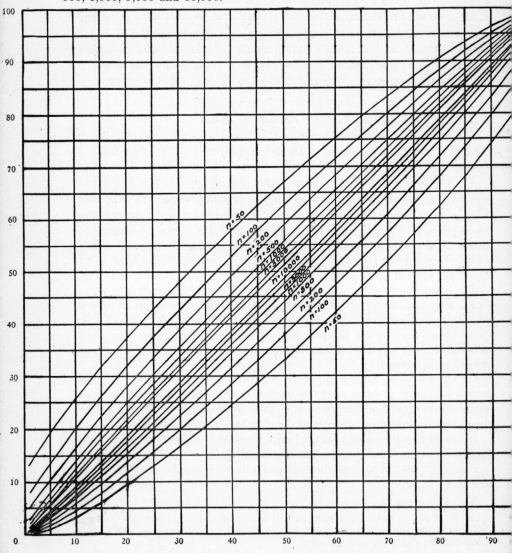

FIGURE 43

Curves giving conservative critical limits of a difference between two percentages in the same sample for the two probability levels .95 and .99.

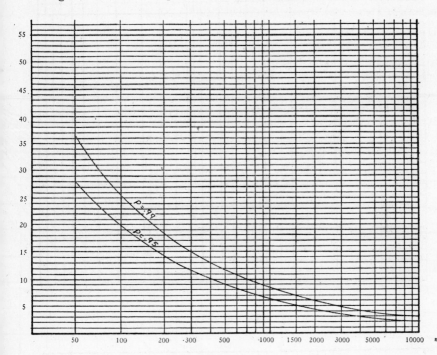

cent and 23.5 per cent. If we apply this procedure to a great many samples, getting a pair of confidence limits each time, and making the statement in each case that the confidence limits include the population value between them, then, under ideal conditions of random sampling, about 99 per cent of our statements will be correct. Under conditions of representative sampling, at least 99 per cent of our statements can be expected to be correct in the long run.

To illustrate the use of Figure 43, suppose the "yes" and "no" percentages to a given question in a sample of 3,000 cases are 38 per cent and 32 per cent, respectively. It is seen in Figure 43 that by taking $n = 3,000$, the critical difference is about 4½ per cent. Hence the 6 per cent difference in the sample can be regarded as significant at the 0.99 probability level.

To illustrate the use of Figure 44, suppose the "yes" percentage to a certain question in a poll of 3,000 cases is 52 per cent, while the "yes" percentage to the question in a second poll of 800 cases is 48 per cent. Taking $n_2 = 3,000$ and $n_1 = 800$, it is seen that the critical difference is about 5 per

FIGURE 44

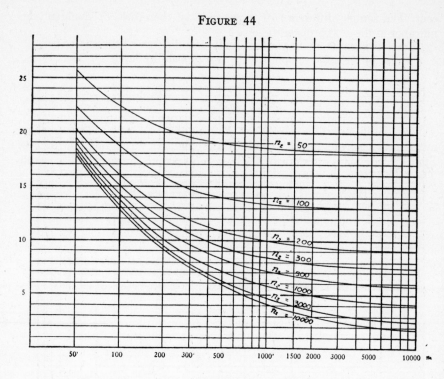

$n_z = 50$
$n_z = 100$
$n_z = 200$
$n_z = 300$
$n_z = 500$
$n_z = 1000$
$n_z = 3000$
$n_z = 10000$

FIGURE 45

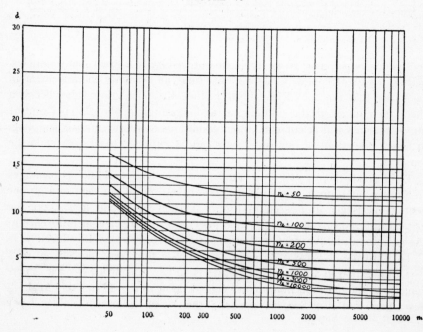

$n_z = 50$
$n_z = 100$
$n_z = 200$
$n_z = 500$
$n_z = 1000$
$n_z = 3000$
$n_z = 10000$

cent. The sample difference of 4 per cent is, therefore, of doubtful significance at the 0.99 probability level.[3]

APPENDIX V

MAPS

Sources of maps for sampling.[1] During the past few years, excellent maps have been developed for cities and counties throughout the United States. These maps offer one of the best sampling media thus far discovered. The following is a digest of the more important sources of maps:

1. War Department, Chief Engineer's office. *Topographical maps,* showing all physical objects, topography, houses, rivers, streams, incorporated places, roads; quadrangles, scale, one inch to the mile, three to eight maps cover a county. Complete index not available; eastern and far western states completely covered; dates vary 1900-1939.

2. Interior Department, Geological Survey. *Topographical maps* (identical to Army Engineer's maps) showing all physical objects, topography, houses, rivers, streams, incorporated places, roads; for quadrangles, scale one inch to the mile, three to eight maps cover one county. May be obtained from Geological Survey Office, Department of the Interior; approximately 46 per cent of the United States land area is covered; dates vary 1900-1939; revision continually in progress; price 10 cents.

3. Census Bureau, Geographer's Office. 1940 census maps and plans.
   (a) *Outline maps,* showing all minor civil divisions in outline, corresponding 1930 census data can be made to accompany each map. No physical objects shown, one map for each state, map sizes and scales vary, complete United States coverage, dated 1933 or later as of 1930. Minor Civil Divisions, no revisions due until after completion of 1940 census. Price 10 cents.
   (b) *Enumeration District maps,* showing all census and civil divisions and enumeration districts, all physical objects except buildings, corresponding 1930 census data available. One map for each county in rural areas, district in suburban areas, and ward or census tract in urban areas. Map sizes and scales vary considerably: complete United States coverage, dated 1940 and revised. No more revisions due until after 1940 census is published. Not for sale, may be photostated on requisition at about $1.00 each. Each section, block, ward, enumeration district is described as of 1940 in volumes entitled *Plans of Division* for 1940 census. Sources; same as *Outline Maps.*

4. Public Roads Administration, Highway Planning Survey maps.
   (a) *General Highway and Transportation Maps*
   (b) *County Base Maps*

[3] If instead of calculating $\bar{d}$, the difference of the two sample percentages p_1 and p_2, we calculate the difference $\bar{d}' = 100(sin^{-1} \sqrt{\bar{p_1}/100} - sin^{-1} \sqrt{\bar{p_2}/100})$ then we have an exact (not conservative) critical limit for $\bar{d}'$, to a close approximation, at the 0.99 probability level. Nomograms based on $\bar{d}'$ for testing the significance of the difference between percentages in two different samples have been prepared by Joseph Zubin, *Jour. Amer. Stat. Assn.,* 1939, 34, ·539-544.

[1] By J. Stevens Stock.

(c) *School Bus Route Maps*
(d) *Postal Route Maps*
(e) *Traffic Flow Maps*

These five series of maps show all physical and civil objects and divisions by type or kind. All houses by type. One map for each rural county to 27 maps for large urban counties; scale, one inch to the mile in rural places and four inches to the mile in urban places, detailed incorporated places not shown, maps 36 inches wide by varying lengths; complete legends; date 1936 to present. United States coverage in progress. Used in 1940 census. Available from State Directors of Bureau of Public Roads. A sixth series of maps in this source is the *State General Highway Map*, one map for each state. Four miles to the inch. Maps for rural sections show practically all the detail of the county maps. This series is probably the most important single source for unincorporated areas.

5. Public Roads Administration, *State Transportation Maps* published in collaboration with the Geological Survey of the United States Department of the Interior. These maps show, in scale of 4 miles to the inch, the state highway and Federal-aid road system and all county connecting roads. All cities and towns and county boundaries are shown, as well as all state and Federal parks. Each state requires one to thirty-six sheets. For sale at Government Printing Office for 20 cents a sheet.

6. The United States Department of Agriculture, *Land Use and Soil Survey Maps*, showing great detail of culture, roads, houses, and other buildings, as well as soil type. Some maps cover whole counties; some cover several counties. Complete descriptive text accompanies each map. Scale, one inch to the mile.

7. Rand McNally publishes or can supply maps showing all streets for almost all principal cities in the United States.

8. All members of the American Association of Directory Publishers (offices in all principal cities) publish maps for all urban places covered by city directories.

9. County surveyors can usually supply maps of their counties and small cities and towns within their counties. Flat maps which are kept for official tax purposes may be reproduced at small charge by photostat.

10. State Bureaus of Public Roads in each state publish road maps for each county in their respective state. Price is usually 50 cents. Accuracy, date, detail varies.

11. Small incorporated areas in most states, in cooperation with WPA, have just completed city or borough maps. Free distribution in most places. Available from the Road Commissioner in each place. Proposed streets are often shown in the same legend as existing streets. Usual scale, four inches to the mile.

12. Fire insurance companies often publish maps for small cities and towns, showing much detail besides the complete water system.

13. Chambers of Commerce or Boards of Trade and City Engineers in large cities publish accurate, up-to-date census-tract maps, made in cooperation with the United States Census Bureau.

14. Hearne Brothers, 17 Cadillac Square, Detroit, Michigan, publish elaborate, up-to-date maps of all large cities, showing all streets and street numbers for the city and its environs. Scale, approximately one inch to the mile. Price $15.00.

FIGURE 46

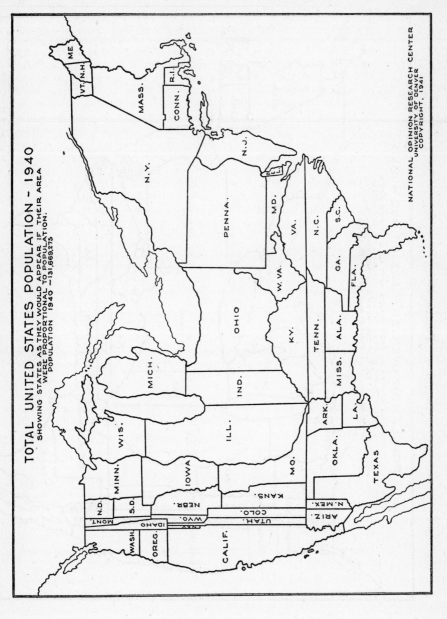

TOTAL UNITED STATES POPULATION - 1940
SHOWING STATES AS THEY WOULD APPEAR IF THEIR AREA
WERE PROPORTIONAL TO POPULATION.
POPULATION 1940 —131,669,275

NATIONAL OPINION RESEARCH CENTER
UNIVERSITY OF DENVER
COPYRIGHT, 1941

FIGURE 47

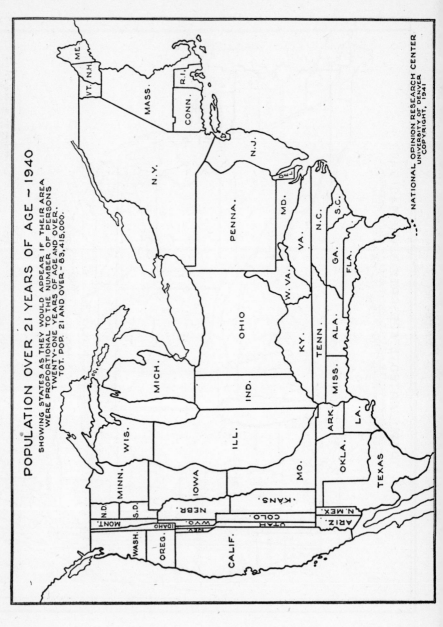

POPULATION OVER 21 YEARS OF AGE ~ 1940

SHOWING STATES AS THEY WOULD APPEAR IF THEIR AREA
WERE PROPORTIONAL TO THE NUMBER OF PERSONS
TWENTY-ONE YEARS OF AGE AND OVER.
TOT. POP. 21 AND OVER ~ 83,415,000.

NATIONAL OPINION RESEARCH CENTER
UNIVERSITY OF DENVER
COPYRIGHT, 1941

FIGURE 48

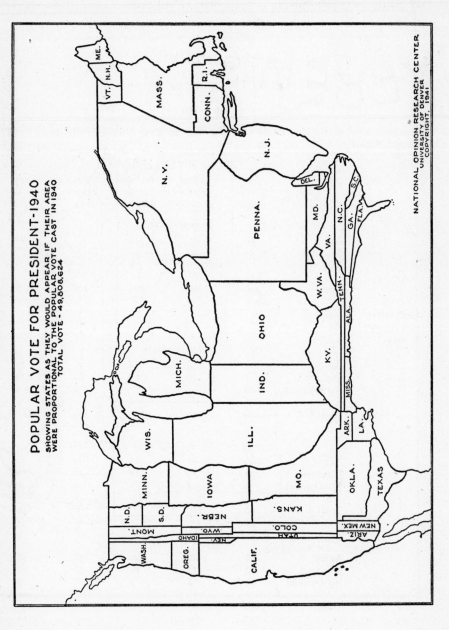

POPULAR VOTE FOR PRESIDENT-1940

SHOWING STATES AS THEY WOULD APPEAR IF THEIR AREA
WERE PROPORTIONAL TO THE POPULAR VOTE CAST IN 1940
TOTAL VOTE - 49,806,624

NATIONAL OPINION RESEARCH CENTER
UNIVERSITY OF DENVER
COPYRIGHT, 1941

Distorted maps. The three maps reproduced above were prepared by Harry Field, Director of the National Opinion Research Center of the University of Denver.[2] They bring out in particularly vivid fashion some of the characteristics of the population in this country.

APPENDIX VI

Tables on Intensity of Opinion[1]

Table 101

Comparison of Four Intensity Devices in Consistency of Differentiation of Attitudes toward Russia

		Degree of Trust of Russia				
		VERY SUSPI-CIOUS	FAIRLY SUSPI-CIOUS	NEUTRAL OR NO OPINION	FAIRLY TRUST-FUL	VERY TRUST-FUL
		Sureness Rating				
Send fewer supplies to Russia	Agree	68	56	44	41	22
	Disagree	31	44	52	58	78
	No Opinion	1	0	4	1	0
	Total	100	100	100	100	100
		Thermometer				
	Agree	61	56	52	27	19
	Disagree	37	40	41	72	76
	No Opinion	2	4	7	1	5
	Total	100	100	100	100	100
		Verbal Self-Rating on Strength of Feeling				
	Agree	66	61	63	40	22
	Disagree	34	36	34	58	78
	No Opinion	0	3	3	2	0
	Total	100	100	100	100	100
		A Priori or Logical Scale				
	Agree	79	59	51	42	37
	Disagree	17	38	46	56	63
	No Opinion	4	3	3	2	0
	Total	100	100	100	100	100

[2] The editor is grateful to Mr. Field for permission to reproduce the maps here. Copies can be obtained by writing the National Opinion Research Center.

[1] These tables refer to Dr. Katz's study of Intensity, Chapter 3, pages 63 f.

	VERY SUSPI- CIOUS	FAIRLY SUSPI- CIOUS	NEUTRAL OR NO OPINION	FAIRLY TRUST- FUL	VERY TRUST- FUL

Sureness Rating

German	32	23	6	9	8
Russian	33	44	60	62	67
No Difference	20	21	26	21	14
No Opinion	15	12	8	8	11
Total	100	100	100	100	100

Which gov't has done more for its people?

Thermometer

German	31	16	6	12	5
Russian	27	36	54	61	73
No Difference	26	38	28	16	20
No Opinion	16	10	12	11	2
Total	100	100	100	100	100

Verbal Self-Rating on Strength of Feeling

German	28	25	6	6	14
Russian	40	26	37	60	66
No Difference	25	39	49	24	6
No Opinion	7	10	8	10	14
Total	100	100	100	100	100

Logical Scale

German	29	27	15	12	14
Russian	35	20	34	49	70
No Difference	26	47	33	27	8
No Opinion	10	6	18	12	8
Total	100	100	100	100	100

Sureness Rating

More	21	32	36	48	61
Less	37	21	12	37	8
As Is	29	38	43	39	20
No Opinion	13	9	9	6	11
Total	100	100	100	100	100

Would you like more or less New Deal?	VERY SUSPI-CIOUS	FAIRLY SUSPI-CIOUS	NEUTRAL OR NO OPINION	FAIRLY TRUST-FUL	VERY TRUST-FUL
	Thermometer				
More	20	24	28	43	61
Less	33	30	18	13	5
As Is	38	37	49	36	32
No Opinion	9	9	5	8	2
Total	100	100	100	100	100
	Self-Rating on Strength of Feeling				
More	33	26	23	49	48
Less	38	26	9	6	14
As Is	20	41	57	37	32
No Opinion	9	7	11	8	6
Total	100	100	100	100	100
	Logical Scale				
More	35	35	24	36	46
Less	33	24	8	18	10
As Is	21	34	49	41	39
No Opinion	11	7	19	5	5
Total	100	100	100	100	100

TABLE 102

Comparison of Four Intensity Devices in Consistency of Differentiation of Attitudes toward Social Reform[2]

Degree of Feeling on Nationalizing Industry

	STRONGLY FAVOR	MODER-ATELY FAVOR	NEUTRAL OR NO OPINION	MODER-ATELY OPPOSE	STRONGLY OPPOSE
	Sureness Rating				
Yes	66	56	48	35	29
No	30	40	43	58	71
No Opinion	4	4	9	7	0
Total	100	100	100	100	100

[2] The figures are the percentages of the intensity groups falling into the response categories on the left. Thus in the first part of the table the figure 66 means that 66 per cent of the rating supporters of industry answered "Yes" to question of limiting incomes.

	STRONGLY FAVOR	MODER-ATELY FAVOR	NEUTRAL OR NO OPINION	MODER-ATELY OPPOSE	STRONGLY OPPOSE

Should we
limit incomes
to a maximum
of $200
a week?

Thermometer

	STRONGLY FAVOR	MODER-ATELY FAVOR	NEUTRAL OR NO OPINION	MODER-ATELY OPPOSE	STRONGLY OPPOSE
Yes	65	52	47	29	22
No	32	42	45	68	71
No Opinion	3	6	8	3	7
Total	100	100	100	100	100

Self-Rating on Strength of Feeling

	STRONGLY FAVOR	MODER-ATELY FAVOR	NEUTRAL OR NO OPINION	MODER-ATELY OPPOSE	STRONGLY OPPOSE
Yes	69	51		27	33
No	29	44		67	62
No Opinion	2	5		6	5
Total	100	100		100	100

Logical Scale

	STRONGLY FAVOR	MODER-ATELY FAVOR	NEUTRAL OR NO OPINION	MODER-ATELY OPPOSE	STRONGLY OPPOSE
Yes	83	58		47	34
No	15	37		48	55
No Opinion	2	5		5	11
Total	100	100		100	100

Sureness Rating

	STRONGLY FAVOR	MODER-ATELY FAVOR	NEUTRAL OR NO OPINION	MODER-ATELY OPPOSE	STRONGLY OPPOSE
More	44	38	39	17	9
Less	15	12	9	28	61
As Is	33	43	44	46	26
No Opinion	8	7	8	9	4
Total	100	100	100	100	100

Would you
like more
or less
New Deal?

Thermometer

	STRONGLY FAVOR	MODER-ATELY FAVOR	NEUTRAL OR NO OPINION	MODER-ATELY OPPOSE	STRONGLY OPPOSE
More	48	42	28	20	7
Less	16	13	8	31	58
As Is	29	39	52	43	27
No Opinion	7	6	12	6	8
Total	100	100	100	100	100

	STRONGLY FAVOR	MODER-ATELY FAVOR	NEUTRAL OR NO OPINION	MODER-ATELY OPPOSE	STRONGLY OPPOSE
Self-Rating on Strength of Feeling					
More	39	36		24	20
Less	17	13		20	36
As Is	37	45		47	38
No Opinion	7	6		9	6
Total	100	100		100	100
Logical Scale					
More	53	33		41	19
Less	13	10		15	42
As Is	27	47		36	30
No Opinion	7	10		8	9
Total	100	100		100	100

APPENDIX VII

BIBLIOGRAPHY OF RESEARCH, 1936-1943[1]

Allport, F. H. Toward a Science of Public Opinion. *Pub. Opin. Quart.*, 1937, 1, no. 1, 7-23.

———. Polls and the Science of Public Opinion. *Pub. Opin. Quart.*, 1940, 4, 249-258.

Bean, Louis H. *Ballot Behavior: a Study of Presidential Elections.* Washington, D.C.: American Council on Public Affairs, 1940, 101 pp.

Belden, Joe. Measuring College Thought. *Pub. Opin. Quart.*, 1939, 3, 458-462.

Benson, E. G. Three Words. *Pub. Opin. Quart.*, 1940, 4, 130-134.

——— and Perry, P. Analysis of Democratic-Republican Strength by Population Groups. *Pub. Opin. Quart.*, 1940, 4, 464-472.

Benson, L. E. Studies in Secret-Ballot Technique. *Pub. Opin. Quart.*, 1941, 5, 79-82.

Bingham, W. V. and Moore, B. V. *How to Interview.* New York: 1934.

Blankenship, A. B. Influence of the Question Form on the Response in a Public Opinion Poll. *Psych. Rec.*, 1940, 3, 345-424.

[1] This bibliography indicates only a selected list of recent technical references. It does not cover references prior to 1936. Research on attitude measurement is deliberately omitted since it has been listed elsewhere.

Results of the Gallup and *Fortune* Polls and also of the British Institute of Public Opinion and the Canadian Institute of Public Opinion are published in each issue of the *Public Opinion Quarterly*. This compilation was begun in the March 1940 issue of the *Quarterly*. Previous Gallup results were brought together in the July 1938 and October 1939 issues of the *Quarterly*.

————. Choice of Words in Poll Questions. *Sociol. and Soc. Res.*, 1940, 25, 12-18.

————. Does the Question Form Influence Public Opinion Poll Results? *J. Appl. Psychol.*, 1940, 24, 27-30.

————. Pre-testing a Questionnaire for a Public Opinion Poll. *Sociometry*, 1940, 2, 263-270.

————. The "Sample" Study in Opinion Research. *Sociometry*, 1940, 2, 271-276.

Cahalan, D. and Meier, N. C. The Validity of Mail Ballot Polls. *Psych. Rec.*, 1939, 3, 2-11.

Cantril, H. Experiments in the Wording of Questions. *Pub. Opin. Quart.*, 1940, 4, 330-332.

————. America Faces the War: a Study in Public Opinion. *Pub. Opin. Quart.*, 1940, 4, 387-407.

————. The Prediction of Social Events. *J. of Abn. and Soc. Psych.*, 1938, 33, 364-389.

————. *The Invasion from Mars*. Princeton Univ. Press, 1940.

————. Public Opinion in Flux. *Annals of Amer. Acad. Pol. and Soc. Sci.*, March 1942, 136-151.

———— and Harding, J. The 1942 Elections: A Case Study in Political Psychology. *Pub. Opin. Quart.*, 1943, 7, 222-241.

———— and Rugg, D. Looking Forward to Peace. *Pub. Opin. Quart.*, 1940, 4, 119-121.

————, Rugg, D., and Williams, F. America Faces the War: Shifts in Opinion. *Pub. Opin. Quart.*, 1940, 4, 651-656.

Chambers, M. M. and Bell, H. M. *How to Make a Community Youth Survey*. Washington, D.C.: American Council on Education, 1939, 45 pp.

Cook, S. W. and Welch, A. C. Methods of Measuring the Practical Effects of Polls of Public Opinion. *J. Appl. Psychol.*, 1940, 24, 441-454.

Copeland, Herman A. Validating Two Tests for Census Enumeration. *J. Appl. Psychol.*, 1937, 21, 230-232.

Cottrell, Leonard S., Jr., The Case Study Method in Prediction. *Sociometry*, 1941, 4, 358-370.

Crespi, L. and Rugg, D. Poll Data and the Study of Opinion Determinants. *Pub. Opin. Quart.*, 1940, 2, 273-276.

Crossley, A. M. Experiments in Polling Technique. *Pub. Opin. Quart.*, 1941, 5, 83-86.

————. Straw Polls in 1936. *Pub. Opin. Quart.*, 1937, 1, 24-25.

————. Operating Plan of a Presidential Poll, with Annotations Based on the Election. *Market Research*, Jan. 1937, 11-14.

————. Measuring Public Opinion. *J. of Marketing*, 1937, 1, 272-274.

————. Methods Tested during the 1940 Campaign. *Pub. Opin. Quart.*, 1941, 5, 83-86.

Edwards, A. L. Four Dimensions in Political Stereotypes. *J. of Abn. and Soc. Psychol.*, 1940, 35, 566-572.

Farber, Maurice Lee. Prison Research: Techniques and Methods. *J. of Soc. Psychol.*, 1941, 14, 295-310.

Ferguson, Leonard W. A Study of the Likert Technique of Attitude Scale Construction. *J. of Soc. Psychol.*, 1941, 13, 51-57.

Field, Harry H. and Connelly, Gordon M. Testing Polls in Public Election Booths. *Pub. Opin. Quart.*, 1942, 6, 610-616.

Fromme, Allan. On the Use of Certain Qualitative Methods of Attitude Research: a Study of Opinions on the Methods of Preventing War. *J. of Soc. Psychol.*, 1941, 13, 429-459.

Gallup, George. The Public Rings the Bell. *Market Research*, Feb. 1937, 3-4.

———. Putting Public Opinion to Work. *Scribners*, Nov. 1936, 100, 36-39.

———. Reporting Public Opinion in Five Nations. *Pub. Opin. Quart.*, 1942, 6, 429-436.

———. Question Wording in Public Opinion Polls. *Sociometry*, 1941, 4, 259-268.

——— and Rae, S. F. *The Pulse of Democracy*. New York: Simon and Schuster, 1940, 290 pp.

——— and Rae, S. F. Is There a Bandwagon Vote? *Pub. Opin. Quart.*, 1941, 4, 244-249.

——— and Robinson, C. American Institute of Public Opinion—Surveys, 1935-38. *Pub. Opin. Quart.*, 1938, 2, 373-398.

Gosnell, H. F. How Accurate Were the Polls? *Pub. Opin. Quart.*, 1937, 1, 97-104.

———. The Improvement of the Present Public Opinion Analysis. In D. Waples (ed.) *Print, Radio and Film in a Democracy*. Chicago: Univ. of Chicago Press, 1942, 118-132.

——— and deGrazia, S. A Critique of Polling Methods. *Pub. Opin. Quart.*, 1942, 6, 378-390.

——— and Pearson, N. M. The Study of Voting Behavior by Correlational Techniques. *Amer. Sociol. Rev.*, 1939, 4, 809-815.

——— and Pearson, N. M. Relation of Economic and Social Conditions to Voting Behavior in Iowa, 1924-1936. *J. of Soc. Psychol.*, 1941, 13, 15-35.

Harding, John. A Scale for Measuring Civilian Morale. *J. Soc. Psych.*, 1941, 12, 101-110.

Harriman, Philip L. An Objective Technique for Beginning the Interview with Certain Types of Adults. *J. Appl. Psychol.*, 1935, 19, 717-724.

Hartmann, George W. Contradiction between the Feeling-Tone of Political Party Names and Public Response to Their Platforms. *J. Soc. Psych.*, 1936, 7, 336-357.

———. Field Experiment on the Comparative Effectiveness of Emotional and Rational Political Leaflets in Determining Election Results. *J. Abn. and Soc. Psych.*, 1936, 31, 99-114.

Hayes, S. P. Homogeneity in Voters' Attitudes in Relation to Their Political Affiliation, Sex, and Occupation. *J. Sociol.*, 1938, 9, 141-160.

Henderson, H. An Early Poll. *Pub. Opin. Quart.*, 1942, 6, 450-451.

Herring, E. P. How Does the Voter Make Up His Mind? *Pub. Opin. Quart.*, 1938, 2, 24-35.

Hulett, J. E., Jr. Interviewing in Social Research: Basic Problems for the First Field Trip. *Social Forces*, 1938, 16, 358-366.

Jacob, P. E. Influence of World Events on U. S. "Neutrality" Opinion. *Pub. Opin. Quart.*, 1940, 4, 48-65.

Katz, D. The Public Opinion Polls and the 1940 Election. *Pub. Opin. Quart.*, 1941, 5, 52-78.

———. Do Interviewers Bias Poll Results? *Pub. Opin. Quart.*, 1942, 6, 248-268.

———. Three Criteria: Knowledge, Criteria, Significance. *Pub. Opin. Quart.*, 1940, 4, 277-284.

——— and Cantril, Hadley. Public Opinion Polls. *Sociometry*, 1937, 1, 155-179.

——— and Cantril, Hadley. An Analysis of Attitudes toward Fascism and Communism. *J. Abn. and Soc. Psych.*, 1940, 35, 356-366.

Kirkpatrick, Clifford and Stone, Sarah. Attitude Measurement and the Comparison of Generations. *J. Appl. Psychol.*, 1935, 19, 564-582.

Lambert, G. B. and Cantril, Hadley. Informing the Public: A Test Case. *Pub. Opin. Quart.*, 1943, 7, 457-466.

Lazarsfeld, P. F. Repeated Interviews as a Tool for Studying Changes in Opinion and Their Causes. *Bull. Amer. Statis. Assn.*, 1941, 2, 3-7.

———. The Change of Opinion during a Political Discussion. *J. Appl. Psychol.*, 1938, 23, 131-147.

———. Panel Studies. *Pub. Opin. Quart.*, 1940, 4, 122-128.

——— and Fiske, M. The "Panel" as a New Tool for Measuring Opinion. *Pub. Opin. Quart.*, 1938, 2, 596-612.

——— and Robinson, W. S. Some Properties of the Trichotomy "Like, No Opinion, Dislike" and Their Psychological Interpretation. *Sociometry*, 1940, 3, 151-179.

Link, H. C. An Experiment in Depth Interviewing. *Pub. Opin. Quart.*, 1943, 7, 267-279.

Link, H. C. and Freiberg, A. D. The Problem of Validity vs. Reliability in Public Opinion Polls. *Pub. Opin. Quart.*, 1942, 6, 87-98.

Lundberg, George. *Social Research*. Particularly chap. 6. New York: 1942.

Lurie, W. A. Statistics and Public Opinion. *Pub. Opin. Quart.*, 1937, 1, 78-83.

Madga, Charles and Harrison, Tom. *Mass Observation*. London: 1937, 64 pp.

Mosteller, F. and McCarthy, P. J. Estimating Population Proportions. *Pub. Opin. Quart.*, 1942, 6, 452-458.

Meier, N. C. and Levinski, R. J. Occupational Variation in Judging Trends in Public Opinion. *Pub. Opin. Quart.*, 1938, 2, 442-449.

Menefee, Selden C. The Effect of Stereotyped Words on Political Judgments. *Amer. Soc. Rev.*, 1936, 1, 614-621.

Miller, D. C. The Measurement of National Morale. *Amer. Soc. Rev.*, 1941, 6, 487-498.

Murphy, Gardner and Likert, Rensis. *Public Opinion and the Individual*. New York and London: Harpers, 1938, 316 pp.

Pace, C. Robert. Factors Influencing Questionnaire Returns from Former University Students. *J. Appl. Psychol.*, 1939, 23, 388-397.

Robinson, Claude. *Straw Votes: a Study of Political Prediction.* New York: Columbia Univ. Press, 1932.

——. Recent Developments in the Straw Poll Field. *Pub. Opin. Quart.,* 1937, 1, no. 3, 45-56, and no. 4, 42-52.

——. Current Research of the American Institute of Public Opinion. *Pub. Opin. Quart.,* 1938, 2, 274-275.

Rogers, Lindsay. Do the Gallup Polls Measure Public Opinion? *Harpers,* 1941 (November), 183, 623-632.

Roper, E. Wording of Questions for the Polls. *Pub. Opin. Quart.,* 1940, 4, 129-130.

——. Sampling Public Opinion. *Amer. Stat. Assn. Jour.,* 1940, 35, 325-334.

——. Checks to Increase Polling Accuracy. *Pub. Opin. Quart.,* 1941, 5, 87-90.

——. Classifying Respondents by Economic Status. *Pub. Opin. Quart.,* 1940, 4, 270-273.

——. Neutral Opinion on the Court Proposal. *Pub. Opin. Quart.,* 1937, 1, no. 3, 17-20.

Roslow, Sydney and Blankenship, A. B. Phrasing the Question in Consumer Research. *J. Appl. Psychol.,* 1939, 23, 612-622.

——, Wulfeck, Wallace H., and Corby, Philip G. Consumer and Opinion Research: Experimental Studies on the Form of Question. *J. Appl. Psychol.,* 1940, 24, 334-346.

Rugg, Donald. A Study of the No-Opinion Vote in Public Opinion Polls. Doctor's Thesis, 1941, Princeton University Library.

——. Experiments in Wording Questions: II. *Pub. Opin. Quart.,* 1941, 5, 91-92.

—— and Cantril, H. War Attitudes of Families with Potential Soldiers. *Pub. Opin. Quart.,* 1940, 4, 327-330.

Schanck, R. Test Tube for Public Opinion: a Rural Community. *Pub. Opin. Quart.,* 1938, 2, 90-95.

Sletto, R. F. Pretesting of Questionnaires. *Amer. Soc. Rev.,* 1940, 5, 193-200.

Stagner, Ross. The Cross-Out Technique as a Method in Public Opinion Analysis. *J. Soc. Psych.,* 1940, 11, 79-90.

——. A Comparison of the Gallup and Fortune Polls Regarding American Intervention Policy. *Sociometry,* 1941, 4, 239-258.

Stephan, F. F. Weighted Proportions and Poll Reliability. *Pub. Opin. Quart.,* 1940, 4, 135.

Studenski, P. How Polls Can Mislead. *Harpers,* 1939, 180 (December), 80-83.

Thomsen, Arnold. What Voters Think of Candidates before and after Election. *Pub. Opin. Quart.,* 1938, 2, 269-273.

Travers, R. M. W. Who Are the Best Judges of the Public. *Pub. Opin. Quart.,* 1942, 6, 628-633.

Updegraff, R. R. Democracy's New Mirror. *Forum,* 1940, 103 (January), 11-14.

Vernon, P. E. A Study of War Attitudes. *Brit. J. of Med. Psychol.*, 1942, 271-291.

Warner, L. The Reliability of Public Opinion Surveys. *Pub. Opin. Quart.*, 1939, 3, 376-390.

Wechsler, J. Interviews and Interviewers. *Pub. Opin. Quart.*, 1940, 4, 258-261.

Wilks, S. S. Confidence Limits and Critical Differences between Percentages. *Pub. Opin. Quart.*, 1940, 4, 332-338.

———. Representative Sampling and Poll Reliability. *Pub. Opin. Quart.*, 1940, 4, 261-270.

Williams, Douglas. Basic Instructions for Interviewers. *Pub. Opin. Quart.*, 1942, 4, 634-641.

Young, Pauline V. *Scientific Social Surveys and Research.* New York: Prentice-Hall, 1939, 619 pp.

INDEX